Sustainable Development Goals Series

The **Sustainable Development Goals Series** is Springer Nature's inaugural cross-imprint book series that addresses and supports the United Nations' seventeen Sustainable Development Goals. The series fosters comprehensive research focused on these global targets and endeavours to address some of society's greatest grand challenges. The SDGs are inherently multidisciplinary, and they bring people working across different fields together and working towards a common goal. In this spirit, the Sustainable Development Goals series is the first at Springer Nature to publish books under both the Springer and Palgrave Macmillan imprints, bringing the strengths of our imprints together.

The Sustainable Development Goals Series is organized into eighteen subseries: one subseries based around each of the seventeen respective Sustainable Development Goals, and an eighteenth subseries, "Connecting the Goals", which serves as a home for volumes addressing multiple goals or studying the SDGs as a whole. Each subseries is guided by an expert Subseries Advisor with years or decades of experience studying and addressing core components of their respective Goal.

The SDG Series has a remit as broad as the SDGs themselves, and contributions are welcome from scientists, academics, policymakers, and researchers working in fields related to any of the seventeen goals. If you are interested in contributing a monograph or curated volume to the series, please contact the Publishers: Zachary Romano [Springer; zachary.romano@springer.com] and Rachael Ballard [Palgrave Macmillan; rachael.ballard@palgrave.com].

Neeraj Gill • Norman Sartorius
Editors

Mental Health and Human Rights

The Challenges of the United Nations Convention on the Rights of Persons with Disabilities to Mental Health Care

Springer

Editors
Neeraj Gill
School of Medicine and Dentistry
Griffith University
Gold Coast, QLD, Australia

Norman Sartorius
Association for the Improvement of
Mental Health Programmes
Geneva, Switzerland

ISSN 2523-3084 ISSN 2523-3092 (electronic)
Sustainable Development Goals Series
ISBN 978-3-031-52178-2 ISBN 978-3-031-52179-9 (eBook)
https://doi.org/10.1007/978-3-031-52179-9

This Springer imprint is published by the registered company Springer Nature Switzerland AG
The registered company address is: Gewerbestrasse 11, 6330 Cham, Switzerland

Preface

This book is inspired by real-life stories of people with lived experience of mental illness and of their family members. Their reports make it clear that the protection of human rights is a long-neglected priority in health care in general and for people with mental illness in particular and that it is timely and essential to act now.

We presented their stories to panels composed of psychiatrists, legal experts, public health specialists as well as people with lived experience of mental illness and their family/carers during the World Psychiatric Association (WPA) World Congresses of Psychiatry in 2021 and 2022. The panels attracted much interest and a multitude of comments during the congresses which made us decide to present this series of case histories and commentaries in the form of a book. We are grateful to the many who participated in these discussions and supported the idea to produce a book containing case stories and commentaries by all stakeholders in the process of mental health care in different countries and cultures.

We thank all the contributors to this book, who provided their written commentaries on the case stories and description of the application of the CRPD in the mental health legislation of their region/country. We are also grateful to those who participated in our panel discussions on the CRPD in the World Congresses of Psychiatry including Dr Rosemary Keyes (Australia), Ms Anita Abu Bakar (Malaysia), Mr Agus Sugianto (Indonesia), Dr Rebecca Brendel (USA), Professor Saul Levin (USA) and Prof Emeritus George Szmukler (UK). We would like to thank Dr Amritash Rai and Asso Prof Shuichi Suetani from Australia who helped to formulate some of the case histories, and Dr Calina Ouliaris and Dr Michael Evans from Australia who helped editing some chapters. Finally, we acknowledge Ms Smitha Diveshan and Ms Catherine Mazars from Springer Nature, who provided us with guidance and support throughout the process of producing this book.

We hope that this book will further the awareness of the importance of considering the best ways of applying the CRPD in mental health care with a view to protect and promote the human rights of people with mental illness. We also hope that this book and the case history method will be used in teaching and training and in thinking about ways to improve mental health laws, policy, and practice.

Gold Coast, QLD, Australia — Neeraj Gill
Geneva, Switzerland — Norman Sartorius

Contents

About the Authors

John Allan MBBS, FRANZCP, PhD, GAICD, is the Executive Director of Mental Health Alcohol and other Drugs Branch in Queensland Health and holds a conjoint position with the University of Queensland, Australia. He has previously been Chief Psychiatrist in both Queensland and New South Wales. He is a national leader in mental health policy and an experienced clinician, researcher, and teacher.

He currently focuses on mental health system reform, clinical service improvement, reduction in restrictive practices, human rights, recovery-oriented practice, and smoking reduction strategies.

He is a former President of the Royal Australian and New Zealand College of Psychiatrists and a foundation member and current co-chair of Equally Well Australia. He co-coordinates the World Psychiatric Association Alternatives to Coercion Working Group.

Michaela Amering is a psychiatrist and Professor at the Division of Social Psychiatry of the Medical University of Vienna/Austria. The main focus of her clinical, teaching, and research activities is on the situation of persons with a diagnosis of schizophrenia and their families and friends and communication with them in "Trialogue," including experiences in the USA, the UK, Germany, and Ireland. She is involved working at the European Psychiatric Association (EPA), the World Association for Psychosocial Rehabilitation (WAPR), and the World Psychiatric Association (WPA), where she enjoys Honorary Membership as a Fellow. She is an Honorary Fellow of the European Society of Social Psychiatry (ESSP) and of the World Association of Social Psychiatry (WASP). She is a board member of the Austrian Association of Social Psychiatry, recipient of the 2020 Austrian

Award for Innovation in Social Psychiatry and is the 2021 winner of the EPA Constance Pascal–Helen Boyle Prize for Outstanding Achievement by a Woman in Working to Improve Mental Health Care in Europe.

Erik Lukas Bode is currently studying psychology (MSc) with a focus on clinical psychology and clinical neuroscience at the University of Bielefeld. He works as a research assistant in the working group "Emotional Neuroscience" at the Department of Psychiatry and Neurosciences at Charité - Universitätsmedizin Berlin. His research interests lie mainly at the interface between behavioral neuroscience and clinical psychology, with a focus on learning theories and motivation as the basis of decision-making in the context of substance use disorders.

Eka Chkonia , MD, PhD, received her training in Psychiatry at Tbilisi State Medical University.

She is a program director in psychiatry at Tbilisi State Medical University (TSMU USMD program) and the clinical director at the Central Psychiatric Hospital (Tbilisi Mental Health Center).

She is actively involved in mental health reform in Georgia and leads research projects in psychiatry and neuroscience.

She is an honorable member of the World Psychiatric Association, vice chair of the European Psychiatric Association (EPA) Council of NPAs, and a board member of the EPA. As a principal author and coauthor with her local and international colleagues, she published 126 research papers in peer-reviewed journals. She headed the working group on national treatment guidelines and protocols for depression, bipolar disorders, and borderline personality disorders.

Michael Evans MD is a junior medical doctor in Australia working at Gold Coast University Hospital. He completed a Doctor of Medicine (MD) at Griffith University, Gold Coast in 2021. Michael is currently planning to pursue training as a psychiatrist and has an academic interest in the relationship between human rights and mental health in Australia. He has published an article on the need for transparency and accountability in the use of forensic orders in Australia. Michael is hoping to pursue a PhD following his clinical fellowship and combine clinical medicine with academic research and education.

Benoît Eyraud PhD, Université Lumiere Lyon 2, CNRS (Centre Max Weber), France, is a sociologist and anthropologist and an expert on welfare and civic law as well as participatory action research. He is the scientific lead of a program of citizen research on the exercise of the human rights of people made vulnerable by old age and disability.

Neeraj Gill , MBBS, MD (Psychiatry), FRANZCP, DrPH, is a Professor of Psychiatry at the School of Medicine and Dentistry, Griffith University, Gold Coast, Australia, and Professor, Public Mental Health at the Mental Health Policy Unit, Health Research Institute, The University of Canberra, ACT, Australia. He is a psychiatrist at the Gold Coast Health, Australia. He is the Secretary of the World Psychiatric Association (WPA) Section on Psychiatry, Law and Ethics and the Regional Vice President, Oceania, for the World Federation for Mental Health (WFMH). He was an elected Director on the Board of the Royal Australian and New Zealand College of Psychiatrists from 2020-2023.

His previous appointments include Clinical/Medical Director of mental health services of district mental health services and Acting Chief Psychiatrist of Queensland. In 2019, he served as the psychiatrist member of the Independent Health Advice Panel (under the so-called Medevac Laws). He was a member of the Queensland Mental Health Review Tribunal from 2018 to 2024.

He was awarded the degree of Doctor of Public Health (DrPH) by the University of New South Wales, Sydney, Australia, based on his doctoral thesis on "human rights of people with mental disabilities." He has published many academic papers on human rights, mental health law, and Indigenous Australian social and emotional well-being.

Oye Gureje , MBBS, MSc, PhD, DSc, FRCPsych, FRANZCP, FWACP, is a Professor of Psychiatry and Director, WHO Collaborating Centre for Research and Training in Mental Health, Neuroscience, Drug and Alcohol Abuse, University of Ibadan, Nigeria. He was a member of the WHO International Advisory Group for ICD Revision and chaired the Work Groups on Somatic Distress and Dissociative Disorders as well as of Cultural Guidance for

ICD-11. He has also been a Board Member of the World Psychiatric Association, the Chair of its Task Force on Brain Drain, as well as serving in other leadership roles, including as a member of the Ethics Committee. He served as President of the Association of Psychiatrists in Nigeria and of the African Association of Psychiatrists and Allied Professions. He plays a leading role in mental health policy development in Nigeria as the Chair of the Federal Ministry of Health's Mental Health Action Committee. A recipient of many awards, he is a Fellow of the Nigerian Academy of Science, Fellow of the Nigerian Academy of Medicine, and was, in 2008, conferred with Nigeria's highest award for academic achievement, the Nigeria National Order of Merit, by the country's President for his contributions to medicine.

Silvana Galderisi , MD, PhD, is full professor of Psychiatry, Director of the Emergency Unit of the Department of Mental Health of the University of Campania Luigi Vanvitelli; Coordinator of the Outpatient Unit for Anxiety and Psychotic Disorders and of the Rehabilitation Program for severe mental disorders.

She is Chairperson and founding member of the European Group for Research in Schizophrenia (EGRIS), President of the Italian Society for Psychopathology, Past President of the European Psychiatric Association, Chairperson of the Standing Committee on Ethics of the World Psychiatric Association (WPA), and Co-chair of the WPA Working Group "Implementing alternatives to coercion in Mental Health Care."

She is board member of the European Scientific Association on Schizophrenia and other Psychoses and of the Italian Society of Biological Psychiatry. She is Honorary Fellow of the World Psychiatric Association-WPA, Honorary Member of the Polish Psychiatric Association and of the Hungarian Psychiatric Association, International Distinguished Fellow of the American Psychiatric Association, International Advisor of the Japanese Society of Psychiatry and Neurology, and Honorary Fellow of the European Society of Social Psychiatry.

Her research activity focuses on Schizophrenia pathophysiology, treatment, and outcomes, with particular reference to the domains of negative symptoms and cognition and their impact on psychosocial outcomes. She is an author/coauthor of more than 400 publications, in national and international journals and books, and a member of the Editorial Boards of several international psychiatric journals. She is Editor-in-Chief of Schizophrenia Bulletin Open, and handling editor of the British Journal of Psychiatry Open.

Prof Galderisi has been awarded the "2023 EPA Constance Pascal – Helen Boyle Prize for Outstanding Achievement by a Woman in Working to Improve Mental Health Care in Europe."

Helen Herrman is Professor Emeritus of Psychiatry at Orygen and the Centre for Youth Mental Health, The University of Melbourne, and Director of the World Health Organization (WHO) Collaborating Centre in Mental Health, Melbourne. She is former president of the World Psychiatric Association (WPA–2017–2020) and the International Association of Women's Mental Health. She is appointed an Officer of the Order of Australia.

Her research and development interests as psychiatrist and public health physician include promoting mental health, community mental health care, and women's mental health. Previously, she was Professor and Director of Psychiatry in St. Vincent's Health Melbourne, and for a year acted as regional advisor in mental health for the WHO's Western Pacific Region. She led the WPA's action plan 2017–2020, concerned with supporting the contribution of psychiatrists to global mental health. Publications include the report as chair of "*The Lancet*-WPA Commission: time for united action on depression" published in 2022.

Cecile Hanon is a consultant in adult and old age psychiatry, in the Regional Resource Center of Old Age Psychiatry, Corentin Celton Hospital, Assistance Publique des Hôpitaux de Paris (APHP), Université de Paris, France. She is currently in charge of a mobile team of Old Age Psychiatry.

She studied Medicine and from 1990 to 1996 and specialized in Psychiatry since 2000. She has a PhD in Ethics and Philosophy, and a member of the Center of Clinical Ethics of APHP.

She is the associated editor of the French journal "Information Psychiatrique" and director of the book collection "Polémiques", Ed John Libbey Eurotext. Within the European Psychiatric Association, she is a board member, the Chair of the EPA Committee on Education and the Co-Chair of the Section of Old Age Psychiatry. She is a member of the WPA Old Age Psychiatry section.

She participates to the works of the "Contrast" collective in 2015–2017, then joins the "Capdroits scientific and citizen approach," that reflect on the conditions for exercising rights and supporting decision-making to improving the appropriation of the fundamental rights of vulnerable people. She is a member of the WHO Collaborating Center of Lille, France, with a specific interest in e-mental health and QR tool kit.

Andreas Heinz is Professor of Psychiatry and Director of the Department of Psychiatry and Psychotherapy at Charité - Universitätsmedizin Berlin, Campus Mitte, Germany. He studied medicine, philosophy, and anthropology at Ruhr-Universität Bochum, Freie Universität Berlin, and Howard University, Washington, DC. He received his doctorate from Ruhr-Universität Bochum in 1988 and from the Institute of Philosophy at the University of Potsdam in 2013. He habilitated in psychiatry and psychotherapy in 1998 and in philosophy in 2022. His research focuses on learning mechanisms in mental illness and the impact of social exclusion on mental health. He is a member of clinical and scientific committees, including the Ethics Advisory Board of the World Psychiatry Association, the Leopoldina, and the Academy of Sciences and Literature in Mainz. Between 2019 and 2021, Andreas Heinz was president of the German Society for Psychiatry, Psychotherapy Psychosomatics and Neurology (DGPPN). Currently, he is speaker of the Collaborative Research Center (Transregio) 265: "Loss and Recovery of Control over Drug Use," funded by the German Research Foundation (DFG) and head of other DFG- and BMBF-funded projects.

Melissa Gül Halil is a clinical psychologist (MSc) and psychotherapist-in-training, specializing in cognitive behavioral therapy. She works as a research associate in the working group "Emotional Neuroscience" at the Department of Psychiatry and Neurosciences at Charité - Universitätsmedizin Berlin. Her research interests are mainly in the area of addiction research, participative research, intercultural psychology, reward and memory systems, and habit formation.

Nasser Loza Immediate Past President of the World Federation for Mental Health (WMFH) (2023–2025), completed his psychiatric training at the Institute of Psychiatry & the Maudsley Hospital in London. He became a member of the Royal College of Psychiatrists in 1987 and a fellow of the College in 1995. He served as the Secretary General for Mental Health, Egypt (2006–2011), Chairman of the Scientific Council of The Arab Board of Medical Specializations (2012–2017), and Honorary Fellow of the Royal College of Psychiatrists (2014). He is a member of the editorial board of The Arab Journal of Psychiatry and The British Journal of Psychiatry (International), and served as the Chairman of the Middle East Division of the Royal College of Psychiatrists (2013–2017). Dr. Loza is the Founder and President of the Egyptian Society for The Rights of People with Mental Illness, and the Director of The Behman Hospital, the Maadi Psychology Centre, and practices at several Behman Consultations Clinics in Cairo, as well as the International Clinic in London.

Marlen Abigain Gómez Mendiola has a degree in Forensic Science from the National Autonomous University of Mexico (UNAM). She has participated in the writing of two book chapters as coauthor, about forensic mental health. Currently, she is a Master's student in Public Mental Health at National Autonomous University of Mexico, with the line of research on variables that influence the decision-making of judges, defense lawyers, and prosecutors in cases with not guilty by reason of insanity defense. In 2017, she worked as a technical consultant at the Public Defender's Office of the Reclusorio Preventivo Varonil Oriente. Currently, she is a research assistant at the Ramón de la Fuente Muñiz National Institute of Psychiatry (INPRFM), Mexico City, Mexico.

Sabine Müller is physicist, philosopher, and medical ethicist in the Department of Psychiatry and Neurosciences of the Charité - Universitätsmedizin Berlin, Germany. Her main research areas are ethical issues of psychiatry, neurosurgery, and neurology. She has coordinated the international, interdisciplinary research project "Psychiatric Neurosurgery: Ethical, legal, and societal issues."

(Please note that the official name of the Charité is in German; it must not be translated to English.)

Mohan Isaac is a Clinical Professor, Faculty of Health and Medical Sciences, University of Western Australia, Perth, Australia. He is also a Visiting Professor at the National Institute of Mental Health and Neurosciences, Bangalore, India, where he was formerly the Head of the Department of Psychiatry for many years.

Nicolás Martínez-López is Professor of Clinical Ethics and Biomedical Research Ethics and Bioethics Dilemmas at the National Autonomous University of Mexico (UNAM). He is an Honorary member of the Mexican Council of Neurosciences and the Mexican Association of Legal Psychology and Criminal Law, and he is Secretary of the Editorial Committee of the Law and Health Collection of Tirant Lo Blanch and Director of the Department of Forensic Psychiatry Research of the Mexican Council of Neuroscience. In 2022, he received the "Lifetime Achievement award Forensic Psychiatry" for his contributions to forensic psychiatric from the American Society of Hispanic Psychiatric.

Tarek A. Okasha Professor of Psychiatry and Director of the World Psychiatric Association Collaborating Centre for Training and Research in Psychiatry—Okasha Institute of Psychiatry, Faculty of Medicine, Ain Shams University, Cairo, Egypt. President Egyptian Alzheimer Society and Editor-In-chief "Middle East Current Psychiatry" Journal. Chairperson of the Higher Council of Universities Committee in Egypt for the promotion of Assistant

Professors and Professors in Psychiatry, World Psychiatric Association Presidential Commendation. Member and honorary member of many international associations and organizations and published more than 85 papers in national and international journals, contributed in 30 national and international books and supervised more than 90 master's degree and doctorate degree thesis.

Balram Pandit is the Medical Superintendent, St Giles' Hospital, and National Advisor Mental Health under the Ministry of Health and Medical Services, Fijian Government, Fiji. He completed his MD in Psychiatry at Patna Medical College, Patna, India, and advance psychiatric training (2010–2013) at the Institute of Medical Sciences, BHU, Varanasi, India. He became member of the Indian Psychiatric Society (IPS) in 2008 and a life fellow in 2021. While serving as an academic, Postgraduate Programme Coordinator, and Head of the Discipline of Psychiatry (2013–2022) at Fiji National University, he developed comprehensive MMED-Psychiatry Programme to meet the contextual training needs in Pacific Island Nations. He is a member of the National Advisory Council on Mental Health, National Medicine and Therapeutics Committee, and Fiji National Health Research Ethics Review Committee. He is chairman of the National Clinical Services Network for psychiatry. He is an international corresponding member of the Royal Australian and New Zealand College of Psychiatrists and member of the International Psychogeriatric Association, Indian Epilepsy Association, Pasifika Medical Association, Fiji Medical Association, and Global Neuropsychiatric Association. He has published several book chapters and research articles.

Soumitra Pathare is a consultant psychiatrist, and the Director of the Center. In the past, he has provided technical assistance to the Ministry of Health and Family Welfare, Government of India in drafting India's new Mental Health Care Act 2017, which takes a rights-based approach to mental health care. He was also a member of the Mental Health Policy Group appointed by the Government of India to draft India's first National Mental Health Policy released in October 2014. He has served as a

WHO consultant in many low- and middle-income countries (Botswana, Seychelles, Lesotho, Samoa, Vanuatu, Eritrea) assisting them in drafting and implementing mental health legislation and national mental health policy.

Soumitra is also the Co-director of SPIRIT (an implementation research project on suicide prevention funded by NIMH) and the co-lead on Outlive! (a youth suicide prevention project funded by Comic Relief, UK).

Maria Rodrigues is a researcher, educator, and development practitioner who focuses on the intersection between mental health, social justice, and cross-cultural peacebuilding. She has supported the World Psychiatric Association as a consultant since 2019, especially contributing to its working group on Implementing Alternatives to Coercion in Mental Health Care and facilitating meetings of its working group on Partnerships with Service Users and Family Carers. Her research and consultancy work has additionally contributed to tool kits, policy, and strategic documents for StrongMinds Uganda, Victoria Health, the National Indigenous Australians Agency, Relationships Australia and Amnesty International.

Norman Sartorius currently the President of the Association for the Improvement of Mental Health programs worked with the World Health Organization for more than 25 years having been the Founding Director of the World Health Organization' Division of Mental health. After that, he was the President of the World Psychiatric Association and of the European Psychiatric Association.

Professor Sartorius has also been the Professor of Psychiatry in Zagreb (Croatia) Prague (Czechia) and Geneva (Switzerland) and a visiting or honorary Professor at the universities of London, and several other universities in the USA and in China.

His current major areas of interest are the problems related to the comorbidity of mental and physical disorders, the fight against stigma related to mental illness and the education of psychiatrists, particularly in its postgraduate period.

Martha Kane Savage Born in the USA, Martha Kane Savage is also a New Zealand citizen, and is Professor of Geophysics at Victoria University of Wellington. She completed her PhD 1987 Geophysics, Univ. Wisconsin, Madison; MS 1984 Geophysics, Univ. Wisconsin, Madison; BA 1979 Physics, Swarthmore College.

In 2017, her son died in a Japanese hospital after being mechanically restrained for 10 days, and she has since campaigned for an end to the practice. She is an Honorary member of the WPA and is serving on the Working Group on Developing Partnerships with Service Users and Family Carers, on the WPA Working Group Implementing Alternatives to Coercion in Mental Health Care, and on the Working Group on WPA Volunteering.

Assina Seitz is a dynamic professional with a diverse background spanning psychology, journalism, and public relations. She holds a Bachelor of Science in Psychology from Fresenius University of Applied Sciences and a Bachelor of Arts in Journalism from DEKRA Media University Berlin.

Throughout Assina's career, she has showcased a strong commitment to both academia and practical experience. Notably, she has contributed significantly to the field of psychiatry and psychotherapy at Charité - University Hospital Berlin. As a working student, she provided invaluable support to the Medical Director and Chair of the Department, undertaking administrative tasks, assisting in publication processes, and spearheading initiatives such as the establishment of the Charité Coaching School. Their role also involved co-therapist duties in group therapy sessions for transcultural male immigrants, demonstrating a dedication to inclusive mental health care.

In addition to their clinical work, Assina has been actively engaged in research, serving as a student research assistant for the Collaborative Research Center TRR 265 at Charité - University Hospital Berlin. Outside of academia and health care, she has gained valuable experience in various industries, including public relations and marketing.

Nermin Mahmoud Shaker Professor of Child and Adolescent Psychiatry, Faculty of Medicine, Okasha Institute, Ain Shams University, Cairo, Egypt, and Deputy Head of Research Unit, General Secretariat of Mental Health and Addiction Treatment. Member of Egyptian Child and Adolescent Psychiatry Association (ECAPA), Egyptian Association of Child and Adolescent Mental Health (EACAMH), Egyptian Psychiatric Association (EPA), MedSPAD Research Committee, Pompidou Group, Council of Europe. Has 37 publications as papers and book chapters, supervised more than 40 doctorate and master degree thesis.

Jill Stavert is Professor of Mental Health and Capacity Law at Edinburgh Napier University, where she leads the Centre for Mental Health Practice Policy and Law Research. Her areas of research and expertise are international, European, and national human rights and mental health and mental capacity law and related law, policy and practice review, and reform. Jill's recent work has included being a member of the Scottish Mental Health Law Review (Scott Review) Executive Team, investigating views and experiences of the Mental Health Tribunal for Scotland and the impact of COVID-19 and related restrictions on law, policy, and practice relating to persons with mental disabilities. Previously, she was an expert advisor to the Scottish Independent Review of Learning Disability and Autism in the Mental Health Act and a member of the Deprivation of Liberty and Supported Decision-Making Working Groups in the Scottish Government review of the Adults with Incapacity (Scotland) Act. She is currently contributing to the mental health and capacity law reform programme in Scotland.

Charlene Sunkel is the Founder and CEO of the Global Mental Health Peer Network. She is a global voice for the rights of people with lived experiences of mental health conditions. She has published widely on issues related to mental health and human rights, stigma, and the needs of people with mental illness in low- and middle-income countries. Ms. Sunkel had been involved in several Lancet Commissions and co-chaired the Lancet Commission on Ending Stigma and Discrimination in Mental Health. Ms. Sunkel had been involved in the review and drafting of various policies and legislation in South Africa and provided technical assistance to national and international mental health-related documents. She serves on a number of international boards and committees, and previously been on the South African Presidential Working Group on Disability and Ministerial Advisory Committee on Mental Health. Ms. Sunkel is the former Principal Coordinator for the Movement for Global Mental Health. She is a faculty member of the Indian Law College. She received a number of national and international awards for her work, with the latest being the Pardes Humanitarian Prize in Mental Health.

Simon Surguladze MD, PhD, DSc, received his training in Psychiatry at Tbilisi State Medical University. At different times he worked as a Head of Department at M. Asatiani Institute of Psychiatry, Associate Professor at Tbilisi State University, and Chief Psychiatrist of Georgia. He took part in numerous projects implementing reforms of psychiatric services. He is one of coauthors of the first edition of Mental Health Law in Georgia (1997). Since 1997 he has been based at King's College London Institute of Psychiatry, working in a field of neuroscience of cognitive and emotional processes in people with psychiatric disorders. As a principal author and in collaboration with colleagues, Dr. Surguladze published 76 research papers in peer-reviewed journals. In parallel to his work at King's he led several projects in Georgia that were funded by European Funds, e.g., Cordaid, Royal Society UK, European Union Framework Program 7, The Wellcome Trust. He currently holds the posts of a Psychiatrist at Home Treatment Service at South London and Maudsley NHS Trust and Senior Visiting Lecturer at King's College London Institute of Psychiatry, Psychology & Neuroscience.

Xiaoping Wang is the director of the Mental Health Institute at Central South University. He is also the director of the Department/Faculty of psychiatry of the Second Xiangya Hospital at Central South University and the director of China's National Clinical Research Center for Mental Disorders. He obtained his PhD degree at Hunan Medical University in 1995. He then joined the psychiatric residency program at Institut National

Marcel Riviere in France between 1997 and 1998. He completed clinical fellow of Forensic Psychiatry in the Department of Psychiatry at the University of British Columbia in Canada in 2004 and then went to complete the POST program of forensic psychiatry in the Department of Psychiatry at Melbourne University in 2005. He has been the vice-president and secretary general of the Chinese Society of Psychiatry and a Standing Committee Member of the Chinese Psychiatrist Association since 2015. Prof Wang has been the president of the Chinese Society of Neuroscience and Psychiatry since 2020. Prof Wang engages in the research fields of forensic psychiatry and the legal rights of individuals living with mental disorders. He has published 40+ peer-reviewed scientific papers in many academic journals. Prof Wang has joined and led many national scientific projects. He is one of the principal investigators of China's National Brain Projects.

Shaoling Zhong is an assistant research fellow at the Affiliated Brain Hospital of Guangzhou Medical University in China. She holds a Doctor of Medicine degree from Central South University and has furthered her research experience with a one-year visiting position at the University of Oxford. Dr. Zhong has led and contributed to some national and provincial research projects in China, resulting in several high-impact peer-reviewed publications. She serves as an editorial board member for both BMC Psychiatry and BMC Public Health journals. Her research is focused on identifying the intricate connections between mental disorders and criminality.

Part I

The United Nations Convention on the Rights of Persons with Disabilities

Introduction

1

Neeraj Gill and Norman Sartorius

Contents

The United Nations (UN) Convention on the Rights of Persons with Disabilities (CRPD) is an international treaty that embeds the human rights of people with disabilities into international law (United Nations, 2006). There has been a significant discussion and debate on the application of the CRPD to mental health care. The CRPD challenges traditional mental health legislation, for example, through articles affirming that people with disabilities have equal legal capacity as others (Article 12), that the existence of disability cannot be grounds for deprivation of liberty (Article 14) and that every person with disabilities has a right to respect for his or her physical and mental integrity on an equal basis with others (Article 17). Furthermore, the CRPD makes it legally binding for the States Parties to protect and promote social, economic, and cultural rights of people with disabilities, which have often been ignored in domestic legislations. For example, the CRPD requires the States Parties to recognize the right to the highest attainable standard of health through accessible health services (Article 25).

The application of the CRPD in the field of psychiatry is not as straightforward as its application in the instance of people with physical impairments, diseases, and disabilities. To open the debate on how best to apply the rules of the CRPD in the field of mental health, the World Psychiatric Association (WPA) organized a series of sessions in which psychiatrists, public health specialists, people with lived experience and carers examined case histories in order to determine what would be best for the person with the mental health condition and how the steps to be taken mesh with the principles the CRPD. The sessions discussing cases were organized in the framework of the World Congresses of Psychiatry and generated much interest both in those attending

N. Gill (✉)
School of Medicine and Dentistry, Griffith University, Gold Coast, Australia

Mental Health Policy Unit, Health Research Institute, University of Canberra, Canberra, Australia

Mental Health and Specialist Services, Gold Coast Health, Gold Coast, Australia
e-mail: neeraj.gill@griffith.edu.au

N. Sartorius
Association for the Improvement of Mental Health Programmes, Geneva, Switzerland
e-mail: sartorius@normansartorius.com

N. Gill, N. Sartorius (eds.), *Mental Health and Human Rights*, Sustainable Development Goals Series, https://doi.org/10.1007/978-3-031-52179-9_1

the sessions and those witnessing the sessions virtually.

The persons invited to participate in these discussions were from low-, middle-, and high-income countries from different continents and from countries differing in their legal traditions. Rather than starting with a theoretical discussion, the group was invited to consider issues arising in the life stories of a series of persons who experienced mental illness. In view of the interest which the case history sessions received, we decided to continue the exploration of the applicability of the CRPD in this way and sent 14 case histories to experts—including some of the experts who were attending the meeting during the World Congress and some others and asked them to provide written commentary on what the course of action would be in those scenarios in their country and what should be done in those cases to protect and promote human rights of people with mental illness. The first section of this book presents these case histories (13 describing stories of individuals and 1 a services development story) and the comments made by the participants in the project.

There was a remarkable consensus among commentators from different parts of the world regarding human rights of people with mental illness. However, there were also some important differences in opinion, possibly related to the commentators' background, lived experience, and country of origin. Therefore, it was decided to include a series of eight descriptions of countries with different legal traditions partially explaining the differences in the way in which the CRPD would be employed in mental health care.

Finally, there is a section illustrating the work of non-governmental organizations related to the CRPD by the description of three such organizations—one professional and two non-professional and their work relevant to human rights. This includes a chapter based on the WPA's work to promote alternatives to coercion in mental health care and the description of two organizations working to promote human rights of people with mental illness, as a reminder that there are many similar organizations doing extremely valuable work which is not very well known.

In the concluding chapter, we have tried to bring together the main issues raised by the experts and by the study of relevant legislation and suggestions for further work on the protection of human rights of people with mental illness and the provision of care. We draw the conclusion that there is a need for a realistic interpretation of the CRPD, and education and training of healthcare workers in the requirements of the CRPD. In addition, we point towards the need for all governments to allocate the resources required to improve social and health services to adopt and implement the principles of the CRPD to protect and promote the rights of people with mental illness.

Reference

United Nations. (2006). Convention on the Rights of Persons with Disabilities, adopted on 13 December 2006, GA Res 61/106, UN Doc A/Res/61/106 (entered into force 3 May 2008). Retrieved from https://www.un.org/development/desa/disabilities/convention-on-the-rights-of-persons-with-disabilities.html

The Application of the CRPD and Other International Human Rights Instruments in Mental Health Care

2

Neeraj Gill and Norman Sartorius

Contents

Supplementary Information The online version contains supplementary material available at https://doi.org/10.1007/978-3-031-52179-9_2.

N. Gill (✉)
School of Medicine and Dentistry, Griffith University, Gold Coast, QLD, Australia

Mental Health Policy Unit, Health Research Institute, University of Canberra, Canberra, ACT, Australia

Mental Health and Specialist Services, Gold Coast Health, Gold Coast, QLD, Australia
e-mail: neeraj.gill@griffith.edu.au

N. Sartorius
Association for the Improvement of Mental Health Programmes, Geneva, Switzerland
e-mail: sartorius@normansartorius.com

N. Gill, N. Sartorius (eds.), *Mental Health and Human Rights*, Sustainable Development Goals Series, https://doi.org/10.1007/978-3-031-52179-9_2

2.1 Pre-CRPD International Human Rights Instruments - The International Bill of Rights

The modern human rights framework was adopted by the United Nations (UN) in 1948 through the Universal Declaration of Human Rights (UDHR) (United Nations 1948). It sets out the basic human rights and fundamental freedoms that should be universally protected. However, as a declaration, it was not legally binding. The International Covenant on Civil and Political Rights (ICCPR) (United Nations 1966a) and the International Covenant on Economic, Social and Cultural Rights (ICESCR) (United Nations 1966b) were the treaties, adopted in 1966, entered into force in 1976, which made it obligatory for ratifying countries to protect and promote human rights. While this International Bill of Rights (consisting of UDHR, ICCPR and ICESCR) is universally applicable and may have contributed to making a difference in lives of people with disabilities, there was no specific mention of people with disabilities in these documents.

2.2 Other Pre-CRPD International Human Rights Conventions

In addition to the International Bill of Rights, the international human rights legal framework also includes:

- International Convention on the Elimination of All Forms of Racial Discrimination (ICERD), adopted in 1965, entered into force 1969 (United Nations 1965).
- Convention on the Elimination of All Forms of Discrimination against Women (CEDAW), adopted in 1979, entered into force 1981 (United Nations 1979).
- Convention against Torture and Other Cruel, Inhuman or Degrading Treatment or Punishment (CAT), adopted in 1984, entered into force in 1987 (United Nations 1984).
- The Convention on Rights of the Child (CROC), adopted in 1989, entered into force 1990 (United Nations 1990a).
- International Convention on the Protection of the Rights of All Migrant Workers and Members of their Families (ICMW), adopted in 1990 (United Nations 1990b).
- International Convention on the Protection of All Persons from Enforced Disappearance (CPED), adopted in 2006 (United Nations 2006).

Note must also be taken of the numerous optional protocols to these instruments that have been entered into. Of special note in this regard is the Optional Protocol to the Convention Against Torture (OPCAT) (United Nations 2002), which was adopted in 2002 and came into force in 2006 and seeks to implement non-judicial measures to prevent torture and uphold the rights of individuals who are detained. The subcommittee on prevention established thereunder is granted wide-ranging powers, including the ability to make supervisory visits to places of detention (including locked psychiatric wards) and to make recommendations (Ouliaris et al. 2024).

2.3 Other Relevant Human Rights Declarations, Resolutions and Principles

In addition to the above conventions and covenants, which are legally obligatory and hence termed ‘hard law’, international human rights law includes soft law in the form of various declarations, resolutions or principles (Jones 2005), including:

- The Declaration on the Rights of Mentally Retarded Persons, 1971
- The Declaration on the Rights of Disabled Persons, 1975
- The World Programme of Action Concerning Disabled Persons, 1982
- The Principles for the Protection of Persons with Mental Illness and for Improvement of Mental Health Care, 1991 (United Nations 1991)
- The Standard Rules on the Equalization of Opportunities for Persons with Disabilities, 1993 (United Nations General Assembly 1993)

Mental health and human rights are both concerned with social justice and social responsibility (Dudley et al. 2012). Mental health and human rights are inextricably related in three ways, as described by Mann et al. (1994) in the context of health, and elaborated by Gostin and Gable in the context of mental health (Gostin and Gable 2004):

- Mental health policy could either protect or adversely affect human rights
- Human rights violations adversely affect mental health
- Positive promotion of both mental health and human rights mutually reinforce each other

Despite this central importance of the relationship between human rights and mental health, and even though the modern international human rights framework was developed in 1948, it was only in 1991 that the rights of persons with mental illness specifically received international acknowledgement. This was through the Principles for the Protection of Persons with Mental Illness and the Improvement of Mental Health Care, also called the Mental Illness Principles or MI Principles, adopted by UN General Assembly Resolution 46/119 of 17 December 1991 (Perlin and Szeli 2012; United Nations 1991). The MI Principles included:

1. Promotion of mental health and prevention of mental disorders
2. Access to basic mental health care
3. Mental health assessment in accordance with internationally accepted principles
4. Provision of the least restrictive type of mental health care
5. Self-determination
6. Right to be assisted in the exercise of self-determination
7. Availability of review procedures
8. Automatic period review mechanisms
9. Qualified decision-makers
10. Respect of rule of law

The 'MI Principles' was the first UN resolution to recognize the right to treatment of mental illness as a human right. However, the MI Principles did not have a legally binding status in terms of international law (Callard et al. 2012).

2.4 The United Nations Convention on the Rights of Persons with Disabilities

The United Nations Convention on the Rights of Persons with Disabilities (CRPD) is an international treaty that was adopted by the United Nations General Assembly in New York on 13 December 2006 after a process of negotiations among various stakeholders including UN representatives, organizations working in the field and service-user and carer bodies (United Nations 2006). It entered into force on 3 May 2008. It specifically sets out human rights of persons with disabilities in international law to ensure that people with disabilities are not 'forgotten' when human rights protections are applied in countries. The CRPD incorporates contemporary human rights discourse, which includes economic, social and cultural rights as well as civil and political rights. It has been described as representing a paradigm shift in the implementation and practice of disability rights by metamorphosing the status of a person with disability from 'an object' of charity, medical treatment and social protection to 'a subject' with rights, capable of claiming those rights, making choices and actively participating in society (Bartlett 2014; United Nations 2006).

Article 3 of the CRPD highlights its general principles, i.e. respect for inherent dignity, individual autonomy and independence of persons; non-discrimination; full and effective participation and inclusion in society; respect for difference and acceptance of persons with disabilities as part of human diversity and humanity; equality of opportunity; accessibility; equality between men and women; and respect for the evolving capacities of children with disabilities as well as respect for the right of these children to preserve their identities (United Nations 2006).

In contrast with the previous declarations by the UN, for example, the MI Principles (United Nations 1991) which were non-binding in nature (Perlin and Szeli 2012), the CRPD has been considered to be a powerful machinery against discrimination of the people with mental disabilities. For example, Article 4 of the CRPD requires States Parties to take measures to modify or abolish discriminatory laws, regulations and practices as well as to provide programmes to protect and promote the rights of persons with disabilities (Szmukler et al. 2014; United Nations 2006). It highlights the general obligations of the States Parties to promote the full realization of all human rights and fundamental freedoms for all persons with disabilities, without discrimination on the basis of disability. To this end, it requires the States Parties to adopt appropriate legislative, administrative and other measures for the implementation of the rights recognized in the Convention. This may include creating legislation as well as modifying or abolishing existing laws, regulations, customs and practices that constitute discrimination against persons with disabilities; and to take into account the protection and promotion of the human rights of persons with disabilities in all policies and programmes (United Nations 2006). However, the majority of violations of the rights of people with mental illness in most countries occur because their governments have not provided sufficient resources for mental health care or social services. It remains to be seen if the adoption of the Convention changes that.

There has been a great deal of debate and controversy regarding the implications of the CRPD on the clinical practice of mental health care and psychiatry. The CRPD has been hailed as 'the dawn of a new era' in disability rights (United Nations 2006). Some practitioners in the field of mental health have described the CRPD as providing an invaluable new trajectory and horizon for human rights protection and promotion in mental health (Mezzina et al. 2019). Other experts, while acknowledging the many merits of the human rights framework adopted by the CRPD, have also pointed to the 'ambiguities' and 'inconsistencies' in the actual text of the convention, or to the fact that the convention is 'silent' when it comes to forms of involuntary psychiatric treatment (Callaghan and Ryan 2014; Dawson 2015; Freeman et al. 2015). Still others have claimed that the convention would leave many people with mental health conditions worse off by interfering with efforts to protect them and called it a 'problem child of international human rights law' (Appelbaum 2019).

While many countries have revised domestic mental health laws to align with the legislative requirements set out in the CRPD, it is unlikely that any domestic legislation can be said to be totally compliant with the CRPD. There is a paucity of credible and reliable evidence of changes in the mental health care and respect for human rights of people with mental illness in signatory countries since the CRPD came into force. This book is the first comprehensive exploration of the opportunities and challenges arising in the practical application of the CRPD to mental health care and human rights of people with mental illness in relation to the international legislation.

2.5 Challenges of the CRPD to Mental Health Care

2.5.1 CRPD and the Civil and Political Rights

Most traditional mental health legislation did not comply with the CRPD articles which require respect for legal capacity, liberty and integrity of persons with disabilities on an equal basis with others (Callaghan and Ryan 2014). The conventional mental health legislation of most countries appears to violate various articles of the CRPD (Szmukler et al. 2014). These include Article 4 ('no discrimination of any kind on the basis of disability'), Article 12 (a 'person shall enjoy legal capacity on an equal basis with others in all aspects of life') and Article 14 ('the existence of a disability shall in no case justify deprivation of liberty') (Szmukler et al. 2014). As a result, various countries around the world have amended or are currently in the process of re-fashioning their mental health legislation to comply with the CRPD (Callaghan and Ryan 2012).

According to some academics, the mere existence of exclusive legislation for involuntary treatment for mental illness is discriminatory, leading to violation of Article 4 of the CRPD ('no discrimination of any kind on the basis of disability'), and they have called for a blanket ban on any involuntary treatment of mental illness and for total abolition of mental health legislation (Minkowitz 2010; Szmukler et al. 2014). Other experts have argued in favour of a 'fusion law' that would apply to everyone regardless of their physical or mental illness and which would only permit involuntary treatment when the person's decision-making capacity for a specific treatment decision is impaired and supported decision-making has failed. Supporters of fusion law argue that this is in line with the CRPD (Szmukler et al. 2014). Some have claimed that the current mental health legislations should be amended to have more reliance on the 'capacity assessment' rather than the 'risk' criteria for involuntary treatment (Callaghan and Ryan 2012).

Article 12 has been at the centre of rekindled debate regarding involuntary psychiatric treatment. There is a range of interpretations of this article. Article 12(2) requires the States Parties to recognize that persons with disabilities enjoy legal capacity on an equal basis with others in all aspects of life. Article 12(3) then requires the States Parties to take appropriate measures to provide access to the 'support' that persons with disabilities may require in exercising their legal capacity. Article 12(4) of the CRPD specifies that any measures relating to the exercise of legal capacity must respect the rights, will and preferences of the person; be proportionate and tailored to the person's circumstances; be free of conflicts of interest and undue influence; apply for the shortest amount of time possible; and be subject to safeguards and monitoring by a competent authority.

The CRPD Committee, through General Comment 1 on Article 12 in 2014, called for a shift from substitute decision-making to supported decision-making; and from the 'best interest' paradigm to 'will and preferences of the individual' paradigm (United Nations Committee on the Rights of Persons with Disabilities 2014). The Committee interpreted the CRPD as prohibiting involuntary treatment under any situation and urged the States Parties to abolish all substitute decision-making regimes, such as guardianship and involuntary psychiatric treatment (United Nations Committee on the Rights of Persons with Disabilities 2014). Critics have called this interpretation radical or absolutist, by pointing to circumstances where the right to refuse treatment and right to health conflict with each other and have called for a more realistic interpretation (Dawson 2015; Callaghan and Ryan 2014; Freeman et al. 2015). It has been argued that Article 12(4) of the CRPD allows for involuntary treatment when it is required as the last resort, for short periods, with strong safeguards (Gill 2019).

A few case vignettes in section 1 of this book raise the question of whether involuntary psychiatric treatment or substitute decision-making may be utilised as the last resort. This issue is also discussed at length in section 2, with chapters from different regions of the world showcasing different legal traditions and how they have responded to the challenges of the CRPD.

2.5.2 Different Viewpoints Among the UN Agencies, WHO and WPA

Even amongst different United Nations bodies, there are contradictory opinions regarding whether involuntary psychiatric interventions can ever be justified under contemporary human rights standards—a disagreement sometimes known as the 'Geneva impasse' (Martin and Gurbai 2019). For example, the UN CRPD Committee and the Special Rapporteur on the right of everyone to the enjoyment of the highest attainable standard of physical and mental health have called for an absolute end to all forced psychiatric treatment and confinement. In contrast, the UN Human Rights Committee (HRC) and the UN Subcommittee on Prevention of Torture and Other Cruel, Inhuman or Degrading Treatment or Punishment (SPT) have recognized that deprivation of liberty or detention of people with disabilities should only be used when it is absolutely necessary to prevent serious harm to the individual or injury to others, as last resort measure with strong safeguards (Guilloud 2019).

The World Health Organization (WHO) has called for complete elimination of all coercive interventions in mental health care services (World Health Organization 2019, 2023), whereas the World Psychiatric Association (WPA) while recognizing the need for coercive interventions as the last resort to uphold the right to health, calls for promoting alternatives to coercion in mental health care, with an emphasis on the protection and promotion of human rights (Herrman et al. 2022; World Psychiatric Association 2020a, b). Nevertheless, the WHO and the WPA, while acknowledging those differences, have recognized common ground between the two organizations, endorsing rights-based recovery-oriented approaches to promote non-coercive interventions in mental health care (Gill et al. 2024).

2.5.3 CRPD and the Economic, Social and Cultural Rights

Most countries' mental health laws continue to focus on the practice of involuntary treatment and what are known as 'negative rights', which include the civil rights to refuse treatment and freedom from arbitrary detention (Gostin and Gable 2004; McSherry 2010). The CRPD also includes economic, social and cultural rights including the right to life (Article 10), independent living and inclusion and participation in community (Article 19), home and family (Article 23), education (Article 24), health (Article 25), habitation and rehabilitation (Article 26), work and employment (Article 27), adequate standard of living and social protection (Article 28) and participation in cultural life (Article 30). Human rights advocates and legal experts have highlighted the need for positive rights to be enshrined into law (Gostin and Gable 2004; McSherry 2010; Perlin and Szeli 2012). They argue that in order to help operationalize the right to the highest attainable standard of mental health, the legislative framework must facilitate access to treatment for all people with mental health issues (McSherry 2014). It has been recognized that economic, social and cultural rights are more fundamental, and their promotion paves the way for protection of civil and political rights (Gill 2019). A few case histories in this volume and some chapters about legal traditions of different countries highlight the need to promote the economic, social and cultural rights of people with mental illness. These case histories point towards the human rights violations of people with mental illness due to inadequate resources in social and mental health care sector, thus highlighting the need for proper resources to respect the right to the highest attainable standard of physical and mental health, the right to employment, the right to social inclusion and participation, and other positive rights.

2.6 Sustainable Development Goals (SDGs) and Mental Health

Adopted by the United Nations (UN) in 2015, the *2030 Agenda for Sustainable Development* outlined 17 Sustainable Development Goals (SDGs) to drive urgent action in areas such as poverty, equality, health, education, sustainability and the environment (United Nations General Assembly 2015). The SDGs are a progression of the Millennium Development Goals (MDGs) from 2000 and broaden the remit of improvement (United Nations 2015). The MDGs had no mention of disability or mental health. Within the 17 SDGs, there are both direct and indirect goals, targets and indicators relating to mental health. The SDG 3 details the goal to ensure healthy lives and promote well-being for all at all ages (United Nations General Assembly 2015). There are three targets within SDG 3 directly related to mental health (Patel et al. 2018):

- Target 3.4: By 2030, reduce by one third premature mortality from non-communicable diseases through prevention and treatment and promote mental health and well-being.
- Target 3.5: Strengthen the prevention and treatment of substance abuse, including narcotic drug abuse and harmful use of alcohol.
- Target 3.8: Achieve universal health coverage, including financial risk protection, access to quality essential healthcare services and access to safe, effective, quality and affordable essential medicines and vaccines for all.

In the annual SDG reports from 2016 to 2023, there is direct mention of mental health in five out of eight of the reports (United Nations 2021, 2023a). Mental health and well-being depend on a complex interplay between biological, psychological and social determinants of health (Alegría et al. 2018). Therefore, many SDGs are directly or indirectly related to global mental health. SDGs 1, 2 and 6 call for the eradication of poverty, hunger and poor sanitation (United Nations General Assembly 2015). Malnutrition and physical illness secondary to poverty, hunger and gastrointestinal disorders from poor sanitation have direct impact on brain development and function creating a predisposition to mental illness and a worsening of pre-existing conditions (Dybdahl and Lien 2018). Quality education (SDG 4) can lead to both psychological and social benefits such as enhanced self-esteem, skills to navigate a complex sociocultural landscape and financial independence (Alegría et al. 2018). SDGs 5, 10 and 16 call for equality peace and justice. Inequality and gender discrimination, war and conflict, displacement and refugee status are some examples of triggers for worsening mental health and well-being (Dybdahl and Lien 2018). SDG 8, 9 and 11 relate to economic growth, infrastructure and sustainable communities—each of these promotes mental health through financial stability and access to a thriving and supportive community (Alegría et al. 2018). SDG 7, 12, 13, 14 and 15 outline goals relating to sustainability and the environment—the longevity and health of our planet is paramount to ensuring the safety and recovery of individuals living with mental illness and the promotion of mental well-being (Kumar et al. 2023).

Each year since implementation, the UN Secretary-General presents an annual SDG progress report in addition to an independent Global Sustainable Development report published every 4 years (United Nations 2023a). The 2023 SDG annual report raises an alarming concern that the world is falling far behind the 2030 agenda—highlighting the impact of COVID-19, the war in Ukraine and climate-related disasters (United Nations 2023b).

2.6.1 Sustainable Development Goals and the CRPD

The CRPD and the SDGs have many shared priorities (Gómez et al. 2022; Wescott et al. 2020). The social, economic and cultural rights of people with disabilities enshrined in the CRPD directly complement the global development efforts of the SDGs. Global development can only occur with equitable allocation of the resources and inclusion of people with capability deprivation due to poverty and disability (Sen 1999). However, there remains a gap between aspiration and reality, as multiple SDGs are running behind targets just as many human rights of people with disabilities, including mental disabilities remain unrealized. Approximately 80% of more than one billion people with disabilities in the world live in the developing countries (World Bank and World Health Organization 2011). The WHO Mental Health Gap Action Program (mhGAP) calls for scaling up services for mental disorders in low- and middle-income countries (World Health Organization 2008). A need for international cooperation has been recognized by the CRPD, Article 32 as well as the SDG 17.

The CRPD can be utilized to implement monitor the progress of SDGs to ensure that people with disabilities, including mental disabilities are not excluded or ignored in policy, planning and practice of health and social services (Bornman 2023). The CRPD provides a trajectory for social inclusion and full participation of people with disabilities, which is crucial to achieve 'society for all' where no one is left behind, as declared by the SDGs.

2.6.2 The UN Resolution on Mental Health and Psychosocial Support, 2023

The UN adopted a resolution on mental health and psychosocial support for sustainable development on 26th June 2023 (United Nations 2023c). This is a landmark development as it is the first time that the UN General Assembly has adopted a resolution on mental health and explicitly recognized the importance of psychiatry and other mental health professions in providing quality treatments and support to people with psychosocial disabilities. It brings together the principles of the CRPD and the SDGs, reaffirming the human rights and fundamental freedoms of people with disabilities, including psychosocial disabilities and that the promotion of mental health and well-being is an essential component of universal health coverage. The resolution urges the Member States to promote and improve mental health services by integrating a human rights perspective into mental health and community services and to adopt, update and implement laws and policies to eliminate stigma, discrimination, abuse, social exclusion, unlawful deprivation of liberty, institutionalization and overmedicalization. It calls upon the Member States to invest in community-based mental health services, integrated with primary health care. It encourages the Member States to include mental health and psychosocial support needs in emergency preparedness and response plans recognizing the need to address psychological trauma in humanitarian emergencies including disasters and armed conflict.

The resolution draws attention to the important issue of a robust mental health workforce by encouraging the Member States to scale up efforts to recruit and retain competent and skilled community health workers and mental health professionals and to provide incentives to have an equitable distribution of qualified health workers especially in rural and underserved areas, by providing appropriate remuneration and safe working conditions. It also encourages full, effective and meaningful participation of persons with psychosocial disabilities and their representatives in planning and implementation of laws, policies and service delivery. The resolution urges the Member States to address the social, economic and environmental determinants of health, including mental health by addressing the barriers arising from underdevelopment, poverty and inequalities. It specifically urges the Member States to adopt prevention strategies to address depression and suicide, especially among young people through multisectorial strategies including antenatal and postnatal care for new mothers; promoting mental health of parents and caregivers; provision of early childhood and school-based programmes to support socioemotional life, resilience and healthy relationships and programmes to prevent online and offline bullying and violence. This resolution also recognizes the needs and vulnerabilities of migrants, refugees, displaced persons, women and girls, persons with disabilities and older persons, and Indigenous Peoples and other marginalized populations requiring special focus on their mental health promotion and well-being. The resolution highlights the need for international cooperation to work together to promote mental health and uphold the inherent dignity and human rights of persons with psychosocial disabilities. It calls upon the Member States to improve research capacity, academic collaboration and the knowledgebase and skills of primary and specialized health workers to deliver evidence-based and culturally appropriate mental health and psychosocial support services.

The resolution requires the UN Secretary-General to provide a progress report on its implementation, in consultation with the Member States, the WHO and other relevant agencies and stakeholders in 2 years in September 2025.

Together, the CRPD, the SDGs and the UN Resolution on Mental Health and Psychosocial Disabilities provide a horizon and vehicle for mental health promotion and protection of human rights of persons with psychosocial disabilities, reaffirming mental health as an integral part of universal health coverage.

2.7 Terminology

2.7.1 Illness, Impairment and Disability

While the CRPD does not define 'disability', Article 1 of the CRPD states: 'Persons with disabilities include those who have long-term physical, mental, intellectual or sensory impairments, which in interaction with various barriers, may hinder their full and effective participation in society on an equal basis with others.' The use of term disability in the CRPD defines disability as the result of interactions between persons with impairment and environmental barriers that hinder their full and effective participation in society (United Nations 2006). A person with an illness may not always have an impairment which may lead to disability. Similarly a mental illness may or may not produce a 'mental impairment' or 'mental disability' (Rudnick 2014; Szmukler et al. 2014).

The WHO International Classification of Impairments, Disabilities and Handicaps (1980) considered disability as 'a restriction or lack (resulting from an impairment) of ability to perform an activity in a manner or within the range considered normal for a human being' (World Health Organization 1980, p. 143). According to this definition, an illness (including a mental illness) may cause an impairment in functioning, and such an impairment can cause a disability if it leads to a lack of ability to perform an activity. The World Health Organization has, in the course of discussions about the definition of terms, also introduced the term handicap which refers to the social disadvantages caused by the disability. Thus, for example, a person who has a *disease* may experience an *impairment,* for example, an amputation of a finger which makes it impossible to use certain apparatus *(disability)* which may lead to a loss of employment *(handicap)*. In modern discourse, handicap has been removed and disability is the term used in a more comprehensive and less precise manner. Although there is no standard, universally accepted definition of 'mental disability', at minimum, it can be safely assumed that people with 'long-term' or recurrent mental illness may be included among persons with impairments which lead to disabilities as per Article 1 of the CRPD (Perlin and Szeli 2012; Rudnick 2014; Szmukler et al. 2014). The meaning of 'long term' is also not clear—how long is long term? Therefore, it must be recognized that not all persons with a mental illness have an impairment which produces a disability at all times.

In this book, we have included case vignettes of people with acute mental distress as well as severe and persistent mental illness, who may or may not meet the criteria for long-term mental impairments. It is envisaged that while the CRPD would be applicable to only those with long-term mental impairments (*which in interaction with various barriers, may hinder their full and effective participation in society on an equal basis with others),* the application of the CRPD to mental health policy and law will change mental health practice in such a way that would result in better mental health care and human rights standards of all people with mental illness, whether or not they have a 'disability'. Individual chapter authors and commentators on case vignettes in this book have used various terms like mental illness, mental disorders, mental health conditions, mental disability and psychosocial disability. The lack of consensus about the language to use in organizing care and protecting the human rights of people affected by mental illness has been and continues to be a major obstacle to success of the Convention.

2.7.2 Patient, Client, Consumer, Service-User and Persons with Mental Disabilities

The other significant semantic issue is the term used for persons living with mental illness or those affected by its consequences. A variety of terms—for example, patients, clients, people with lived experience, people with mental health conditions, consumers and service-users—have been used in the literature for persons with mental illness. There is no consensus satisfying everybody, and it is generally agreed that people with mental illness or its consequences are the ones who should decide what terms should be used. While this principle is accepted, it does represent a difficulty in the relevant literature. Having acknowledged the above issues, all of the above terms, i.e. 'patient', 'client', 'consumer', 'service-user' and 'person with a mental disability' have been used interchangeably by different authors in this book.

2.8 Conclusion

In view of the variety of issues described above it is best to take a pragmatic attitude and view the CRPD as an instrument which can help to advance autonomy and supported decision-making provisions, intensify the development and application of alternatives to coercion, and support the realization of economic, social and cultural rights, for example, housing, employment, social inclusion, early access to treatment and voluntary care (Gill 2019; Bernadette McSherry and Wilson 2015). Upholding the spirit of the CRPD, therefore, goes well beyond law reform, into the realm of improving service provision and social attitudes (Carney and Beaupert 2013). The paradigm shift signalled by the CRPD involves a fundamental shift in epistemological and ontological understanding of human rights of people with disabilities (Series 2019). Such paradigm shift will neither be without impediments, nor easy to implement. While it is important to ensure that 'progressive realisation' (as allowed by Article 4(2) of the CRPD) does not become a justification for inaction, a stalemate cannot be permitted between the diverse stakeholders from different geographical, cultural, economic and political backgrounds and with contradictory opinions and ideologies (Bartlett 2014). *A 'crucial conversation' needs to take place, when stakes are high, opinions vary and emotions run strong* (Patterson et al. 2002). It is difficult to imagine a conversation more crucial, than the one initiated by the CRPD. It will involve international, inter-disciplinary and public debate; a social movement for awareness-raising and reform; and rational arguments against hostile inertia or cognitive dissonance of people in different camps holding extreme views. We hope that this book will help to promote this crucial conversation and provide practical ways forward to implement the principles of the CRPD for protection and promotion of the human rights of people with mental illness.

References

Alegría M, NeMoyer A, Falgàs Bagué I, Wang Y, Alvarez K (2018) Social determinants of mental health: where we are and where we need to go. Curr Psychiatry Rep 20(11):95. https://doi.org/10.1007/s11920-018-0969-9

Appelbaum PS (2019) Saving the UN convention on the rights of persons with disabilities–from itself. World Psychiatry 18(1):1

Bartlett P (2014) Implementing a paradigm shift: implementing the convention on the rights of persons with disabilities in the context of mental disability law. In: Torture in healthcare settings: reflections on the special rapporteur on Torture's 2013 thematic report. Centre for Human Rights and Humanitarian Law, American University Washington College of Law, Washington, pp 169–180

Bornman J (2023) Communication, disability, and human rights: exploring the role of the sustainable development goals. In: Handbook of speech-language therapy in sub-Saharan Africa: integrating research and practice. Springer, Cham, pp 559–580

Callaghan S, Ryan CJ (2012) Rising to the human rights challenge in compulsory treatment—new approaches to mental health law in Australia. Aust N Z J Psychiatry 46(7):611–620. https://doi.org/10.1177/0004867412438872

Callaghan SM, Ryan C (2014) Is there a future for involuntary treatment in rights-based mental health law? Psychiatry Psychol Law 21(5):747–766

Callard F, Sartorius N, Arboleda-Flórez J, Bartlett P, Helmchen H, Stuart H et al (2012) Mental illness, discrimination and the law: fighting for social justice. Wiley, Chichester

Carney T, Beaupert F (2013) Public and private Bricolage-challenges balancing law, services and civil society in advancing CRPD supported decision-making. UNSWLJ 36:175

United Nations Committee on the Rights of Persons with Disabilities (2014) General comment 1. Convention on the rights of persons with disabilities. Committee on the rights of persons with disabilities. https://documents-dds-ny.un.org/doc/UNDOC/GEN/G14/031/20/PDF/G1403120.pdf?OpenElement

Dawson J (2015) A realistic approach to assessing mental health laws' compliance with the UNCRPD. Int J Law Psychiatry 40:70–79

Dudley M, Silove D, Gale F (2012) Mental health, human rights, and their relationship: an introduction. In: Dudley M, Silove D, Gale F (eds) Mental health and human rights: vision, praxis, and courage. Oxford University Press, pp 1–49

Dybdahl R, Lien L (2018) Mental health is an integral part of the sustainable development goals. Prevent Med Commun Health 1.

Freeman MC, Kolappa K, de Almeida JMC, Kleinman A, Makhashvili N, Phakathi S et al (2015) Reversing hard won victories in the name of human rights: a critique of the general comment on article 12 of the UN convention on the rights of persons with disabilities. Lancet Psychiatry 2(9):844–850

Gill NS (2019) Human rights framework: an ethical imperative for psychiatry. Aust N Z J Psychiatry 53(1):8–10

Gill N, Drew N, Rodrigues M, Muhsen H, Morales G, Savage M, Pathare S, Allan J, Galderisi S, Javed A, Herrman H, Funk M (2024) Bringing together the WHO QualityRights initiative and the WPA position statement on implementing alternatives to coercion in mental health care—a common goal for action. BJPsych Open 10(e23):1–7

Gómez LE, Morán ML, Navas P, Verdugo MÁ, Schalock RL, Lombardi M et al (2022) Using the quality of life framework to operationalize and assess the CRPD articles and the Sustainable Development Goals. J Policy Pract Intellect Disabil 21:e12470

Gostin LO, Gable L (2004) The human rights of persons with mental disabilities: a global perspective on the application of human rights principles to mental health. Maryland Law Rev 63(1):20–121

Guilloud SD (2019) The right to liberty of persons with psychosocial disabilities at the United Nations: a tale of two interpretations. Int J Law Psychiatry 66:101497

Herrman H, Allan J, Galderisi S, Javed A, Rodrigues M (2022) & WPA task force on implementing alternatives to coercion in mental health care. Alternatives to coercion in mental health care, WPA Position Statement and Call to Action

Jones M (2005) Can international law improve mental health? Some thoughts on the proposed convention on the rights of people with disabilities. Int J Law Psychiatry 28(2):183–205. https://doi.org/10.1016/j.ijlp.2005.03.003

Kumar P, Brander L, Kumar M, Cuijpers P (2023) Planetary health and mental health nexus: benefit of environmental management. Ann Glob Health 89(1):49.

Mann J, Gostin L, Gruskin S, Brennan T, Lazzarini Z, Fineberg H (1994) Health and human rights. RTs:1–6

Martin W, Gurbai S (2019) Surveying the Geneva impasse: coercive care and human rights. Int J Law Psychiatry 64:117–128

McSherry B (2010) The right of access to mental health care: voluntary treatment and the role of law. In: McSherry BW, Weller P (eds) Rethinking rights-based mental health laws. Hart Publishing, Oxford, pp 379–396

McSherry B (2014) Mental health laws: where to from here. Monash UL Rev 40(1):175–197

McSherry B, Wilson K (2015) The concept of capacity in Australian mental health law reform: going in the wrong direction? Int J Law Psychiatry 40:60–69

Mezzina R, Rosen A, Amering M, Javed A (2019) The practice of freedom: human rights and the global mental health agenda. In: Advances in psychiatry. Springer, Cham, pp 483–515

Minkowitz T (2010) Abolishing mental health laws to comply with the convention on the rights of persons with disabilities. In: McSherry B, Weller P (eds) Rethinking rights-based mental health law. Hart publishing, Oregon, pp 151–177

Patel V, Saxena S, Lund C, Thornicroft G, Baingana F, Bolton P et al (2018) The Lancet Commission on global mental health and sustainable development. Lancet 392(10157):1553–1598. https://doi.org/10.1016/s0140-6736(18)31612-x

Patterson K, Grenny J, McMillan R, Switzler A (2002) Crucial conversations: tools for talking when stakes are high. Tata McGraw-Hill Education, New York

Perlin ML, Szeli E (2012) Mental health law and human rights—evolution and contemporary challenges. In:

Dudley M, Silove D, Gale F (eds) Mental health and human rights: vision, praxis, and courage. Oxford University Press, Oxford
Ouliaris C, Gill N, Castan M, Sundram S (2024) OPCAT: how an international treaty regarding torture is relevant to the Australian mental health system. Australian & New Zealand Journal of Psychiatry 00048674231221419
Rudnick A (2014) What is a psychiatric disability? Health Care Anal 22(2):105–113. https://doi.org/10.1007/s10728-012-0235-y
Sen A (1999) Developement as freedom. Oxford University Press, New York
Series L (2019) Disability and human rights. In: Routledge handbook of disability studies. Taylor & Francis, New York
Szmukler G, Daw R, Callard F (2014) Mental health law and the UN convention on the rights of persons with disabilities. Int J Law Psychiatry 37(3):245–252. https://doi.org/10.1016/j.ijlp.2013.11.024
United Nations (1948) The universal declaration of human rights. United Nations. http://www.un.org/en/documents/udhr/
United Nations (1965). International Convention on the Elimination of All Forms of Racial Discrimination, A/RES/44/25 C.F.R.
United Nations (1979) Convention on the Elimination of All Forms of Discrimination against Women
United Nations (1966a) International covenant on civil and political rights.
United Nations (1966b) International covenant on economic, social and cultural rights.
United Nations (1984) Convention against Torture and Other Cruel, Inhuman or Degrading Treatment or Punishment.
United Nations (1990a) Convention on the Rights of the Child, A/RES/44/25 C.F.R
United Nations. (1990b). International Convention on the Protection of the Rights of All Migrant Workers and Members of Their Families
United Nations (1991) Principles for protection of persons with mental illness and for the improvement of mental health care (MI Principles)
United Nations (1993) United Nations general assembly: Vienna declaration and program of action. New York Retrieved from. http://www.ohchr.org/EN/ProfessionalInterest/Pages/Vienna.aspx
United Nations (2002) Optional protocol to the convention against torture and other cruel. Inhuman or Degrading Treatment or Punishment
United Nations (2006) Convention on the Rights of Persons with Disabilities, adopted on 13 December 2006, GA Res 61/106, UN Doc A/Res/61/106 (entered into force 3 May 2008). https://www.un.org/development/desa/disabilities/convention-on-the-rights-of-persons-with-disabilities.html
United Nations (2015) The Millennium development goals report 2015. https://www.un.org/millenniumgoals/2015_MDG_Report/pdf/MDG%202015%20rev%20(July%201).pdf
United Nations (2021) The sustainable development goals report 2021. https://unstats.un.org/sdgs/report/2021/The-Sustainable-Development-Goals-Report-2021.pdf
United Nations (2023a) The 17 goals. https://sdgs.un.org/goals
United Nations (2023b) The Sustainable Development Goals Report 2023: Special edition. https://unstats.un.org/sdgs/report/2023/The-Sustainable-Development-Goals-Report-2023.pdf
United Nations (2023c) UN General Assembly Resolution A/RES/77/300. Adopted 26th June 2023: Mental Health and psychosocial support. https://digitallibrary.un.org/record/4014613?ln=en#record-files-collapse-header
United Nations Committee on the Rights of Persons with Disabilities (2014) General Comment No. 1 (2014). Article 12—equal recognition before the law. 11th session, March 31–April 11, 2014. https://documents--dds-ny.un.org/doc/UNDOC/GEN/G14/031/20/PDF/G1403120.pdf?OpenElement
United Nations General Assembly (2015).Transforming our world: the 2030 agenda for sustainable development. https://documents-dds-ny.un.org/doc/UNDOC/GEN/N15/291/89/PDF/N1529189.pdf?OpenElement
Wescott HN, MacLachlan M, Mannan H (2020) Disability inclusion and global development: a preliminary analysis of the United Nations Partnership on the Rights of Persons with Disabilities programme within the context of the Convention on the Rights of Persons with Disabilities and the Sustainable Development Goals. Disability CBR Inclusive Dev *31*(4):90–115
World Bank and World Health Organization (2011) World report on disability. World Health Organization, Geneva. https://www.who.int/publications/i/item/9789241564182
World Health Organization (1980) International classification of impairments, disabilities, and handicaps: a manual of classification relating to the consequences of disease, published in accordance with resolution WHA29. 35 of the Twenty-ninth World Health Assembly, May 1976.
World Health Organization (2008) mhGAP: Mental Health Gap Action Programme: scaling up care for mental, neurological and substance use disorders. World Health Organization, Geneva
World Health Organization (2019). WHO QualityRights initiative - improving quality, promoting human rights. Retrieved from https://www.who.int/mental_health/policy/quality_rights/en/
World Health Organization (2023) Mental health, human rights and legislation: guidance and practice. In Mental health, human rights and legislation: guidance and practice
World Psychiatric Association (2020a) Implementing alternatives to coercion: a key component of improving mental health care. Retrieved from, Position Statment. https://www.wpanet.org/_files/ugd/e172f3_635a89af889c471683c29fcd981db0aa.pdf
World Psychiatric Association (2020b) Implementing alternatives to coercion in mental health care. Retrieved from, Discussion paper from the Task Force. https://3ba346de-fde6-473f-b1da-536498661f9c.filesusr.com/ugd/e172f3_3702b1a4202c458b85451e6d74075cbc.pdf

Part II

The Application of the CRPD and Related Regulations in Mental Health Care Practice: Issues Arising

3 Issues Arising in the Application of the CRPD in Practice - Case Histories

Neeraj Gill, Norman Sartorius, Charlene Sunkel, Martha Savage, Michaela Amering, Michael Evans, Oye Gureje, Cecile Hanon, Andreas Heinz, Mohan Isaac, Nicolás Martínez-López, Sabine Müller, Soumitra Pathare, and Assina Seitz

Neeraj Gill wrote the case histories, with input from Norman Sartorius, Charlene Sunkel and Martha Savage. All the other authors, including Charlene Sunkel and Martha Savage provided commentaries on the case histories. Michael Evans helped in the organization of the work and preparation of the chapter. Neeraj Gill and Norman Sartorius edited the commentaries and prepared conclusions.

N. Gill (✉)
School of Medicine and Dentistry, Griffith University, Gold Coast, Australia

Mental Health Policy Unit, Health Research Institute, University of Canberra, Canberra, Australia

Mental Health and Specialist Services, Gold Coast Health, Gold Coast, Australia
e-mail: neeraj.gill@griffith.edu.au

N. Sartorius
Association for the Improvement of Mental Health Programmes, Geneva, Switzerland
e-mail: sartorius@normansartorius.com

C. Sunkel
Global Mental Health Peer Network, Paarl, South Africa
e-mail: charlene.sunkel@gmhpn.org

M. Savage
School of Geography, Environment and Earth Science, Victoria University of Wellington, Te Herenga Waka, Wellington, New Zealand
e-mail: Martha.Savage@vuw.ac.nz

M. Amering
Clinical Division of Social Psychiatry, Department of Psychiatry and Psychotherapy, Medical University of Vienna, Vienna, Austria
e-mail: michaela.amering@meduniwien.ac.at

M. Evans
School of Medicine and Dentistry, Griffith University, Gold Coast, Australia

Mental Health and Specialist Services, Gold Coast Health, Gold Coast, Australia
e-mail: michael.evans4@health.qld.gov.au

O. Gureje
WHO Collaborating Centre for Research and Training in Mental Health, Neuroscience, Drug and Alcohol Abuse, Department of Psychiatry, University of Ibadan, Oyo, Nigeria
e-mail: ogureje@com.ui.edu.ng

C. Hanon
Regional Resource Center of old age Psychiatry, APHP, University of Paris, Paris, France
e-mail: cecile.hanon@aphp.fr

A. Heinz · S. Müller · A. Seitz
Klinik für Psychiatrie und Psychotherapie, CCM, Charité—Universitätsmedizin Berlin, Berlin, Germany
e-mail: andreas.heinz@charite.de; Mueller.sabine@charite.de; assina.seitz@charite.de

M. Isaac
School of Medicine, University of Western Australia, Perth, Australia

N. Martínez-López
Clinical Epidemiology Laboratory, Ramón de la Fuente Muñiz National Institute of Psychiatry (INPRFM), Mexico City, Mexico

S. Pathare
Centre for Mental Health Law and Policy, Indian Law Society, Pune, India
e-mail: spathare@cmhlp.org

N. Gill, N. Sartorius (eds.), *Mental Health and Human Rights*, Sustainable Development Goals Series, https://doi.org/10.1007/978-3-031-52179-9_3

Contents

3.1 Introduction to Case Histories

As mentioned earlier, the case history method was adopted in this book to explore ways to protect and promote human rights of persons with mental illness and to understand how the Convention on the Rights of the Persons with Disabilities (CRPD) can be applied in real-life scenarios in clinical practice (United Nations, 2006). To explore complex issues raised by the CRPD, the World Psychiatric Association (WPA) brought together psychiatrists, persons who experienced mental illness and persons who provided formal and informal care to people with mental illness, to discuss what could be the best way to act in different frequently occurring situations and examine whether the best course of action for the person with an impairment and those around them is in harmony with the CRPD requirements. The persons invited to participate in these discussions were from different countries ranging from low-, middle-, to high-income countries, A commentator with lived experience of mental illness from South Africa and commentator who was a family/carer from New Zealand provided service-user and carer lived experience voices. Psychiatrists who provided commentary had expertise in law, ethics, and/or public health in addition to clinical psychiatry. The psychiatrist commentators were from Australia, Austria, France, Germany, India, Mexico, and Nigeria.

The discussants were presented life stories of 13 persons and a public mental health scenario. The case histories are deliberately kept brief and aim to raise different kinds of questions regarding desirable and undesirable actions in each situation.

The participants in the case history exploration were asked the following questions:

1. What should have been done in this case? Were there any other options to act and if so, in which order?
2. How does the context, e.g., the wealth/resources of the country, ease of access to health services, the number and qualifications of staff working in mental health services, or availability of medications influence the order of actions?
3. In what way would the CRPD require different action from that taken and how could the differing demands or actions be reconciled?

In some vignettes, specific questions were asked regarding how to ensure that mental health care was compliant with the provisions of CRPD and human rights-based care. While there was a strong consensus among commentators about most issues, there were some disagreements. We hope to generate discussion and debate about whether that points toward the need to update views and practice to be compliant with the CRPD or whether that sheds light on conflicts and controversies in interpretation and application of the CRPD. It is possible that readers from different backgrounds and various regions of the world will disagree with the commentators and may have a different interpretation and recommendation for the course of action in certain vignettes and that will make them examine the best way to help people with mental health conditions in harmony with the CRPD and related legislation.

This collection of case histories misses certain important themes, which we hope to include in subsequent discussions about the CRPD using the case history method. For example, there is only one vignette related to a person below the age of 18 and we realize the need for a more thorough discussion on application of the CRPD in the care provided to children and adolescents. Similarly, there is only one vignette related to the rights of the elderly people with disabilities related to conditions in the elderly, e.g., dementia. While drug and alcohol use issues are incorporated in a few of these case vignettes, those are not the specifically dealt with and there should be more elaborate discussion on conflicts and controversies related to the intersection of human rights with drug and alcohol use disorders. Intellectual disability is another area that requires further exploration.

We hope that such case histories and others described in the local environment will be produced and used in further work related to the application of the CRPD and in efforts to protect the human rights of people with mental illness.

3.2 Case History 1: A Young Man Imprisoned for Symptoms of Mental Illness

John is a 23-year-old man who lives with his mother in a small town in South Africa. He was diagnosed with schizophrenia 2 years ago and was prescribed antipsychotic medications. He ceased his medication within a few months, due to side effects. He had informed his psychiatrist of the side effects but was told that he had to remain on the medication.

Soon after stopping the medication, he started to experience psychotic symptoms. He started hearing voices and seeing people outside the windows of his home. He got very agitated and started to smash the windows at home. His mother was very frightened and had no option other than calling the police. The police arrested John and charged him with wilful damage to property.

Despite his mother informing the public lawyer of John's mental health issues, this was never introduced in court as part of his defence, and he was convicted and sentenced. In prison, he was stigmatized and bullied by other prisoners because of his psychiatric diagnosis. The prison did not have proper mental health care or medications, and his condition deteriorated. His mother ended up supplying his medication to the prison.

After 6 months, John was released on parole. He returned to university and graduated, only to find that no one would employ him because he had a criminal record, this caused further distress and depression.

Further specific questions in addition to the standard questions:

- Would the introduction of an insanity plea and diversion from the prison system to the health system be justified under the CRPD?
- Would court-ordered forced treatment be justified if John refused treatment in prison?

3.2.1 Commentary

3.2.1.1 Charlene Sunkel, Service-User Representative, South Africa

First and foremost, this matter should never have been dealt with as a criminal matter but rather should have recognized and acknowledged that John's actions could have resulted from his mental health frame of mind at the time of the incident and that would have been substantiated by his known history with a diagnosis of schizophrenia. Unnecessarily taking a legal route could have had a significant impact on John's emotional state and obstructed his possibilities for recovery to where he could return to building a career as a young person and to becoming an independent and self-sufficient adult who is able to thrive in society.

Another important aspect was his mother's level of understanding of her son's mental health condition and how to support and help him. At the point where John received his diagnosis, the psychiatrist should have adequately informed his mother about John's condition and how to apply de-escalation techniques should a situation arises where he becomes agitated and potentially aggressive. John at the same time should have been included in these conversations to help his mother understand from his own perspective about what he experienced and how he would like to be treated when he has a relapse or finds himself in emotional crisis. Families should always be included in the treatment and recovery plans of a loved one (unless explicitly objected by the person (patient)).

The process of John having been taken to hospital needs a lot of rethinking and transformation. Communication with the person is often the first failure of attempts to help a person who is experiencing an emotional crisis or relapse, as it often denies the person to be involved in decision-making or providing for supported decision-making if required. In my experience in South Africa and under its Mental Health Care Act, when a person is deemed a danger to him/herself or others and is refusing treatment, the involvement of the South African Police Service comes into effect, whereby the police's role is mainly to assist in escorting the person to a general hospital with a psychiatric ward where this person will be assessed and where it will be determined if necessary to implement involuntary admission. Yet, before all this, it rarely happens that a conversation takes place with the person to ask basic questions of which the most important one is "how can I/we support and help you," rather the decision is instantaneously taken away from the person by activating an involuntary admission process without any form of communication or engagement with the person. At this point, a conversation could de-escalate a volatile situation and lead to voluntary admission instead of coercion. The second flaw in the system is the involvement of the police (unless of course a crime has been committed), which only promotes stigma and associates mental health conditions with crime.

Misdemeanor crimes, such as in John's case (breaking windows) and where the act was potentially related to a mental health condition and where a history of a mental health condition exists, should avoid involvement of the justice system and rather directed to the mental health system. For such a system to be efficient and effective, a collaborative coordination between key role players of cases should be implemented, including family support and empowerment programs and peer support services; and justice and health systems, to identify and distinguish between a crime and a mental health crisis, and facilitate accordingly.

Unfortunately, in South Africa, (formal) Peer Support Work does not exist within the mental health system, which could be valuable in helping to close the human resources gap.

3.2.1.2 Martha Savage, Family/Carer Representative, New Zealand

1. Other options and order in which they should have been done:
   (a) John's psychiatrist should have worked with him to try to find alternative medicines or helped him to stop medicine more slowly so that he could have returned to treatment when things started going wrong. He could have been taught warning signs and techniques to avoid obeying the voices if they started and he could have been given a peer mentor to help him if things were going badly.
   (b) John's mother should have been trained in warning signs and in de-escalation procedures and given information on whom to call if John had problems.
   (c) In New Zealand, there would have been a Mental Health Crisis team that John's mother could have called for help. They would have evaluated John and calmed him down and they might have persuaded him to go to a hospital for treatment. The police should not have charged John—they should have taken him to a hospital with a psychiatric unit or a Mental Health Crisis team for evaluation.
   (d) The defense lawyer should have used John's psychiatric state as a defense for his behavior. John's mother should have tried to get them to drop the charges.
   (e) The prison should have had a forensic psychiatry unit where John could have been given better treatment. They should have been able to get medicine for him.

(f) Employers should not have discriminated against John for his criminal record or his disability.
(g) Now, he could still try to find a more enlightened employer. He could volunteer at something related to his interests to get more experience and a "foot in the door" and to give him a purpose while he continues to apply for jobs. He and his mother should get counselling to help him.

The state breached John's right to access to justice. The police breached John's right to a high standard of health by taking him to jail instead of to a mental health facility. The prison breached several human rights: freedom from exploitation, violence, and abuse; and the right to the enjoyment of the highest attainable standard of health without discrimination on the basis of disability. This was breached by not having adequate facilities for people with psychosocial disabilities. See above for what should have been done. As mentioned above, the prison should have dedicated mental health professionals and a forensic unit. The prison might have done better with more staff, but the country could have saved a lot more money by keeping John out of prison in the first place.

- Would the introduction of insanity plea and diversion from prison system to health system be justified under the CRPD?

  Yes. Particularly in regard to proportionality of the crime. A few windows broken for the "crime" of not continuing medicine should not justify a prison term.

Would court-ordered forced treatment be justified in case John refused treatment in prison?

This does not seem to be relevant since the prison doesn't even seem to have any mental health treatment systems available. But if forced treatment could be given instead of prison and the crime had been greater, it could be a good option to give John the choice of prison or treatment.

3.2.1.3 Andreas Heinz, Sabine Müller und Assina Seitz

Klinik für Psychiatrie und Psychotherapie, CCM, Charité—Universitätsmedizin Berlin, Berlin, Germany

First, John like any other patient on medication and upon whom no acute legal restrictions are imposed has every right to stop his medication. His psychiatrist should have discussed with John the potential problems and perspectives of ceasing medication and, in case John still wants to stop taking medication, agreed with him upon a helpful way to gradually phase out medication. Long-term application of dopamine D2-receptor blocking neuroleptics induces an increase in both the number and sensitivity of dopamine D2-receptors (Silvestri et al. 2000; Samaha et al. 2007). Any abrupt cessation of medication therefore carries a risk of triggering another psychotic episode, even stronger than the first one due to the counter adaptive upregulation of dopamine D2-receptors. Therefore, medical doctors must listen to their patients and inform them about helpful ways to reduce medication in case patients want to stop taking the drug.

Several consecutive actions violate John's human rights, including lack of any assessment whether the damage he caused was perpetuated in a psychotic state of mind, thus reducing his ability to understand the current situation and to act in accordance with social expectations and with the law. Moreover, just smashing windows is a minor offence. His psychotic illness was never introduced in court as part of defense and therefore it was not considered when sending John to prison, without offering him any health care options, in violation with UN CRPD Article 25.

Finally, after his release, he is discriminated because of his past imprisonment. Again, the imprisonment itself is highly doubtful, he received no adequate medical treatment, the mitigating effects of his mental disorder when perpetrating the property destruction were not considered, and now he is even discriminated due to having been imprisoned. So, several aspects of discrimination add up in this case.

The case shows that the "insanity plea" and a diversion from the prison system to the health care system might ameliorate some but not all the problems encountered by John. In a health care system, his mental disorder could be treated adequately provided that there are different treatment choices and not only coercion to take medication. Diversion to the health care system has by some, but not all on board, understood as a potential or real violation of Article 14, which requires that "the existence of a disability shall in no case justify a deprivation of liberty." In John's case, deprivation of liberty was carried out under a legal system that is equal for all persons with and without disabilities. Therefore, there was no violation of this article; however, John was punished extremely hard, out of proportion to the alleged offence and was denied any adequate medical service, thus violating Article 25 of the UN CRPD.

In Germany, court-ordered forced treatment is permitted only in rare situations according to decisions of the Federal Constitutional Court of Germany and accordingly reformed laws. Particularly, forced treatments are not allowed with the only aim of preventing harm to third persons, because then confinement is seen as sufficient to reduce the danger. However, the German laws allow involuntary treatment if there is lack of insight due to a mental disorder in two situations: first, to prevent harm from the person herself; second, to restore insight. Insight in these circumstances is defined according to the capacity to consent to a medical treatment, which requires insight in the potentials and dangers of the treatment as well as in the risks of non-treatment, plus it requires an ability to act according to this insight.

3.2.1.4 Michaela Amering, Psychiatrist, Austria

This should have played out differently, for sure. John's doctor should have been able to react to the fact that John had a right to all the necessary information and probably extra support for his plan to stop his medication. And a more active management to deal with the reported unwanted effects of the medication in the first place might have resulted in John's decision to continue the medication or reduce safely. With or without considering the CRPD, his right to adequate health care seems to have been violated.

In addition, one wonders whether John and his mother have been offered the information and support that would have put her in a position to call a mental health crisis or emergency team instead or along with the police.

Whether such harsh prison sentence for such a minor offense must be considered a discrimination depends on the reasoning for this hopefully unusual decision and John should certainly have had best legal support to negotiate or fight this decision and/or enter a court-diversion scheme, which might or should exist for an offence of this nature and context.

However, once in prison his rights as a prisoner to health and mental health care have been violated. At this point, I wonder whether the CRPD obligations from Article 26 Rehabilitation and Article 27 Work and Employment might help this very unfortunate situation, which seems a result of prior rights violations.

3.2.1.5 Oye Gureje, Psychiatrist, Nigeria

The first thing that should have been done in John's case was to find the appropriate medication that would cause him less troubling side effects that resulted in the cessation of medication. Perhaps, if the right medication or the least problematic dose had been worked out in partnership with him, he might not have had a relapse that resulted in the violent episode that led to the involvement of the police. Working out an appropriate medication and dosage would involve engagement with the patient and might take time, conditions that might not be easy in settings where the clinician is under intense time pressure because of case load or where there is a limited number of drugs to choose from.

John's mother turned to the police when confronted with the crisis of John's acute relapse as she had no other recourse. If she had been in a setting where more a comprehensive and agile mental health service was available, this would not have been necessary. A crisis assessment and treatment team with appropriate level of staffing would arrive at the scene and arrange for John to be taken to a treatment facility rather than to a police detention center.

The police, in responding to John's behavior, did not consider the possibility that his illness might have been responsible for the manifest violence and that the appropriate action to take was to transfer him to a health facility where he could receive treatment. The judge, in deciding on how to respond to John's violent behavior, also did not consider the role John's clinical condition could have played in his behavior. The judge could have sought a medical opinion and use such opinion to make the appropriate decision which would have been to ask that John be availed treatment. These shortcomings most likely reflect a general lack of awareness and training by law officers or, perhaps, an absence of codified laws to protect persons with mental illness.

Prisons are rarely a good place to receive appropriate and adequate care by persons with mental illness. However, the situation in which John found himself in the facility to which he was sentenced appeared to be even worse than the average with him having no access to medications to treat his condition. His experience of bullying is a direct assault on his right to be treated with dignity.

Finally, the series of unfortunate events to which John was exposed culminated in his not being able to gain employment. Crucially, this was not even because of his illness, from which he had made good recovery, but from the incarceration which he was clearly undeserving. While it is common that, in many jurisdictions, laws exist to protect persons with history of mental illness from being denied access to employment for which they were otherwise qualified, the same is not quite true for persons with history of criminal conviction. Thus, John would not have been protected from this denial of right to gainful employment even if a law specifically targeting persons with mental illness existed in his setting since his illness was not the basis of his being denied employment.

3.2.1.6 Cecile Hanon, Psychiatrist, France

John should have been listened to when he said he was experiencing side effects and offered an alternative treatment in order to promote adherence with medication, in accordance with the principle of autonomy and beneficence. It is the patient who knows what is good for him, better than the doctor. Not listening to the patient led to a breakdown in treatment and a psychotic relapse.

Being seen as guilty and incarcerated affected John's human rights. As he was unable to meet with a mental health professional in prison, he suffered a loss of opportunity to access care, and stigmatization from fellow inmates.

The CRPD requires the right to health protected as well as the right to autonomy and freedom from discrimination and hence John should have received proper treatment.

In France, there are consultation services in all prisons, and for some regions, there are hospitalization units outside of detention centers.

Would court-ordered forced treatment be justified in case John refused treatment in prison?

Initially, depending on his symptoms and agitation, this may be necessary. Once he has calmed down, it will be important to discuss with John to ensure compliance, and depending on his tolerance, to prescribe a suitable drug that he will tolerate well without side effects.

3.2.1.7 Nicolás Martínez-López, Forensic Psychiatrist, Mexico

In the first place, the diagnosis was timely and there was adequate adherence to treatment; however, John had side effects that, due to their manifestation and apparent lack of solution by the psychiatrist, led to the abandonment of treatment. Up to this point, John clearly has adequate cognitive capacity and like anyone else he was free to withhold medication in recognition of his legal capacity in the convention.

When John's symptoms that lead to agitation and aggression qualify as a psychiatric emergency and need attention in a medical service. By not having this and being reported for damage to property and not establishing criminal responsibility, he is judged as fully capable at the time of the alleged offence; a situation that leads to unjustified deprivation of liberty.

Different reasonable adjustments could have been made from calling emergency services for his care in the health sector, the policeman, with appropriate training in mental health, suggested taking John to a clinic for his emergency care, to home-based services where the psychotic crisis John presented could be treated at home.

Finally, given the form of resolution of the case, the stigma that prevails over John is not only for having schizophrenia, but also for having a criminal record, violating his human right to work and recognition of his legal capacity.

3.2.1.8 Soumitra Pathare, Psychiatrist, India

This case vignette highlights how the unnecessary criminalization of mental health symptoms has long-term deleterious effects on the lives of persons with mental illness leading to exclusion and preventing effective rehabilitation in society.

John had caused non-personal violence under the influence of symptoms of mental illness. Legal systems need to look at other alternatives to dealing with such situations rather than handing down a criminal conviction and prison sentence. John could have been diverted from the criminal justice system to the healthcare system with a probation order. If necessary, the probation order could have mandated his admission to hospital for treatment, followed by discharge and ongoing treatment and support in the community.

Such approach (court-diversion approach) would be entirely consistent with the CRPD's requirements to provide "accommodation" for persons' disabilities in all areas of life. In this case, there would be no need to invoke an insanity plea. The court while recognizing that the person had perpetrated violence could use the probation and health care system to provide effective care and rehabilitation to John as well as future protection of society from such violence.

While the availability of human and other resources in different countries does impact how people are treated for mental illness, I would argue that low resource settings should be particularly keen to move people away from the criminal justice system to the healthcare system. The criminal justice system with its associated court procedures and incarceration of people with mental illness is frequently more expensive than investing the same resources in improving access to and quality of mental health services.

In the vignette, he was sent to prison and the question is whether forced treatment in prison is appropriate. This depends on a number of factors—for example, does John have the capacity to make decisions or is it impaired to an extent that he cannot be expected to provide informed consent? Was support provided to John to understand the treatment options (and the refusal of treatment) and the likely outcome of these different treatment (incl refusal) options? Are the mental health services in the prison of adequate quality?

3.2.1.9 Mohan Isaac, Psychiatrist, Australia

In the first instance, John's relapse of symptoms could have been prevented by appropriately dealing with the distressing side effects of antipsychotic medications that he experienced. While the psychiatrist's advice was right that John had to continue antipsychotic medications, he could have creatively applied principles of "shared decision making" and persuaded John to continue on another antipsychotic with less, different, or no side effects.

While John's mother could not be blamed for seeking police assistance, the police should have taken John to a treatment center (with his past history of mental illness) for restarting treatment and should not have arrested him or charged him for an offence.

The public lawyer entrusted with John's case failed miserably by not informing the court about his mental illness, his past treatment for mental illness, and John's non-adherence to past treatment instructions and medications. Due to the lawyer's ignorance?/neglect?/lack of concern?/poor judgment?/systemic/legislative issues, John had to experience the triple whammy of being jailed, being bullied and stigmatized because of his mental illness and being unemployed due to criminal record although qualified. His rights as an individual as well as a mentally ill person were violated.

Poor awareness and appreciation of the proper ways of managing "treatment non-adherence" in persons with severe mental disorders and lack of concern about their right to treatment, rather than the context of inadequate wealth/resources of the country or number of staff influenced the course of events in John's management. The insanity plea should have been introduced, and John's care should have been diverted from the prison system to the health care system.

I firmly believe that in John's case, a period of court-ordered, mandatory treatment (until John attained adequate insight and capacity to make appropriate treatment choices) would be most appropriate and justified.

3.2.2 Concluding Comments on Case History 1

3.2.2.1 Neeraj Gill and Norman Sartorius

This case history discussion highlights how the criminalization of mental health symptoms has long-term deleterious consequences on the lives of persons with mental illness leading to social exclusion and preventing effective rehabilitation in society. There was remarkable overlap among comments by practicing psychiatrists including those with a special interest in medical ethics, service user, and carer commentators from different parts of the world. However, there were some important differences and disagreements, which merit consideration.

The importance of strong therapeutic alliance, peer support, shared decision-making, and/or supported decision-making was highlighted. It was recognized that John wanted to cease medication despite psychoeducation and medical advice and that the psychiatrist needed to respect John's autonomy, his will, and preference and find a helpful way to gradually phase out medication to avoid abrupt cessation. John and his mother could have been taught the early warning signs of a relapse, de-escalation procedures, and ways to implement early interventions.

There were different opinions about the course of action to deal with John's outburst secondary to his psychotic relapse involving the Mental Health Crisis team or police, for acute response and involuntary psychiatric treatment and containment in a hospital.

There was consensus that this should have been managed by a "health system response" rather than by a justice system response. Some commentators recommended the use of "insanity plea" while one commentator argued for a probation order to mandate hospital treatment, without having to use insanity plea. It was argued that the court-diversion approach would be entirely consistent with the CRPD's requirements to provide "accommodation" for persons' disabilities in all areas of life. It was also argued that in low resource settings, it is particularly important to move people away from the criminal justice system to the healthcare system.

Finally, structural stigma and discrimination due to history of mental illness or criminal conviction were criticized by all commentators, who highlighted the rights to social inclusion and participation, rehabilitation, and work and employment as per the CRPD.

3.3 Case History 2: A Woman Locked Up in a Mental Asylum for 40 Years

Yukiko is a middle-aged woman in Japan. She was diagnosed with schizophrenia at the age of 17. She believed that people on TV were talking about her. She was admitted in a mental hospital for a month, treated and discharged on regular oral medication.

Thereafter, she was symptom-free for almost a year, but she and her family were stigmatized in the community due to her mental illness. Then, she fell and hurt her leg, refused to let her mother attend to the wound and became very agitated. She was committed to a mental hospital again at the age of 18.

Yukiko spent the next 40 years of her life in that mental institution. She was released at the age of 58, when the mental hospital was evacuated in the wake of a natural disaster. On re-evaluation, a community psychiatrist found that she never needed institutionalization. On inquiry, the nursing staff revealed that she was a model patient, although always insisting to be discharged. On several occasions, she tried to escape from the hospital. In view of the fact that until 1980, the family's request was required for a discharge (and Yukiko's brothers were not ready to take her back because they were busy with their families and business), she could not be released from the hospital.

Further specific questions:

- Is such prolonged institutionalization a thing of the past, and does it nowadays happen only in certain countries?
- What should psychiatrists do when the lack of resources in the community prevents the application of correct treatment in the community and follow-up?

3.3.1 Commentary

3.3.1.1 Charlene Sunkel

There is a great emphasis globally on taking a person-centered approach to mental health that means to not primarily focus on the person's mental health condition, but a rather holistic view of the person and that includes responding to physical health conditions or concerns expressed by the individual. The person's mental health condition must never be the primary focus of addressing every physical problem that the person seeks treatment for. Unfortunately, persons with mental health conditions are often not taken seriously when they express other health concerns. Therefore, Yukiko's complaints about her hurting leg should have been attended to and not dismissed as part of symptoms or past history with her mental health condition.

In terms of the community and family and how or what they perceived as "normal" or "acceptable" prevented her from claiming her own identity and making her own choices. Ignorant perceptions, stigma, and discrimination can have a devasting impact on a person's life—and in Yukiko's case, robbed her of 40 years of her life, and opportunities of her youth, and her liberty and security, by unnecessarily detaining her in an institution. Awareness and destigmatization campaigns, involving persons with lived experience, can be a start to effect change and correct the misperceptions of those living with a mental health condition and consider the human life that suffers when that person's voice is silenced.

Long-term institutions should not exist by any means, and a deinstitutionalization process should be facilitated to integrate patients into the community with the necessary support and access to services where they live. Unfortunately, deinstitutionalization in many countries failed, mainly because the resources did not follow the patients to the community, resulting in the individuals being abandoned and neglected.

At the time when Yukiko left the institution with nowhere to go as her brothers were reluctant or not willing at all to welcome her back home, community housing should have been available, but also provided her access to a psychosocial rehabilitation or recovery program, to assist her to adapt after such a long-term detention (in 40 years, the society changes a lot as to how we live our daily lives).

This case presents with multiple human rights violations and contradictions of the CRPD—denied autonomy, identity, personhood, liberty and security, decision-making, or supported decision-making, among others. The implementation of the involuntary treatment and detainment offered her no right to appeal such a decision made about her life without her consent.

3.3.1.2 Martha Savage

1. What should have been done in this case? Were there any other options to act and if so in which order?
   (a) She should never have been taken back to hospital just based on her family's evaluation.
   (b) Her case should have been regularly reviewed and she should have been let out when she asked to be discharged.
   (c) Once Japan signed the CRPD, they should have reviewed her case (and all other ones) and released her into the community.
   (d) Her family should have been offered counselling and help so that they would accept her back.
   (e) She needs to be given support as she returns to life in the community, probably with community housing if the family counselling does not work well.

Japan is a high-income country. It has the third highest GDP in the world. It should have enough money to pay for more staff in psychiatric hospitals. In fact, the problem is that they pay for too many people to be hospitalized. They could save a lot of money by treating people in the community. The problem is the attitudes of the hospital, society, and the family because of stigma of mental illness. According to health ministry data as of the end of June 2017, there were an estimated 280,000 psychiatric inpatients—about 60% hospitalized for more than 1 year, considered "long-term stays," and 55,000 for more than 10 years. It is not a thing of the past. Moreover, Japan uses "treatments" that are actually torture, such as tying people to beds with mechanical restraints for days at a time and isolating them in rooms by themselves. However, Japan at least provides some information about the use of restraints in its hospitals, which is not done in most other Asian countries. So, we don't really know how it compares to other high-income countries in Asia.

The CRPD prescriptions would require her to be treated with respect and if she didn't break any laws she should not be held against her will. She would never have been allowed to be hospitalized the second time, and she should have been released as soon as Japan ratified the CRPD.

What can the psychiatrists do when the issues are related to resources in the community?

Psychiatrists can treat patients with respect. They can work to help educate the community, the patient, and the family to learn how to treat each other fairly and with respect. They can lobby the government for more resources.

3.3.1.3 Andreas Heinz, Sabine Müller und Assina Seitz

Personally, I (AH) encountered patients with decades of legal confinement in 1984 when working for a psychiatry complaint center in Berlin. At the time, there was a change in legislation and all legal confinements in Germany from then on had to be decided by a judge, which in the current legal system also requires an independent medical consultant giving their view on the situation. The average duration of stay in German psychiatric hospitals is now down to 3 weeks, with the exception of forensic psychiatry, which treats patients sentenced to have committed a felony and due to the insanity plea have been placed on a forensic ward. In forensic psychiatry, the duration of legally required stay can be up to many years and there is currently a reform movement trying to limit the overall duration of such stays. Additionally, judges must regularly decide whether the stay is to be prolonged or not, which is currently required on an annual basis.

The whole case of Yukiko is an example of blatant violation of human rights, and it shows that such violations occur in wealthy and industrialized countries, too. Since Yukiko posed no physical harm to any person or herself, there was absolutely no reason to put her into a mental health institution in the first place. Previous diagnoses of mental disorders or causing embarrassment to the family are absolutely no reason to infringe on a person's liberty. Just because a patient's family cannot or will not provide their care, or because a patient has no family, cannot be a reason to place the patient in a psychiatric hospital against their will. In such cases, other forms of care should be found, e.g., assisted living in a shared apartment, if regular care is necessary at all.

3.3.1.4 Michaela Amering

This is a heart-rending story, and many psychiatrists around the globe do not live with the awareness that such a thing can be happening today in any country. However, it does remind me of the fate of people stuck in situations of residential care, which they cannot leave for many years because of the social and/or financial situation and the lack of support for change. An exclusive focus on a maintenance paradigm instead of a collaborative commitment for change as formulated for recovery-orientation can also keep people trapped in community care. I am reminded of a patient who told me "you know, I am a lost case, everything has been tried on me and I don't get better." Then, when you look at his treatment history, you can see that the same thing has been tried over and over again and many interventions that could have possibly changed the situation, have not been offered or are not even available for different and rarely good reasons. Another topic of still more often than not serious neglect of the evidence-base is working with and supporting families with a clear need of improving quality and quantity of working with families as formulated, e.g., by EUFAMI. Regarding this horrible story, Article 8 of the CRPD comes to mind which obliges state parties to work toward awareness raising.

3.3.1.5 Oye Gureje

Yukiko was subjected to an inappropriate and protracted period of institutionalized care not because of symptoms of schizophrenia but because her family was unwilling to agree for her to be discharged back to them because they were unprepared to care for her and, possibly, because of the shame of having a sick family member in their midst.

It seems very likely that with a more personalized care consisting of the choice of appropriate medicine, regular follow-up, and case management, Yukiko would probably have had a favorable course of illness. In the course of that illness, short admissions to respond to any relapse or related indication might have been all that would be required. That is, with a better organized system of care, Yukiko would have been able to remain in the community and probably acquire necessary education or training to make a productive member of the society. Such a well-organized system would have detected the inappropriateness of her institutionalization much earlier than after a long period of 40 years. As it turned out, and in view of the poor care available in the facility where she was admitted, her legitimate request for discharge was described as "obsessive" and denied, leading to several attempts to abscond. It is easy to see how she could have found herself in a vicious cycle where those requests and attempt to leave would have been used as further "proof" of her illness and the need to keep her institutionalized despite the evidence that she was otherwise well behaved.

It is a surprise that Yukiko experienced these series of events in a high-income country. The mental health systems of low- and middle-income countries are more likely to be characterized by lack of the resources to deliver good quality care due to shortage of appropriately trained staff to deliver such service. On the other hand, Yukiko's experience is also a demonstration of the fact that persons with mental illness are often at risk of severe disablement that may be more a consequence of social problems of stigmatization and denial of basic human rights. The specifications of the CRPD, if properly implemented, could have prevented the outcome that Yukiko experienced.

Psychiatrists can help in the situation that Yukiko found herself. First, psychiatrists can ensure that patients in their care receive appropriate treatment that could help prevent or reduce the likelihood of relapse or clinical deterioration. When patients are responding to treatment and are clinically stable, they may be more likely to receive adequate family support and less likely to experience abandonment. Second, psychiatrists can advocate for improvement in mental health service to ensure that policies are made and implemented that provide for adequate staffing of the service as well as provision of social services, including housing, to prevent institutionalization. Third, psychiatrists can ensure that service providers and policy makers are aware of and committed to implementing CRPD as a way of promoting and protecting the human rights of persons with mental illness.

3.3.1.6 Cecile Hanon

It is clear that Yukiko did not need to be hospitalized in this way without psychiatric symptoms, with no indication other than that she needed accommodation, or to relieve her family? Who decided that she could not live alone and independently?

The focus on human rights is on the restriction of movement, on her choice of where to live. She should have been assessed for autonomy in order to provide appropriate care. The family's request was required for her discharge, because she was a minor, during the first year of her hospitalization, between the ages of 17 and 18? If not, was she deemed incompetent?

In France, this type of prolonged stay no longer exists. The decrease in hospital capacity has been such for the last 30 years. At present, as far as public psychiatry is concerned, a psychiatric "sector," which represents a geographical area of 70,000 inhabitants, has 15–20 hospital beds. In addition, there is hospital capacity in private psychiatry, which is more expensive and less socially accessible.

3.3.1.7 Nicolás Martínez-López

This is a case that commonly happens in Mexico, unfortunately the stigma that weighs on mental disorders causes the community and the family to confine people with schizophrenia indefinitely.

This case is clearly a violation of her human rights from the lack of recognition of Yukiko's legal capacity, liberty, and freedom from forced treatment despite a high probability that she could follow up voluntarily and make her life outside of the institution.

In Mexico, the number one cause of prolonged institutionalization is intellectual disability, and abandonment has been a constant since the twentieth century. Today we have a reform that aims to prevent that, however, it continues to happen that people with mental disorders are taken to institutions against his will and the family disappears.

In this case, both the family and the health system configured the violations of their human rights for 40 years and the damage should be repaired both morally and economically.

3.3.1.8 Soumitra Pathare

This is a particularly terrible instance where a person's entire life has been destroyed due to actions of the health care system. Unfortunately, this is not something that not only happened in the past but continues to happen even today in many countries.

Mental health professionals involved in her incarceration during her 40 years in hospital could have taken many steps to prevent this from happening. It highlights the need for independent oversight of mental health institutions to prevent such incidents happening in the future. I believe that Yukiko is entitled to compensation by the mental health system for the 40 years of loss suffered by her.

The absence of community facilities is not sufficient justification for inaction of mental health professionals. For instance, the mental health professionals could have got her legal aid during her long stay in hospital, to exercise her right to her family home (which was presumably being denied by her brothers). Mental health professionals could also advocate for a change in the law, so that family's consent is not required for discharge from hospital. Did the mental health professionals attempt to discharge her from hospital in the 40 years that she was there?

The CRPD's emphasis on respecting the will and preferences of the individual does provide sufficient protection to prevent recurrence of such instances. Hence the need to codify into law the need to respect the will and preferences of the individual when providing mental health treatment.

3.3.1.9 Mohan Isaac

In the first instance, Yukiko, with a past history of successful treatment in a mental hospital for schizophrenia should never have been committed again to a mental hospital at the age of 18 when she "hurt her leg" and she was upset/agitated about it. Secondly, she should never have been kept in the mental hospital (for whatever reasons) for the next 40 years. This is a gross violation of Yukiko's human rights.

Yukiko could have been managed as an outpatient for her leg problems. She could have been managed in the community if she had any recurrent symptoms of schizophrenia. There is no evidence that she had any unmanageable symptoms which warranted psychiatric hospitalization. In fact, Yukiko was always a "model patient" and her only "symptoms" were wanting discharge and attempting to escape from the hospital. Her initial mental hospitalization and her family's unwillingness/non-cooperation to participate in her management seem to have contributed to her long stay (40 years) in the mental hospital.

Prolonged, unnecessary institutionalization is certainly not a thing of the past. It continues to occur in many countries in Asia, Africa, Latin America, and Eastern Europe. Unlike other developed, advanced, and rich countries of Western Europe, North America, and countries such as Canada, Australia, and New Zealand where institutionalization of the mentally ill is a story of the past, Japan is an exception where, as the clinical story of Yukiko highlights, long-term institutionalization continues to exist.

Psychiatrists and other mental health professionals have a duty to educate (psychoeducation) and actively involve the family in the ongoing management of the mentally ill person. In settings where community mental health programmes do not exist, psychiatrists have a role to advocate for and help in the development of community resources and services.

3.3.2 Concluding Comments on Case History 2

3.3.2.1 Neeraj Gill and Norman Sartorius

All the commentators agreed that Yukiko should not have been admitted to the psychiatric institution in the first place, and her ongoing incarceration in the mental institution was a gross violation of her human rights. It was discussed that the CRPD's principle of respecting the will and preference of the individual must be adopted in domestic legislation. Strong safeguards against violation of right to autonomy, including independent oversight of the psychiatric institutions was recommended to prevent such human rights violations.

Unfortunately, such atrocities continue to occur in many parts of the world, in rich and in poor countries. The mental health system robbed Yukiko of 40 years of her life and took away her rights to equal legal capacity, liberty, integrity, freedom of movement, social inclusion and participation, employment, and the right to live in the community and to have a family.

There was general agreement that psychiatrists and other mental health professionals, apart from respecting their patients and advocating for them, can educate families and community, and engage in advocacy at a systems level for better-resourced community-based mental health care and social services which respect the human rights of people with disabilities.

3.4 Case History 3: A Teenage Woman Hospitalized for Going Against Social Norms

Aalya is an 18-year-old woman in a Middle Eastern Country. She was picked up by the ambulance staff of a private psychiatric hospital after her parents reported to the psychiatrist in-charge that she was excited, did not stay in any place, was reckless, and engaged in sexual promiscuity. Three ambulance workers went to her male friend's home where she was staying and forcibly brought her to the hospital. Once in the hospital, she was kept in a locked ward for observation. She was abusive, agitated, and angry that she was brought to the hospital against her wishes. Meanwhile, her friend applied to the court against her involuntary detention in the hospital. Failing to provide sufficient psychiatric grounds for detention, the hospital discharged her after 24 h observation period.

The parents reported that Aalya had in the past few years, periods of excitement and was sexually promiscuous which brought disgrace to her parents' reputation in their society. Her parents had previously sought psychiatric intervention because of her behavioral problems, but she never had any treatment. She had sexual relations with her art teacher, a man in his mid-30s, almost double her age. Two days before her involuntary detention, Aalya left home and moved in with this man. Extremely upset with her actions, her parents went to the private psychiatric hospital seeking help and support in her best interest, given that her reckless and promiscuous behavior at the tender age of 18 was, in their opinion, to be harmful for her well-being as well as to her family's reputation.

After discharge, Aalya sued the psychiatrist for ordering her illegal apprehension and detention. The court is considering her complaint at present.

3.4.1 Commentary

3.4.1.1 Charlene Sunkel

Detaining Aalya based on perceived immoral relationships and the perceived shame she brought onto the family, denied her right to have relationships. The court finding that there were insufficient psychiatric grounds for detention may have been a good indication that her decisions about her relationships were not related to a matter of legal incapacity and the inability to make decision about her own life or mental health choices.

The other side of the story is the much older man who she has been involved with, who may have been taking advantage of her, and the blame should not have been solely placed on her. In my experience, I have come across cases where relatives did not approve of the behavior of a person who had a history with a mental health condition and used the diagnosis as a means to enforce involuntary treatment as "punishment"—to prevent such incidents, mental health laws must have mechanisms in place, such as internal appeals processes or the courts (which has been the case for Aalya who had turned to the courts).

One could also argue that the process to detain Aalya, was in no way free of conflict of interest and undue influence, from her family who seem to have been more concerned about their own interests (the shame on the family), instead of considering what support they could provide Aalya to make more responsible choices in her life. It goes to the notion of replacing the "best interest" paradigm with the "will and preferences paradigm." It is also important to acknowledge that when it comes to mental health and ensuring that practices are aligned with human rights, culture does have an impact and approaches should always be culturally sensitive.

3.4.1.2 Martha Savage

(a) In Aalya's youth, she should have been offered a different psychologist if she was not engaging with the one she saw.
(b) Her family should have been part of the counselling, especially if she was not engaging.
(c) Her art teacher should not have entered a sexual arrangement with his student, even if she were no longer his student. The power difference is too great.
(d) When the parents tried to get their adult daughter kidnapped, they should have been offered counselling. This may depend on the age of majority in the country.
(e) The hospital staff should have refused to kidnap Aalya and should not have locked her up.

All the actions (kidnapping, holding Aalya overnight against her will) have breached human rights.

The wealth and resources of the country and number of staff have nothing to do with it. The culture does though. In fact, it would have been better value for money and staff time to have refused to kidnap her or keep her in the hospital against her will. Except that the private hospital can charge the parents and make more money, which may be part of their motivation.

Her rights under CRPD to freedom from oppressive treatment, from arbitrary detention and the right to fair trial and equality before law were all breached.

3.4.1.3 Andreas Heinz, Sabine Müller und Assina Seitz

Aalya does not seem to have any mental disorder and, decisively, there is no serious harm to her health or to other persons. That her behavior is considered undesirable in traditional societies is no evidence for a mental disorder, and therefore any harm that she may experience is due to social conflicts and should not be dealt with in the realm of mental health. Accordingly, medicine and the mental health care system should not have been invoked. This is not to say that Aalya's behavior could also be manifest in conjunction with a mental disorder, for example, mania, however, then the clinical criteria for a bipolar disorder need to be checked and they do not rely on the social unwarrantedness of a certain behavior.

Persons who suffer from and rebel against social norms, which systematically oppress and discriminate them, may need support or psychological counselling on a voluntary basis in case they ask for it. In such cases, it should be supportive and not punitive. All of the actions taken affect her human rights–she should not have been admitted to a hospital. However, it was good that the hospital discharged her after a short observation period. There was no violation of Article 14 of the CRPD, because Aalya does not fall under the category of persons with disability.

3.4.1.4 Oye Gureje

Aalya did indeed need a proper assessment to determine if she had a diagnosable condition for which treatment might be required. However, this should be done in a consensual manner. At 18 years of age, she was an adult and her consent and agreement should have been obtained before any medical intervention was offered. While this might not be an easy process, depending on her level of insight, this should nevertheless be the appropriate way to proceed. This could require the involvement of professionals who could attempt to gain Aalya's trust and cooperation. While the family's concern about their reputation is understandable, this should not lead them to taking actions that would be more appropriately described as punitive. Rather, the goal should be Aalya's well-being and this should be the basis for trying to gain her cooperation. Her cooperation and engagement with professionals would be required not just for a proper assessment of her clinical status but also for any long-term intervention, should any be required.

The forceful removal of Aalya and subsequent involuntary admission was a violation of her right to freedom and an abuse of her right to be treated with respect and dignity. The fact that this lasted for barely 24 h does not detract from that conclusion. Her views and consent were not obtained for the admission, and her objections were ignored.

3.4.1.5 Cecile Hanon

The question that arises here is the role of social control that psychiatry is asked to play. Aalya is "arrested" not for a mental disorder but for deviation from the social norm, for being marginal and damaging the reputation of her family.

Her rights to freedom of movement and freedom of choice were violated by the actions taken by mental health professionals.

3.4.1.6 Nicolás Martínez-López

This case reflects the reality of several countries where there is a moral vision of mental health, that is, they consider psychopathological decision-making that is not in accordance with the standards of a certain culture. For this reason, the practices in psychiatry have suffered from the signaling of the anti-psychiatry movement.

Historically, the involuntary internment of people for being dissidents of a regime or for having ideas or behaviors against "good customs" was carried out due to the high moral burden of the first conceptions of capacity in the psychiatric medical model, which led to the actions of torture that stigmatize the practice of psychiatry in our days. Unfortunately, this vision of mental disorders continues to prevail throughout the world and is overshadowed by various health professionals, hindering and further stigmatizing the practice of psychiatry.

The case of Aalya has all the human rights violations of a person who, due to her behavior described as antisocial by her parents, generated the actions of health professionals and security authorities, conditioning a practice that has led to the widespread stigma of psychiatry. Aalya's actions should not be judged as psychopathological and surely the lawsuit against the staff that admitted her and her parents is reasonable based on the torture of which she was a victim.

3.4.1.7 Soumitra Pathare

The handling of this case demonstrates all that is wrong in the way mental health services in many countries address the needs of people with acute mental health crises.

From the case study, it is not clear what are the provisions of mental health law in the country. If the parents felt that their daughter needed a psychiatric assessment that should have been authorized by a legal authority, e.g., a court or a mental health tribunal. Mental health ambulance services barging into people's homes and forcibly moving them to hospital without any legal authorization amounts to battery and assault.

It is also not clear what procedures were followed by the psychiatrist and the hospital when admitting this individual once they were brought to the hospital by the ambulance staff. For example, whether she was assessed by one or two independent mental health professionals, the sections of the mental health law used to admit her to hospital, and the provisional diagnosis when she was admitted to hospital. It is quite alarming that the hospital was unable to provide sufficient grounds for detaining her in hospital when questioned in court and discharged her within 24 h.

3.4.1.8 Mohan Isaac

All the actions taken such as ambulance staff forcibly taking Aalya to private psychiatric hospital and locking her up for 24 h were in violation of her human rights. Her parents colluded with the private hospital psychiatrist with false reporting of "manic symptoms" to lock her up in the hospital.

Aalya's parents could have contacted her male friend with whom she had moved in. If Aalya's friend had not approached the court against her involuntary detention, she may well have continued in illegal detention for a longer period.

Teenagers/adolescents with behavior problems can be very difficult to manage, all over the world. They are reluctant to engage in psychological/psychiatric assessment and intervention. However, forcible detention in a psychiatric hospital is not the solution. While the parents did whatever they did in her best interest, it is a gross violation of the rights of an individual aged 18 years. Parental concern about "family reputation" in a very traditional and culturally diverse country is understandable but their action to deal with their concern is not acceptable. The problem of Aalya and of her parents also highlights the need for specialized focus on youth mental health services.

3.4.2 Concluding Comments on Case History 3

3.4.2.1 Neeraj Gill and Norman Sartorius

This case is an example of abuse of psychiatry as a means of social control. Commentators agreed that forcibly moving Aalya to psychiatric hospital without any legal authorization amounted to assault; one even called it "kidnapping" and it is hard to argue against those strong allegations. As commentators said, even if there had been grounds for involuntary assessment, that should have only been done with proper paperwork under a mental health act with necessary authorizations. Using a mental health act without any procedural fairness in such cases lends psychiatry to risk of abuse and stigmatization.

This case also points to the potential of conflict between the interests of person with lived experience and the motives of family members. While the family values of Eastern cultures need to be respected, it is important to ensure that family "honour" and culture are not allowed to become grounds for violation of individual rights.

As rightly pointed out by one commentator, while Aalya's human rights have been grossly violated, the CRPD is not applicable in her case as she did not have a mental illness or disability. However, it is envisaged that the CRPD would provide an impetus for a human rights culture within all sectors, including the health system. A mental health system and legislation compliant with the CRPD would have rights protections built in, which would prevent such violations.

3.5 Case History 4: A Man with Mental Illness, Beaten and Restrained by Villagers and then by Service Providers

Ikemba is a 30-year-old single man, who lives with his parents and brothers in a village in Nigeria. He works on the farm with his father.

Two months ago, the family started to notice change in Ikemba's behavior. He would stay up till late at night, often playing loud music. He stopped going to the farm, told his father that he had acquired many acres of land and was going to be elected the head of a group of villages.

He bought a second-hand motorbike with all his saving. He crashed that motorbike into a car, while driving recklessly. He got aggressive at the scene and ended up getting bashed by the crowd. Given his agitated behavior, and claims of being the head of all villages, it was collectively decided by the people who happened to be there that he should be taken to the mental hospital in the city, 200 km from their village. He was put in a van, with his legs and arms shackled, and taken to the mental hospital. His two brothers went with him and stayed with him in the hospital.

This mental hospital has an outpatient department with daily attendance of more than 300 patients. There is one psychiatrist and one other medical officer. The psychiatrist saw Ikemba and ordered Haloperidol 10 mg and Lorazepam 2 mg both intramuscular. He was admitted to the acute ward of 40 inpatients, supervised by one nurse for the whole ward. The psychiatrist had a ward round once a week. Ikemba remained chained to the bed for most of the time, supervised and supported by his brothers. He was switched from intramuscular to oral medication after 3 days, when lithium carbonate was added.

After 1 week, Ikemba's father, the head of the family, insisted on taking Ikemba to a famous faith-healer. There, he was beaten up with a broom and baton which was done as part of an exorcism practice. He was then brought back to the ward and treatment continued. Ikemba got better after 3 weeks' treatment in the hospital and weekly visits to the faith-healer. He was discharged with 2-months' supply of lithium, haloperidol, and benztropine.

Now, Ikemba is mentally stable, but has tremors and rigidity in his body, and drools saliva from his mouth. He is not able to work in the fields and is supported by his family.

3.5.1 Commentary

3.5.1.1 Charlene Sunkel

Ikemba's parents would have been better equipped to support him and access appropriate (available) services if they had more knowledge about mental health and mental health conditions. His parents would also have benefitted from a family and carer support group, and Ikemba himself could have been in a better position to relate and manage his symptoms through peer support that further could have helped him navigate the local mental health system to access services that are based on evidence and what he needs for recovery. In addition, a collaboration between mental health professionals and religious and cultural leaders could have helped eliminate practices that were harmful. Ikemba's decision-making powers were taken away from him, as being chained and beaten would not be a choice any person would make. Being exposed to such practices would be constituted as torture, inhumane, and degrading treatment, which could cause more harm and trauma, and limit possibilities for recovery. Although he did get well after his treatment was continued at the hospital, the concern remains about the long-term impact of the abusive religious and cultural practices he received.

3.5.1.2 Martha Savage

1. What should have been done?
   (a) The family should have tried to get help when Ikemba's behavior first started changing. Without community services, it would have been helpful if there were a phone/remote consultation with a psychiatrist or other trained person who could talk with Ikeda and his family.
   (b) Once at the hospital, they should have tried to talk Ikemba into taking medicine voluntarily.
   (c) It is very good that the family was allowed to be with him in the hospital. He should have been untied since his family was there to keep him out of trouble.
   (d) If he stayed tied up, they should be sure to see that he could move around to avoid the risk of Deep Vein Thrombosis (DVT).
   (e) After he went home, there should be remote access, i.e., online, visits to allow Ikemba and his family to discuss his symptoms and to try to see if there was a way he could reduce the medicine slowly to reduce the symptoms while still staying stable.
2. If human rights are affected, which action should be taken first? How will the context, e.g., the wealth/resources of the country or number of staff influence the order of actions?
   (a) As above—first try voluntary compliance and talk therapy, as early in the process as possible. The poor country does not have enough trained psychiatrists or other mental health workers, which led to lack of access.
   (b) But even rich countries sometimes treat their patients in ways that are as bad or worse than Ikemba was treated. For example, in Japan they give their patients forced medication, tie them down and even put them in seclusion rooms without any access to visits from family.

Further optional questions:

- Was it justified to detain and involuntarily treat Ikemba?

  Yes if he continued to be violent, but they should try to talk him into voluntary treatment.
- Was restraint (chemical as well as physical) justified in this case?

  In the vehicle it was necessary to restrain him, but after that mechanical restraints are too easy to leave on even when they are not necessary. Forced medication is also an issue, but to my mind it is preferable over continual physical restraints.
- Was it justified to let him be physically assaulted in the name of cultural practices?

NO—there is a limit to what one should allow in the name of "culture." There should be discussion with the traditional healers to see if some compromise methods could be tried that respect the traditions without harming the service users.

3.5.1.3 Andreas Heinz, Sabine Müller, Assina Seitz

1. It is not clear, why the afflicted person, Ikemba, was shackled when being driven to the mental hospital. It is reported that he was agitated and aggressive before admission, however, there is no report about continuing aggressive behavior that would justify physical restraint.

   As not unusual in many low- and middle-income countries, but also high-income countries, there was a lack of staff, particularly regarding medical care and psychotherapy. There is a dire need for de-escalation and psychosocial support in repetitive talks with the patient, which did not happen. Chaining Ikemba to the bed is a violation of his human rights and was not justified by any report regarding him posing a danger to himself or others.

The medication with haloperidol 10 mg and Lorazepam 2 mg is inappropriately high; it has been known for several decades that sufficient receptor blockade in a never before treated subject requires only around 3 mg of haloperidol (Heinz et al. 1996). In any case, since there is no report of acute danger that the patient posed to himself or others, and since no other ways to de-escalate the situation were tried out, there is absolutely no justification for compulsory medication in this situation. Lithium carbonate is an adequate medication in the case of mania, which is a likely diagnosis for this patient. Neuroleptic medication is often not indicated in such situations except for emergency reasons.

Taking Ikemba to a faith-healer who beats him constitutes another violation of his human rights; however, it is not reported, whether the patient agreed to this practice or whether this was decided by his family only.

The patient suffers from persisting neuroleptic side effects; most likely, the inappropriately high haloperidol medication was continued, so tremors and rigidity as well as drooling saliva are symptoms of a Parkinsonian syndrome induced by neuroleptics. The patient should have never received the high dose of haloperidol, even though in many hospitals around the world this is a usual and widely used but nevertheless scientifically and medically unjustified dosage. High dosing of neuroleptics also increases the risk for long lasting side effects.

2. Shackling the patient when transporting him to the hospital and shackling him to the bed is absolutely unjustified and a violation of his human rights. Beating the patient in a traditional healing ceremony also violates his human rights. There is a right for adequate treatment guaranteed by the CRPD that would include personal talks, psychosocial/psychotherapeutic interventions on a regular basis, and common talks with the patient and his family. This can be achieved in low- and middle-income countries as well, for example, Prof. Koumaré in the medical hospital Point G in Bamako, Mali, practiced family care and family centered systematic intervention with regular clinical rounds in his hospital in a similar economic setting.
3. The CRPD demands adequate care, which was not provided in this case and which can also be achieved beyond expensive medical interventions by systematically teaching nurses and other healthcare professionals basic psychotherapeutic and de-escalation skills. In addition, family interventions can be provided by training healthcare personnel, as has been documented in Afghanistan (Missmahl et al. 2012).

A key approach is to involve family and friends in the care of patients all over the world, which is specifically relevant in situations where there is a lack of medical care and relatives carry most of the burden of interaction with an afflicted person. Therefore, systematic approaches involving patients and relatives in therapeutic sessions and allowing patients to stay on the hospital grounds in order to take care of the patients during treatment are of key importance to reconcile different demands.

3.5.1.4 Michaela Amering

This sounds like a very typical story of a first manic episode. One wishes there would have been help earlier and closer. Earlier help could have assisted the patient and family in the community with a chance of avoiding violence and maybe even hospitalization as well as being able to help with unwanted effects of medication now. A continuous presence of mental health expertise in the community might also have had an effect in avoiding or changing the behavior of the faith-healer. And one feels for the mental health workers for their immense workload on too few people.

Unfortunately, similar flows of events are well known in high-income countries and much better-resourced mental health systems just as well. Outreach services, home treatment teams, and other crisis alternatives are available in some regions and not in many others, which gives unfairly uneven access across the world and within countries or even cities. Ikemba's story certainly raises this and several other human rights questions. However, the CRPD might not apply as the definition of person with disability might not be met for a person with a short-lived acute mental health crisis.

3.5.1.5 Oye Gureje

The mental health care system available to Ikemba was clearly seriously under-resourced. The available human and material resources for the care of persons with severe mental disorders were grossly inadequate, and the providers in the system were apparently doing the best they could in the circumstance. It seems therefore that, at least regarding the care provided to Ikemba at the service level in which he had presented, no clear alternative option seemed to be feasible. At a higher level of the system, what could have made a difference would be better provision of human and material resources to meet the needs of Ikemba and people like him who might experience similar mental health conditions.

He received antipsychotic medication, an appropriate intervention for his condition. But then developed serious side effects that subsequently constituted a hindrance to him resuming work. A mitigating approach to this outcome would have been the use of a medication with less potential to cause extra-pyramidal side effects or at least an adjustment to the dosage to reduce the side effects. Medications that are less likely to cause serious side effects similar to the ones Ikemba experienced, most notably the second-generation antipsychotics, were probably unavailable to Ikemba's mental health care providers.

Ikemba was a victim of several violations of his human rights. He was shackled to take him to hospital, he was physically abused by the healers and his admission was apparently involuntary with no identified process in place to obtain a second opinion or the opinion of a legal guardian before enforcing admission on him.

The inadequacies in Ikemba's treatment reflect the shortcomings of the mental health systems of many developing countries. In the specific instance of Ikemba, Nigeria has mental health workforce constraints as well as lack of materials and supplies – factors that were no doubt associated with the quality of care that was available to Ikemba.

The recourse to traditional healing is both a reflection of the constraints of resources in the formal health sector and the common belief by patients and their families that healers have the skills to provide cure, getting to the presumed supernatural causes of the illness.

A modern mental health legislation, incorporating the CRPD specifications, is currently not in operation in Nigeria. However, it is unlikely that a strict adherence to the specifications of the CRPD, including those related to involuntary admission, would have been practicable in the country. This is because the human resources to implement them in the public health system are currently not available and their application to services provided by healers may be difficult given that the healers operate outside of the formal sector. One way of preventing the abuse of human rights in the process of care by the healers would be some form of active collaboration with the public health system.

3.5.1.6 Cecile Hanon

Ikemba could have died several times with all the bad treatment he received (beatings, hematomas, and intramuscular injections). Ikemba's coercion is unjust and contrary to the principles of autonomy and beneficence/non-maleficence. The "mentally stable" state that is described is nothing more than major side effects of the treatment, with abrasion of effects and parkinsonian syndrome.

3.5.1.7 Nicolás Martínez-López

In this case, it is evident that Ikemba presented a first outbreak of mania with psychotic symptoms and that in his community, the stigma caused him to be seriously assaulted.

In addition, the lack of resources in the field of mental health shows that the only way out for many patients like Ikemba is to have the available drugs, despite having side effects that make daily life difficult, making them dependent on the others.

Ikemba needs other medications to improve his quality of life, but it is unlikely that he will be able to access those, given the conditions in which he lives. It demonstrates the great disparity in access to mental health care that currently prevails and seems not to have changed since the last century.

These types of circumstances happen in Mexico every day. There are people who take up to 15 years to have a correct diagnosis and adequate treatment, given the lack of mental health care services close to their home and, as in this case, the great lack of information that allows for community awareness.

3.5.1.8 Soumitra Pathare

What this case highlights is the lack of availability of mental health services in many countries which is a violation of Article 25 of the CRPD. When services are available, they are usually not geographically accessible, provided largely in mental hospitals (which tend to be unacceptable to many patients and their families) and of questionable quality (for example, not adequately addressing the side effects experienced by this person). This is one of the reasons why families and service users turn to faith healers—not the only reason, but a significant reason. Many faith healing services violate the rights of persons with mental illness as shown in the example above. Governments have a duty to regulate the faith healing services and faith healers, as much as they have a duty to regulate medical mental health services (protection from cruel, inhuman and degrading treatment, the right to bodily integrity).

The case also highlights the lack of social care support and rehabilitation services in many countries in violation of Article 26 (Right to rehabilitation).

3.5.1.9 Mohan Isaac

Ikemba's change in behavior, aggression, agitation, and grandiose claims about himself are all indicative of his mental illness, which required appropriate assessment and treatment. The family having to take Ikemba 200 km away to a mental hospital reflects the poor status of mental health services in Nigeria. Ikemba's rights were violated when he was taken to the hospital with his legs and arms shackled. He could have been sedated, if facilities for such first aid sedation of aggressive mentally ill persons were available closer to Ikemba's home. That could have avoided shackling his arms and legs during the travel to the mental hospital.

It is not clear from the information provided in the vignette whether Ikemba's consent was obtained for treatment (injection), admission, and further management in the hospital—perhaps not. It is also not clear whether any mental health care legislation exists in Nigeria and if yes, whether the provisions of the legislation were applied for Ikemba's admission and treatment.

It is stated that Ikemba was started on medications and his stay in the hospital was "supervised and supported by his brothers." With his brothers around, why did he have to be "chained to the bed for most of the time," violating his individual rights?

Large number of patients (daily attendance of more than 300 outpatients, 40 patients in the acute ward) and the grossly limited number of staff (one psychiatrist, one medical officer, and one nurse for an acute ward with 40 patients) clearly describe the context of Ikemba's situation.

Family member's faith in alternate systems of healing including in practice of exorcism is quite strong and cannot be easily challenged or changed, even if the patient was beaten up by the healer as part of the intervention. Enhancing mental health literacy in the country may be a solution to prevent unscrupulous rights violation by "faith healers."

3.5.2 Concluding Comments on Case History 4

3.5.2.1 Neeraj Gill and Norman Sartorius

This case highlights the plight of people with mental illness in many low- and middle-income countries with poor mental health literacy in the community and the abysmal lack of social and mental health services due to lack of investment by the governments.

There was consensus that Ikemba was a victim of several violations of his human rights, including being shackled and being physically abused. In addition, the commentators pointed to the fact that the mental health services were so far away, and short-staffed/poorly resourced. The need to enhance mental health literacy was highlighted, to prevent rights violations by the faith healers. The need to regulate faith healing services was emphasized.

The description of the case and the comments also highlight the need to have a system of legal protection of people with mental illness in place, in addition to the prescription of the right to treatment and other prescriptions contained in the CRPD and other UN documents. Such legislation should also protect people with mental illness against disrespect for their human rights in the name of culture.

3.6 Case History 5: A Nurse Locked Up for Suicide Risk

Sue is a 30-year-old married mother of two children (3- and 5-year-old) in Canada and works as a nurse. She has recurrent depressive disorder and has been on antidepressant medications off and on for almost a decade. She stopped taking her antidepressant medication about 6 months ago and has been feeling persistently low in her mood for the past 3 months. She developed severe depression and started feeling suicidal a few weeks ago. She was also having anger outbursts at her children and felt like hurting them at times. As her depression worsened and given the previous history of suicide attempt by overdose and aggressive outbursts directed at her children, her private psychiatrist recommended admission to the local private hospital, to which she reluctantly agreed.

After 3 days in the hospital, Sue felt that she was feeling worse in her mood due to being on the psychiatry ward and requested discharge. It was a weekend, and the psychiatrist responsible for her treatment was not available to be asked to allow her discharge from hospital against medical advice. The nursing staff advised her that she would have to wait till Monday for her psychiatrist to approve her discharge. On hearing this, Sue escalated in her behavior and threatened to cut her wrist if she was kept in the hospital against her wish. The nursing staff invoked Mental Health Act due to her depression, risk of self-harm and risk to her children if discharged home. An ambulance was called, and Sue was transferred to the emergency department (ED) of the public hospital.

By the time she was assessed in ED, Sue had experienced a crisis, became agitated, and screamed objecting to her admission to the emergency department of the public hospital, while she had agreed to be admitted to the private hospital. Given her depression, the history of suicide attempt, current threat to self-harm, and agitated behavior, it was decided to admit her under the Mental Health Act for 24 hours in the locked psychiatric ward of the general hospital for observation. Once on the ward, her condition worsened, as she found herself among a lot of very unwell patients. After the 24 hours assessment period, she was discharged back to the private hospital, a transfer to which she reluctantly agreed as that was a place in better order than the psychiatric department in the public hospital. She was discharged after 2 weeks stay in the private hospital.

3.6.1 Commentary

3.6.1.1 Charlene Sunkel

Right from the start at the point where Sue experienced depression, as a first step and to avoid her condition from becoming a crisis, relatives or friends (if she had any who she could rely on) could have assisted in taking the children in for a couple of days, while a peer support worker or similar community service could provide support and check in with her daily, while updating her treating psychiatrist. Should her condition have deteriorated, hospital admission would have been the next option for her to consider.

It is unclear as to why Sue decided to stop her medication, but again, the reason would have been helpful to find ways for her to prevent a relapse. That is why a partnership between psychiatrist and client should exist, where trust is the foundation and where the client can feel safe to disclose any concerns.

While in hospital, Sue clearly expressed that she was not benefitting from being hospitalized and when told to wait out the weekend, her frustrations turned into desperation. In my experience, how a conversation is initiated with a patient often determines what happens next—a patient (or any person for that matter) wants to feel that his/her concerns are taken seriously. It was not unreasonable to expect Sue to wait until the Monday to be discharged, but in the interim, the question could have been posed to her as to how and what the hospital staff could have done to support her throughout the weekend, e.g., maybe a simple gesture to have her talk with her kids over the phone to cheer her up, or have a peer support worker come see her on the ward.

3.6.1.2 Martha Savage

(a) She should have had more monitoring and support as she stopped her medicine. Very slow decreases in medicine can sometimes help people to stop it more easily than the standard suggestions.
(b) Her husband and/or other adult family members should have been offered counselling and support for how to help her.
(c) She should have received more support when she first started getting depressed, perhaps to re-start her medication or at least talk therapy.
(d) If a person voluntarily admits themselves to a hospital, they should be allowed to leave when they want. If there is some reason not to allow that, then at least psychiatrists should be available on weekends to help evaluate patients who want to leave.
(e) When she was angry, the nurses at the private hospital and later at the public hospital, should have used de-escalation, talking to keep her from spiralling up in anger.
(f) There should be better care on the public ward.
(g) Her family (mainly her husband, but perhaps also her parents if they are involved) should get counselling and help to learn de-escalation techniques and to know what to do if she takes a turn for the worse.

Freedom from arbitrary detention and the right to a fair trial and equality before law were breached. As stated above, Sue could have gone home if the family worked together and had somebody take care of the children for a while. The resources in terms of number of staff might have been a problem with the State hospital and with not having people available to help patients leave when they wanted to. But that was not the country's wealth, but instead the private hospital's desire for profits, that was at stake.

Refusing discharge, even though she was a voluntary patient is not only unethical, but it's also bad practice because it will make her not want to seek help next time.

3.6.1.3 Andreas Heinz, Sabine Müller und Assina Seitz

Sue should have had every right to leave the facility immediately as she went there voluntarily and there was absolutely no legal obligation to stay. Problems within the institution regarding the availability of medical staff to approve a discharge are no reason to infringe on the right of any patient to leave an institution. The latter escalation that includes a threat of Sue to cut her own wrists if held on the ward against her wish appears to be completely triggered by the unlawful situation and any harm to herself apparently could have been avoided by releasing her as should have been required by the local law. Instead, this escalation resulted in admitting her to a public hospital emergency department. The latter could have happened before, because it was reported that Sue had anger outbursts at her children and felt like hurting them at times. If this was not just a feeling but real harm or hurtful behavior toward the children, family consultants should have been contacted and it should have been assessed whether Sue poses a danger to third persons due to a mental disorder. So, within another context, Sue may also have been transferred to a public hospital emergency department; however, this would then have happened on completely different grounds.

In the current case vignette, upon arrival at the emergency department, she was retained for observation for 24 h and discharged back to the private hospital, which was chosen by her in order to avoid involuntary detention at the public hospital. Given that the whole escalation was fostered by unlawful behavior of the private hospital, it is questionable that detention for 24 h in the public hospital was lawful. In any case, it should have been checked by an independent medical specialist and a judge. This being said, most emergency checks on the lawfulness of involuntary detention do not occur immediately. For example, in Germany, any involuntary admission must be checked by a judge within the first 24 h. Also, an independent medical specialist must provide an additional expert opinion. Instead of involuntarily transferring Sue to a public health emergency department, where she was locked up for 24 h, de-escalation and consultation should have taken place in the emergency room and it should have been ascertained whether Sue can be discharged immediately as the only threat to hurt herself was linked to being kept involuntarily. At the same time, it could have been assessed whether there is any danger to her children by involving the family or at least informing family consulting services in the community.

3.6.1.4 Michaela Amering

Again, a case that lends itself more to thinking about positive rights than about freedom rights, as important as the latter undoubtedly are. First, there is the often-lacking specialist services for reducing and/or safely ceasing medication, that might have changed the course. There is the right to home treatment or other alternatives to hospital treatment including support for family and parenting. CRPD Article 23 on respect for home and family spells out a lot of obligations that correspond to unmet needs we see in the community. At this point I would also like to mention CRPD Article 31 on Statistics and Data collection. We do have data that show that these context-dependent decisions regarding coercion show a great variability within similar or even the same mental health systems and there is more to find out how to better understand what brings them about and to use these data to reduce coercion.

3.6.1.5 Oye Gureje

Sue presented with a history and current features that justified immediate medical attention. So, the offer of admission to the private hospital to which she agreed was the right course of action. Given her condition and the likelihood of a high level of impulsivity during the episode, her request to be discharged barely 3 days into that admission and unwillingness to wait for a couple of more days for proper discharge by the psychiatrist is probably clinically understandable. That situation would have required an attempt to counsel her and see whether she could be persuaded to exercise some patience until Monday. It is unclear to what extent the staffing level in the private hospital was appropriate for that task which would have required some time and experience. Invoking the Mental Health Act by the nurse was understandable in the circumstance as that would allow for Sue to be transferred to a setting where a more detailed psychiatric evaluation could be done and a decision to discharge or otherwise made. The decision to transfer only further aggravated the situation as Sue became even more angry. Again, there should have been attempts at de-escalation and it is not clear whether such attempts were made or whether they were simply unsuccessful. If they had been made and had been successful, the need for involuntary admission would probably not have arisen.

The transfer of Sue to the emergency department of the psychiatric hospital and her subsequent involuntary admission constituted abridgment of her rights to freedom and personal choice. The two actions were ostensibly taken to protect Sue from any harm to self or to others (in particular, her children), which are legitimate rights for herself and her children. The abridgement of one right in the other to presumably protect another right could only be justified if the first was a necessary step to the latter. In Sue's case, the necessity for the abridgment of her right to freedom can only be justified if every necessary step was taken to persuade her about the need for voluntary admission but this did not succeed. It is not clear if this was the case.

It seems that there were clear guidelines to the clinicians about what to do in a situation of clinical crisis. The invocation of the Mental Health Act and the involuntary admission seem to have followed specified procedures about handling potentially dangerous situations that the clinicians might be confronted with. Such clear guidelines may reflect a good mental health system and, even though this may not require large resources to implement, may still be more likely to occur in well-resourced settings. On the other hand, the availability of well-trained clinical staff able to handle challenging clinical situations by the application of counselling and de-escalation techniques are more likely in well-resourced settings. Since Sue was a patient in Canada, a high-income country, it could be that resource constraints were not a major factor in the way her condition was handled.

The CRPD prescriptions would require that Sue should not be denied her right to freedom, self-determination, and respect. A strict interpretation of such prescriptions might suggest that the invocation of the Mental Health Act by the nurse and the involuntary admission in the hospital represented denial of those rights and should not have taken place. However, the CRPD also prescribes a right to health. For example, Article 25 states that "States Parties shall take all appropriate measures to ensure access for persons with disabilities to health services that are gender-sensitive, including health-related rehabilitation." The invocation of the Mental Health law and the involuntary admission were "appropriate measures" taken to ensure that Sue had access to health care.

3.6.1.6 Cecile Hanon

Sue is a victim of a lack of health organization, of a difference between public and private care. It is clear that it is not the depressive illness that is at work in the therapeutic escalation, but the disorganization, the lack of adaptation of institutions to people. It is the principle of justice that is not respected here.

3.6.1.7 Nicolás Martínez-López

In this case, Sue could clinically not have a recurrent depressive disorder, she probably suffers from bipolar disorder or comorbidity by borderline personality disorder, however regardless of the diagnosis, clearly the psychiatrist's indication was correct in view of the risk of suicide and aggression toward her children, in fact it was carried out properly in a private institution.

The fact that during hospitalization she presented an episode of agitation due to the refusal of voluntary discharge, the management of shift personnel did not allow the patient to have adequate support, so she was referred to a public service. This situation for me is somewhat different from what happens in my country, Mexico, because if Sue had had this in a private institution she would have been treated inside the hospital where she was and a psychiatrist on duty would have attended the emergency by calling to the treating psychiatrist to consult the decision. This can configure a violation of human rights since in the process an involuntary admission is made due to agitation, even though it seems that all the time Sue had the ability to make decisions.

3.6.1.8 Soumitra Pathare

This is not an uncommon example and indicates poor staff training as well as poor procedures for seeking consultant approval on weekends. It seems the nurses were not trained in de-escalation techniques and allowed the situation to escalate with unfortunate consequences for the patient.

I do not think the CRPD or any international document can protect individuals from human rights abuses if staff are not adequately trained and the regulatory authorities do not take penal action against such medical facilities.

The patient should be compensated for poor service quality by this private mental health service provider.

3.6.1.9 Mohan Isaac

What happened to Sue (being placed under Mental Health Act, transferred to emergency department of a public mental health care hospital, observation in a locked ward as an involuntary inpatient along with many seriously unwell patients) is indeed unfortunate and must have caused her a lot of distress.

The suggestion of invocation of Mental Health Act seemed to have escalated Sue's symptoms, ultimately reaching a crisis point. One cannot but wonder if the crisis resulting in Sue's transfer to public sector could have been prevented or avoided by a more creative and empathetic "shared decision making" by the ward nursing staff. Sue wanted to go home as she was feeling worse in the ward but the nurses wanted her to stay until her psychiatrist could assess her after the weekend. Was there no way of contacting Sue's treating psychiatrist during the weekend? Was the perception of Sue's "risk" by the nursing staff and the action that followed to deal with the risk, disproportionate? In the process, Sue's individual human rights were compromised.

The "risk averse" culture that exists in mental health care settings of many countries including Canada emphasizes and prioritizes risk avoidance, above all other goals of management including the patient's human rights. This may lead to excessive restrictions. Once staff who know a patient for some period of time escalate the patient's risk of self-harm, staff in other settings who do not know the patient well are unlikely to de-escalate the risk, as happened to Sue in the public hospital.

3.6.2 Concluding Comments on Case History 5

3.6.2.1 Neeraj Gill and Norman Sartorius

This case generated disagreement and debate among commentators. Of the opinions gathered in the vignette, most believed that this individual had been mismanaged, that involuntary treatment in this case was a human rights violation under the CRPD and that a less restrictive solution should have been prioritized.

However, a significant point of disagreement was raised by a psychiatrist commentator. The CRPD describes a right to health where access to health services must be ensured for people requiring healthcare. The voluntary admission in this vignette was appropriate and protected the autonomy of the patient. It was argued that discharge against medical advice could have resulted in a worse outcome for this individual. Therefore, one commentator argued that enactment of involuntary treatment under the mental health act was in the best interests of the patient to ensure they continued to receive treatment for their suicidal ideation.

Alternatively, other people who reviewed the case felt that the transfer to an involuntary public service was a stopgap measure enacted due to short staffing and lack of appropriately trained nursing staff over the weekend at the private hospital. These reviewers believed that involuntary treatment in this scenario was a violation of human rights and even called for punitive action against the facility.

It is noteworthy that the CRPD Committee has clarified through General Comment 1 on Article 12 that the "best interest" paradigm must be replaced by the "will and preference of the individual" paradigm. Adherence to CRPD in this case would have required respect for autonomy of the individual and/or supported decision-making, and community/home-based support and treatment. The implementation of the CRPD requires that those who provide care are adequately prepared to do so. The right to treatment can only be realized if the services are competent in the application of treatment. It would be desirable to develop internationally applicable minimum standards for the treatment of mental illness even if, for the time being many countries might find this an additional burden.

3.7 Case History 6: A Young Man with Acute Psychosis Brought to Emergency Department by the Police

Rob is a 20-year-old man in England, who was brought to a hospital emergency department by the police, as he was armed with a knife and tried to stab someone in a public place. On mental status examination, he was found to have acute psychosis, characterized by persecutory delusions that the devil had sent some people to kill him. He said that he heard voices telling him that he had to kill someone because otherwise the devil will kill a million children. Therefore, he tried to stab a man with a knife, after which the people made a citizens arrest and called the police.

In the emergency department, he soon got agitated as he came to believe that the doctors, nurses, and the police were all conspiring against him. He assaulted a nurse and had to be restrained by the hospital security staff.

He was sedated with intramuscular haloperidol and lorazepam and was transferred to the psychiatric inpatient unit after 2 h observation in Emergency Department. On arrival, on the psychiatry ward, he again became aggressive. The security officers physically restrained him, and he was put into solitary confinement in the seclusion room with padded walls and continuous CCTV monitoring. He remained in seclusion overnight and was brought out of seclusion, in the morning.

Specific questions:

- Was it justified to detain Rob under the Mental Health Act?
- Was it justified to involuntarily treat Rob under the Mental Health Act?
- Was seclusion and restraint (chemical and physical) justified in this case?

3.7.1 Commentary

3.7.1.1 Charlene Sunkel

The community in this case was central to dealing with the situation, and the question arises as to their own knowledge of mental health conditions, de-escalation techniques or whether anyone knew a relative or friend who could be contacted to assist and help calm the person down by talking to the person.

Communication with the person, despite psychosis, is always important as the first step in helping the person— ask who can be contacted for supported decision-making, explain observations (e.g., "I can see you are in distress, how can I help or support you"), discuss treatment options (e.g., "what would you feel comfortable with"), and explain what is going to happen (e.g., "we are going to take you to hospital now").

In Rob's case, lives were at risk and he himself could have gotten hurt in the process, or worst-case scenario, should he have hurt someone else, he would have had to live with that guilt for the rest of his life. There was no "presumption of dangerousness," which many oppose as a determining factor for using coercive measures, but the act of aggression was already there and Rob's reasoning for "defending" himself signified that he lost touch with reality, and therefore the use of restraints and involuntary hospitalization was justified. His disability was not the reason for detainment, but it was based on his violent behavior.

What is important is how this [restraints and involuntary admission] is done, e.g., dignity must be at all times maintained, restraints or seclusion must be applied for the shortest possible time and with the strictest protocols in place. Advanced directive is helpful when consent to hospitalization, prescription of medication/s and type/s of restraints are required in case of crisis.

3.7.1.2 Martha Savage

1. Question 1
    (a) In New Zealand, he would have been met at the hospital by a Crisis Action Team who are specially trained in psychiatric care to evaluate people presenting with psychiatric symptoms. These people are also trained in de-escalation techniques and might have been able to calm Rob down so that he would not have assaulted anybody.

(b) There should have been attempts to contact Rob's family to find out if such a situation had happened before and if there were any standing suggestions of what would work best to calm him down.
(c) If he still assaulted somebody, he could be talked to during his restraint and given the choice of whether to take medicine or not.
(d) He should have been transferred to the psychiatric hospital as soon as possible rather than be observed for a couple of hours in an Emergency Department where there are many other problems to deal with and fewer trained people.
(e) When he arrived at the psychiatric hospital, he should have been calmed down with de-escalation techniques. If he needed to go to the seclusion room, he should be visited and checked on every hour or two.
(f) Now, he needs to be evaluated to determine if he is in the right place and what is the right treatment, and whether the law needs to be invoked to keep others safe.

2. Whether any of the actions taken affected human rights, and if so, what else could have been done? How will the context, e.g., the wealth/resources of the country or number of staff influence the order of actions?

   Involuntary medicine is a human rights violation, but that might be mitigated by the need to keep him and others safe. Solitary confinement is also torture in some definitions. Talking to Rob as a human being and finding out what his issues were and discussing whether the voices really had his health in mind would be good. England is not a poor country. Lack of money is no good excuse. They should have adequate numbers of people to talk to him and make sure others are out of his way.

3. In what way would the CRPD prescriptions require different action from that taken and how should the differing demands/actions/situations be reconciled?

   Involuntary medicine and solitary confinement both contravene the CRPD prescriptions. Assault cannot be allowed, but the restraints and solitary confinement should have been done for shorter times.

   - Every person with disability has a right to respect for his or her physical and mental integrity on an equal basis with others' (article 17)—from the beginning if Rob had been treated with respect he might not have gotten agitated and thought people were out to get him.
   - Involuntary confinement: "The existence of a disability shall in no case justify a deprivation of liberty" (article 14).
   - Article 12(4) of the CRPD—Any measures relating to exercise of the legal capacity must respect the rights, will, and preferences of the person; (involuntary medicine doesn't).
   - Be proportional and tailored to the person's circumstances.
   - Apply for the shortest possible time.
   - Be subject to safeguards and monitoring by a competent authority.
   - By not monitoring him and keeping him in solitary confinement overnight, they may have been breaching his civil rights. He should have been monitored to see if he could have been removed from solitary confinement earlier.

   Since he tried to stab somebody, it was justified to detain him. But once at the hospital, there should have been more attempts to try to get him to calm down without seclusion and restraint before the actual assault. He could not be allowed to assault somebody, so some form of coercion was necessary both to take him away from people when he tried to stab members of the public, and when he assaulted people at the hospital. And once it was decided, he needed to be moved, a short period of restraint to get him to the psychiatric hospital would be justified. I think that Rob's treatment was better than he would have received if he had been taken to the jail, so I think detention under the Mental Health Act was justified. There needs to be a legal procedure to see how long he should be detained, and it should not be longer than he would be detained if he committed the same offense without having a psychiatric condition. I am not sure about involuntary treatment, although I think it is preferable to use chemical restraints than long periods of physical or mechanical restraints.

3.7.1.3 Andreas Heinz, Sabine Müller und Assina Seitz

The case vignette of Rob does not describe any attempts of de-escalation of current situation. While the whole situation may be understandable as an emergency, in which there is little time to calm a highly aggressive patient down, this should always be attempted and any physical restrains should only be a last resort to avert severe harm. Applying antipsychotic medication against the will of the patient is forbidden in Germany if it is only done in order to protect the rights of third persons. If there is no advantage for the patient themselves, then only physical restraint and in some cases sedation in order to alleviate the restraint is allowed. Since article 14 of the UN CRPD requires liberty and security of person on an equal basis with others, physical restraints would only be allowed if they are imposed on any highly aggressive person regardless of the presence of a mental disorder or not. If persons with a mental disorder could harm themselves in solitary confinement, the German law allows to avert the potential self-harm by physically restraining the person in case there is no other way available with less infringement on the person's physical integrity.

Some proponents of the UN CRPD suggest that any confinement of aggressive persons with mental disorders in the mental health care system is a violation of the UN CRPD, because it includes laws that specifically aim at persons with disabilities, thus violating article 14 and 17 of the UN CRPD. The Federal Constitutional Court of Germany did not follow this line of reasoning but would allow confinement and sedation if it is necessary to protect the patient from violating themselves. Specific medication is only allowed if either the patient endangers her own health or it is required to restore insight, which is otherwise impaired by the mental disorder.

CCTV monitoring is forbidden in Germany, as it constitutes an infringement in personal integrity. In all cases, a person restrained to a bed, or any other piece of furniture must always be monitored and accompanied by a nurse or other medical staff in the same room. Thus, the patient is always able to talk to a human being. Moreover, physical restraint to a bed or any other device must be reported to a judge within 30 min and must be checked by this representative of the legal system immediately (with inconsistent regulations overnight in different German federal states). Restraint in a room with padded walls, in which a patient can move freely, is understood as a less severe limitation of personal liberty, in this case the patient still needs to be observed continuously by a human being in the same room or at least through a screen.

There is evidence that a lack of staff and crowded wards are both associated with an increase in physical restraint, also, wards that try to generally open their doors compared to those that are always locked tend to have lower rates of physical restraint and violence (Nienaber et al. 2018). So, setting and personal equipment play a large role in reducing physical restraint and coercion in the mental health care system.

3.7.1.4 Michaela Amering

With Rob here I wonder again whether this very dangerous and difficult situation could have been avoided if his right to adequate treatment could have kicked in earlier. If the stigma was lower as CRPD obliges us to fight for and other obstacles to early interventions and support could be overcome, we have reason to assume that the occurrence of situations like the one described could be reduced. However, there will always be people who do attack other people in exceptional states of mind that are the results of different kinds of acute health problems including substance use and acute psychotic states as described here. For other peoples' and their own safety, they need to be kept from carrying through with their violent acts. I want to pose the question: Which place and expertise is necessary to do this best? In Rob's case, the police obviously has taken him to a hospital. The Emergency department seems to have been equipped to medically sedate him, but obviously only for a short time. Questions as to whether this was the right kind of de-escalation are quality and quantity as soon after, more interventions were necessary: restraint done by security officers, solitary confinement in a seclusion room, and CCTV monitoring. Each of the mentioned interventions need to be assessed regarding their medical safety (e.g., need to medically monitor sedated patients; need for assessments that allow a diagnostic and therapeutic management of such an acute state of ill health) as well as regarding their necessity and efficacy (e.g., seclusion with camera versus restraint and communication) and of course resources (e.g., number of people, set of trained experience) and of course their ability to preserve as much of a person's rights and dignity as possible under the emergency circumstances (e.g., communication, choice, advance directives).

3.7.1.5 Oye Gureje

Clinicians have a duty to ensure that the behavior of a person with mental illness that could result in grave danger to the life of the patient or to those of others is controlled as effectively as possible and with due respect to the dignity of the patient in doing this. In this instance, it would appear Rob's illness had placed him in a position where his behavior constituted a risk to the lives of others. Since his illness made him unable to be less likely to appreciate the consequences of his behavior, it would be unfair and in fact a denial of his right to good health care to not respond appropriately to prevent those consequences.

The immediate need was to disarm him. It could be argued that this could be done through de-escalation techniques. Such techniques require the appropriate level of trained staff and an assessment of imminence of danger. They also require an assessment of the point of entry for such de-escalation approaches. In this instance, while it is not clear whether appropriately trained staff was available, it seems that two other conditions might be the basis for using physical restraint in this instance. One was the possibility that the risk of serious harm was imminent and the situation would not permit for de-escalation procedures which might require some time to implement and the immediate outcome of which could not be predicted. Second, the focus of Rob's anger was some unknown forces threatening to perpetrate evil and which Rob was intent on preventing. De-escalation might be more likely to succeed if the object of Rob's anger was known persons or clearly understandable situations.

There is some controversy about whether the CRPD specifications prevent the use of physical restraint under any circumstance. Rob's case is an example of a situation where a total exclusion of the possibility of using physical restraint would be impractical in certain clinical situations where a patient's clinical condition demands that steps be taken to help them avoid serious consequences (e.g., legal liability) that may follow their behavior when such behavior is clearly out of their control.

3.7.1.6 Cecile Hanon

What should have been done in this case? Were there any other options to act and if so in which order?

Rob should have been treated again on arrival in the inpatient unit with soothing, perhaps sedative medication at first, but it is far more distressing to leave him agitated, alone, in isolation without pharmacological treatment. Camera surveillance can also be worrying for a person who feels watched and victim of a plot.

Was it justified to detain Rob under the Mental Health Act?

If he was found to be incapable of consenting to care, Yes

Was it justified to treat Rob involuntarily under the Mental Health Act? Yes

Was seclusion and restraint (chemical and physical) justified in this case? Yes

Whether any of the actions taken affected human rights, and if so, what else could have been done?

Restriction of liberty (represented here by physical restraint and isolation) must be legislated. In France, any infringement of the freedom of movement is regulated by the "juge des libertés et de la détention," which is seized as soon as a measure of constrained care is undertaken. The term "constrained care" refers to hospitalization without consent, imposed treatments (intramuscular injections), and restriction of freedom of movement (isolation room, physical restraint).

In what way would the CRPD prescriptions require different action from that taken and how should the differing demands/actions/situations be reconciled?

The judicialization of psychiatric care is efficient to ensure the respect of the autonomy and freedom of movement of individuals.

3.7.1.7 Nicolás Martínez-López

Rob was having a psychotic episode in which he tried to hurt others, even attempting to kill someone. Consequently, the decision-making of the police can be read in several ways, the first is that they acted correctly and took him to an emergency service, which would indicate that the citizen who was attacked did not file charges of attempted homicide, if not that a lesser sanction is configured; giving the freedom to place it in a health service.

After that, acting in the emergency room would sound somewhat unspecific since the administration of antipsychotics would have been sufficient for the episode, in addition, mechanical restraint and isolation are clearly human rights violations and a practice that the convention determines as torture, so that should not have been exercised.

The second way of visualizing it is the configuration of attempted homicide during the psychotic episode that could lead to not guilty by reason of insanity defense, and later take him from emergency care to a criminal instance so that he can be tried before the complaint against him, which would lead to treatment, probably involuntary.

This case highlights the difficulty of the complete application of Article 12, since if Rob's temporary impairment due to psychosis is not contemplated, it would be determined as a voluntary act of attempted homicide and he would spend time in jail-that should not happen.

3.7.1.8 Soumitra Pathare

Based on the limited details available, I do not see any other alternatives for the health care professionals and police in dealing with this situation. I also do not feel the CRPD is particularly relevant when dealing with the immediate emergency, when the person's life as well as the life and safety of those around him is at risk.

The question of treating Rob "involuntarily" does not arise in my opinion. "Involuntary treatment" implies that Rob was in a state to be able to consent or refuse consent to treatment (which does not appear to be so) and his will and preferences were not respected. This is not the case here.

The Committee on Convention on Rights of Persons with Disabilities in its General Comment 1 (guidance document on Article 12 interpretation) also says "Where, after significant efforts have been made, it is not practicable to determine the will and preferences of an individual, the 'best interpretation of will and preferences' must replace the 'best interests' determinations."

In this particular incident, it may be argued that health care professionals and police were not in a position to determine Rob's will and preference despite efforts and their actions were guided by their best interpretation of Rob's will and preferences.

What happened in the days and weeks leading up to the incident and what happened in the days and weeks after the incident would be more relevant from the CRPD perspective. For example, did Rob have access to good quality mental health services in the period leading up to this emergency? What services were provided to Rob in the days, weeks, and months after this incident?

3.7.1.9 Mohan Isaac

Dealing with problems such as Rob's presentation (armed with knife and attempting to stab others in public indiscriminately, in response to abnormal and bizarre thoughts and perceptions) can always be difficult and demanding. One must make a decision balancing "risks" (in this case, to others) versus "rights" (personal rights of Rob). Protecting the public as well as health care providers from the dangerous actions of an individual acting on abnormal thoughts and perceptions is of utmost importance and urgency. There are no options other than appropriately medicating the person showing abnormal behavior. Restraint and seclusion, if absolutely necessary, should be used under established guidelines and only for the least period required.

Medicating (intramuscular injection) Rob without his consent violated his "human rights," but under the circumstances described in the clinical vignette, perhaps nothing else could have been done. In the larger interest of dealing with a potentially dangerous situation, it was appropriate to detain Rob and treat him without his consent, under the Mental Health Act. While chemical restraint is justifiable, whether seclusion and physical restraint necessary are debatable.

The context (wealth/resources of the country, number of staff) certainly influenced the actions in Rob's case. Unlike John (in South Africa), in case vignette 1, who was arrested, charged, produced before a court and jailed for a lesser offence of smashing windows and damage to property, Rob (in England) was "sectioned" under the Mental Health Act and appropriately treated for his mental illness in a psychiatry inpatient unit. The police, in these two situations (occurring in two different countries) acted and behaved differently.

3.7.2 Concluding Comments on Case History 6

3.7.2.1 Neeraj Gill and Norman Sartorius

This case highlights the need for containment and treatment of mental illness during an acute exacerbation requiring emergency response. All the commentators agreed with the need for involuntary hospitalization in this case. This person had assaulted others and tried to stab someone and hence, deprivation to liberty was not considered to be against the CRPD in this case, as deprivation of liberty was on an equal basis with others. There was agreement about the need for health response, rather than criminal/justice system response in this case, as this young man was considered very unwell requiring treatment, in the interest of his right to health and the community's right for safety. However, many responses pointed toward the need for de-escalation techniques, peer support, and more humane treatment.

It was argued that some may interpret the CRPD as prohibiting all involuntary treatment due to violation of Articles 12 (equal legal capacity), 14 (liberty), and 17 (physical and mental integrity). However, all the commentators, including the service-user representative rejected such absolutist interpretation and argued for promotion of right to health of this individual. There were, however, clear disagreements between the level of legal oversight in the process of involuntary treatment, with some commentators calling for much more robust mechanisms for involuntary psychiatric treatment than the others.

The word treatment may include a variety of interventions, some acceptable and some non-acceptable to those who are to be offered some treatment. The CRPD and other documents should not only consider the right to treatment but also the criteria for the acceptance of the "right treatment" and the right treatment may vary under different circumstances. Without insistence that these matters must be defined and based on scientific research, the rules about treatment are difficult to apply in the best interest of the patient.

3.8 Case History 7: A Young Man Who Developed Mental Illness After Being Assaulted in Prison

Aidan is 25-year-old African American man, born and raised in a socio-economically disadvantaged "ghetto" in metropolitan Chicago. As a child, he suffered from frequent physical abuse from his alcohol abusing father. He dropped out of high school, started smoking marijuana at the age of 13 and started using amphetamines when he was 18 years old. He became a drug-mule to support his amphetamine addiction, was nabbed by the police and incurred charges of drug dealing. He was imprisoned with a 6 months' sentence.

In prison, Aidan was subjected to horribly violent racist abuse. During his first week in prison, he was severely, physically, and sexually assaulted by hardened criminals. He was admitted to the prison hospital for a few days, only to be discharged to the same environment, and he again fell prey to the perpetrators of violent sexual assault. This continued for a few days and he ended up in the prison hospital again. After that admission, he was placed in solitary confinement, "for his own safety." After a few days in solitary confinement, Aidan became mentally disordered. He could not sleep, and when he finally fell asleep, he had nightmares. He had flashbacks of his sexual assault and started to hear voices of people threatening to rape him. He started banging his head against the wall and was admitted to hospital again.

In the hospital, he was diagnosed as having post-traumatic stress disorder, with a differential diagnosis of acute polymorphic psychosis. It was recommended that he should be admitted to the state psychiatric facility but there were no beds available. He could have been admitted to another psychiatric facility but that required additional resources, given that he was a current serving prisoner, and to find such resources would have taken time. He remained in the prison general hospital but had to be moved out of there due to bed-pressure. Ultimately, after inpatient treatment in the prison psychiatric unit, he will have to return to prison to serve his time.

3.8.1 Commentary

3.8.1.1 Charlene Sunkel

The prison system is the one place that should have a stand-alone mental health unit or as a component of their so-called infirmaries. Especially considering how many people with mental health conditions or substance-use disorders end up in the prison system, and who often then become targets of abuse from other inmates, as happened in Aidan's case.

To backtrack, Aidan should have been able to access mental health care services and support as a child, when the school should have been educated or trained in basic mental health to identify children who are potential victims of domestic violence and abuse. The school or education system should have professionals such as psychologists to provide a clinical perspective and recommend an appropriate intervention, which could initiate social work intervention to remove children or try and find alternative approaches to stop the violence at home. But this involves human and financial resources which governments often reject due to budgetary constraints. Considering a lifetime approach, investing in protecting children, may result in large cost savings down the line when the children become productive members of society who contribute socially and economically.

3.8.1.2 Martha Savage

(a) Aidan and his parents should have been given social welfare help and counselling for his father's alcohol problem and for his reaction to it.
(b) Counsellors in middle school or high school could have helped him to get off drugs before he dropped out.
(c) There could be community programs to get dropouts into work or apprenticeships, or to help people overcome their drug habits before they get to the point where they are dealing drugs themselves.
(d) There could be separate facilities for prisons of people who are non-violent and violent.
(e) He could have been sent to a drug rehabilitation program instead of to prison.
(f) The prison should have better control of the prisoners so that they do not abuse each other.
(g) There should be more beds in both the prison hospital and the community hospital.

(h) Now: They should try to move him into a treatment program instead of into prison. Or into a different prison that has better control of its prisoners or has more options for drug rehabilitation. If he must go back to the same prison, they should monitor the other prisoners and move them to another place and provide other sanctions if they continue beatings. They should also try to help his family with counselling.

1. Whether any of the possible actions affect human rights, and if so, what else can be done?
   (a) Putting prisoners in solitary confinement is contrary to the convention against torture.
   (b) The prison is abridging the rights of people to be kept free from abuse by not properly controlling the inmates.
   (c) Any time spent in psychiatric hospital should count as prison time.
   (d) The prisons should have more staff to control prisoners and should try to implement some newer techniques to try to help rehabilitate the perpetrators rather than letting them terrorize the other prisoners or separate the violent and non-violent offenders.
   (e) The US is the most powerful and wealthy country on earth, and they should be able to afford more staff and better programs.

Allowing abuse in prison is against the convention for freedom from abuse. Solitary confinement is against the convention against torture. So the main thing the CRPD requires is more humane treatment of their prisoners.

Prisons should have better psychiatric care in their own facilities. In the US now, a high proportion of the prisoners have psychiatric problems. If a prisoner develops a mental illness from their treatment in the prison, they may need to be transferred to a better facility, but if the prison has its own psychiatric care that may not be necessary. In many ways, prisons in the US are substitutes for psychiatric facilities, but the guards are not properly trained to deal with patients, with predictably bad outcomes. Prisons need wholesale reform.

3.8.1.3 Andreas Heinz, Sabine Müller und Assina Seitz

First of all, Aidan's criminal responsibility should have been investigated by an expert of forensic psychiatry. In Germany, persons who are not criminally responsible because they committed a crime under the influence of acute drug consumption or addiction are not imprisoned but placed in a forensic hospital or a rehab center for treating drug addiction. While the system in Germany certainly has its flaws, failing to provide treatment in forensic hospitals or rehab centers is in violation of Article 25 regarding health care and Article 26 regarding offers of rehabilitation. However, in the German system, it is problematic that even those who are not motivated to undergo any therapy are admitted to these institutions. In theory, such therapeutic offers could also be established within a jail, however, they need to include state of the art mental health care services. Simply providing possibilities for general medical care is not adequate.

Accordingly, the consequences of abuse in jail including posttraumatic stress disorder or an acute psychotic reaction also require that Aidan is provided with the full choice of options of medical care including health care established in his country.

On nationwide levels, it has been shown that reduction of inpatient treatment facilities was linearly correlated with an increase in prison population in Latin America (Siebenförcher et al. 2020). Disregard of acute mental disorders including addiction and their respective impact on a person's behavior is inhumane. Instead of applying the legal system designed for persons without impairment of their decision-making abilities and insight, persons with drug addiction should be provided with the same health care options as persons with all other mental disorders. It is grossly inadequate to apply the same prison sentence if the reprimanded behavior occurred under the influence of drug addiction including acute withdrawal or impairment of decision-making abilities.

In this context, we would like to mention the example of a patient with Parkinson's syndrome, who under the effects of dopaminergic medication developed a psychotic state and set his hospital bed aflame. Again, this patient did not have insight or capacity to consent. It would appear to be grossly inadequate to transfer such a person to a jail instead of providing adequate medication or other forms of treatment in hospital in order to counteract the iatrogenic effects of the previously prescribed medication.

Some institutions working with the UN CRPD argue that replacing a prison sentence by treatment in a forensic hospital on grounds of a disability, in this case a drug addiction would be in violation of Article 14. Compulsory admission to a hospital is still a deprivation of liberty. In this view, mental health care must be provided within the prison system. However, even if this care was to be provided in jail (which definitely was not happening with respect to Aidan), there should also be a reduction or abolition of the prison sentence if mental disorders including drug addiction impair decision-making capacities of a person.

Our experiences in Germany show that it is very unrealistic to assume that prisons can provide the same mental health care as a dedicated institution, and we strongly propose to establish alternative treatment options and institutions for persons who commit a crime under the impact of a severe mental disorder including addiction.

Leaving aside the question of prison or forensic psychiatry, it is clear that Aidan's repeated placement with violent hardened criminals violated Article 17. A prison must protect all prisoners against violence and sexual abuse by fellow prisoners.

3.8.1.4 Oye Gureje

There are some social disadvantages that might have been precursors of Aidan's criminality, such as poverty. These social circumstances are issues that would have required political attention to redress. His incarceration seems to be legally justified, being a consequence of his criminal involvement in drug dealing. However, even if his conviction was legally justified, his confinement with hardened criminals was not. As a first offender, he should have been given a lighter sentence, such as community service or a similar punishment. Incarcerating him with hardened criminals could have set the stage for him to become more rather than less criminally involved following his time in prison. As it happened, he was subjected to serious abuse by the other inmates, an experience that could have made the prison less of a correctional facility for him.

Following the abuse he experienced, a review of his placement ought to have taken place. This experience resulted in his need for hospital admission. Surprisingly, he was sent back to the same environment following his discharge. This was inappropriate. A review of his confinement conditions should have been conducted at that stage, and a less toxic environment found for him even if no other action, such as parole, was possible.

Once he decompensated mentally, a vicious cycle was set in motion for him. The prison hospital was unable to provide the care he needed, and the specialist psychiatric hospital was unable to find him a bed, especially given the extra security requirements needed to accommodate a convict in an open ward. This should have further prompted the prison officials to set in motion the process for a proper review of Aidan's situation. Surely, there ought to be options for dealing with a severely ill first-time convict to have a review of their conviction so that they could receive adequate treatment.

The right of Aidan to be treated with respect and dignity was violated by his fellow inmates who physically abused and sexually assaulted him. His right to health was not respected by the prison authorities who put him at harm's way and did not find the appropriate response to his mental illness so that he could receive adequate treatment. Even as a convict, these rights were sacrosanct and ought not to be denied Aidan.

The inability to find a bed for Aidan in an appropriate specialist hospital reflects resource limitation. That situation is more likely to occur in a low resourced country.

The CRPD specifically prescribes that persons with mental illness, irrespective of whether they are free or serving prison sentence, have the right to adequate and humane treatment. Indeed, in many jurisdictions, special protections are offered to prisoners in view of their vulnerability and confinement.

3.8.1.5 Cecile Hanon

What should be done in this case? Are there any other options to act and if so in which order? In France, there is psychiatric care for prisoners, with outpatient units and the possibility of inpatient care. Aidan's situation is terribly frequent and is linked to the extremely poor conditions of detention, overcrowding and the resulting violence.

Whether any of the possible actions affect human rights, and if so, what else can be done? How will the context, e.g., the wealth/resources of the country or number of staff influence the order of actions.

Of course, the country context comes into play here. Just because one is detained and in breach of the law does not mean that one loses one's status as a human being and one's dignity and right to health.

In what way would the CRPD prescriptions require different action from that taken and how should the differing demands/actions/situations be reconciled? The right to health must be respected here.

3.8.1.6 Nicolás Martínez-López

The reality of people with a dual diagnosis is that they are immersed in the criminal justice system, without clear access to resources for their care and with a vision of criminalizing substance dependence. However, in this particular case, both violence due to skin color and suffering from a mental disorder were the driving force for him to be labelled as guilty of the crime of drug trafficking, without seeing that dependency should be considered as a cause of not guilty by reason of insanity defense, since by altering the decision-making of those who suffer from it, the crimes that they commit are for the purpose of consuming the substance. A modern way out has been the drug courts, which are not able to generate a radical change in the care of people with a dual diagnosis, since crimes like the one in this case are hardly candidates for a therapeutic measure in my country, as they are in other countries like Europe.

Finally, the Nelson Mandela Rules or The United Nations Standard Minimum Rules for the Treatment of Prisoners (McCall-Smith 2016) say:

B. Prisoners with mental disabilities and/or health conditions.

Rule 109

1. Persons who are found to be not criminally responsible, or who are later diagnosed with severe mental disabilities and/or health conditions, for whom staying in prison would mean an exacerbation of their condition, shall not be detained in prisons, and arrangements shall be made to transfer them to mental health facilities as soon as possible.
2. If necessary, other prisoners with mental disabilities and/or health conditions can be observed and treated in specialized facilities under the supervision of qualified health-care professionals.
3. The health-care service shall provide for the psychiatric treatment of all other prisoners who are in need of such treatment.

Therefore, Aidan should have treatment and support outside the prison.

3.8.1.7 Soumitra Pathare

The lack of mental health facilities for treating vulnerable populations such as prisoners has not received sufficient attention of policymakers and the mental health community in most countries. In particular, there are few community drug treatment facilities even in high-income countries. This vignette also highlights intersectionality that is common for so many people—dual diagnosis, ethnicity, and mental illness.

A number of CRPD rights are violated in this case, and the government (prison authorities) have to be held responsible. Failure to prevent sexual abuse (Articles 16 and 17) and the lack of mental health and drug treatment facilities (Articles 25 and 26) are two most obvious examples.

3.8.1.8 Mohan Isaac

Aidan has a right to receive appropriate assessment, diagnosis, and management by a competent mental health professional, as early as possible. As his proper assessment and management for his PTSD/psychosis are indefinitely delayed or denied, his right to receive treatment and care is violated. He also deserves appropriate rehabilitation for his substance use and related problems.

Aidan's racial and socioeconomic background have undoubtedly contributed to his current situation.

3.8.2 Concluding Remarks on Case History 7

3.8.2.1 Neeraj Gill and Norman Sartorius

This case reflects on multiple abject failures present at the interface between the custodial and psychiatric systems and the role of the prison system in the development and mistreatment of mental illness. A noteworthy feature of this vignette is the role of endemic racial bias influencing the imprisonment, abuse, and neglect experienced by this individual.

The consensus opinion of all reviewers was that this individual would have benefited from early intervention with adequate treatment of his father's alcohol misuse, protection from his unsafe living circumstances, and psychological assessment and support during high school. Forensic assessment of his criminal responsibility for his drug charges would have been beneficial. It was identified that the prison system failed to protect this individual and his mental health needs went largely unmet.

The bleak reality put forward by multiple commentators is one of an incidental establishment of the prison system as an unsupported safety net for people living with untreated mental illness. The unanimous opinion of the commentators was that there is an absolute need for dedicated psychiatric assessment units within the prison system and for a formal process to be created to ensure incarcerated persons have access to timely psychiatric assessment, diagnosis, and treatments. Lack of access to subspecialist forensic services was identified as a key aggravating factor in the case discussed.

Reflection on this case calls for a critique on the mistreatment of the prison population and the need for prison reform especially for those who already have, or develop, a mental illness during their incarceration. The need for prison reform is highlighted including the need to establish formalized processes to access specialist mental health care while incarcerated. A harmonization of the rules concerning incarceration and other related measures and the CRPD concerned with human rights of all people, including those who commit crimes is a task that has been given insufficient attention.

3.9 Case History 8: A Man with Mental Illness Refusing Life-Saving Treatment of a Physical Illness

Paul is a 40-year-old single man, who works as junior engineer and lives with his parents in a metropolitan city of Australia. He has a known diagnosis of bipolar affective disorder and has been on lithium for almost 10 years. He has a history of multiple manic and depressive episodes ever since his illness started at the age of 20. His manic episodes were characterized by excessive cheerfulness or irritability, aggression, reckless driving, and financial indiscretion. During depressive episodes, he attempted suicide three times by hanging and medication overdose. He responded well to lithium, and while he had relapses secondary to non-compliance in the beginning, his mental state has been mostly stable for the last 5 years.

Approximately 3 years ago, Paul developed renal insufficiency and his lithium had to be ceased. He was switched over to sodium valproate for mood stabilization. His mental state remained stable, but his renal condition continued to get worse, and he went into chronic renal failure, requiring renal dialysis, three times a week. This had a major impact on his life, as he had to stop work, went on disability support pension and required a non-governmental organization's support. He had to give up playing football which had always been his passion.

After 2 years, Paul decided to stop dialysis. He told his renal physician that his quality of life was very poor, he could not work or play footy, he had few friends and his life now revolved around dialysis. He was very depressed and wanted to die. His parents were very worried about him. A psychiatrist assessed Paul and advised that John was having a relapse of bipolar depression and his wish to die was due to his depression. John was transferred to a locked psychiatric ward and was administered Electro-Convulsive Therapy (ECT) against his wish. His dialysis was continued under sedation. After 12 ECTs, John's mental state improved, he accepted to continue dialysis and was discharged back home.

Six months later, Paul decided to stop dialysis again. This time, a different psychiatrist assessed him and decided that he had capacity to consent for (or refuse) treatment and that his wish and preference should be respected. His parents were distraught. The nephrologist advised that Paul could be placed on the waiting list for renal transplant but said that it might take many years before a transplant could be made. Paul said that he did not want to go on any longer and remained adamant that he should be allowed to stop dialysis and have a dignified death.

3.9.1 Commentary

3.9.1.1 Charlene Sunkel

One can imagine the impact of his physical health situation, considering that work and sports were what brought meaning to his life and by losing the ability to continue engaging in these activities had a significant reduction in his quality of life.

Perhaps more support could have been provided, to try to help him discover other passions that he could focus on that could increase his quality of life and renew his purpose in life. Peer support and/or a clubhouse program could have added a support structure, since he did not have many friends and perhaps felt isolated and lonely—this could have helped him in knowing that he had support and new friends to help him during moments of despair.

Regarding the choice to terminate dialysis—a psychiatrist made the determination that he had the capacity to decide for himself, therefore and in terms of his human rights, as any other person would be able to refuse treatment (termination of dialysis), his wishes should have been respected in this regard.

The question however is, was he asked what and if anything, could be done to support him and help him find meaning in his life, until a transplant is available, and linking him up with peer support services and a clubhouse program, for example.

3.9.1.2 Martha Savage

This is a tricky case, because there is a right to refuse medical treatment, but in this case it may conflict with the right to life and to proper medical treatment if his wish to die comes from his bipolar depression. But there were certainly other options in the past:

(a) The blood lithium values and renal function should have been monitored better. He should be on the minimum level of lithium that would allow his symptoms to be relieved. He might have been able to use a lower dose with extra support, especially if his renal function started to decrease.
(b) There should have been some family counselling all along. If it was not happening earlier, it should have been done each time he expressed the suicidal wish to stop treatment.
(c) There should be a second opinion before he is allowed to stop treatment. There should always be a requirement of more than one opinion before a step that is likely to lead to death is taken. Also, a death due to renal failure is particularly awful and painful, and that fact must be impressed upon Paul.
(d) It should also be realized that if he really wants to die, he could probably easily obtain materials that would make it simpler, shorter, and less painful. So his asking to stop treat-

ment may actually be a call for help. Therefore, now he and his family need more psychological, and/or social worker and/or peer support. He could be encouraged to do alternative activities, such as a less physical sport than footy, or to start another hobby, or part-time work or volunteer work, perhaps even for his footy team. He could get a dog or another pet, or do something else that would involve caring for another (most people adjust to live without personally doing footy when they get older). Medical care gets better and better, and there may be alternatives to transplants from humans in the fairly near future, which could give him a better life if he would only hold on a little longer. Because of the concern that his choice is due to his mental state, there should be some bargaining with him about giving him a certain length of time to try the actions above with the idea that if he is still adamant in (some length of time, such as 1 year), he could stop treatment.

(e) There should be family counselling to be sure that everybody is at peace with whatever decision gets made. They are the ones who will have to live without their loved one if he stops his medication.

Whether any of the possible actions affect human rights, and if so, what else can be done? How will the context, e.g., the wealth/resources of the country or number of staff influence the order of actions? As mentioned above, the right to life and the right to refuse medical care are in conflict here. The best thing would be to provide more resources to monitor/provide extra support and try the suggestions above. Australia is rich; it should be able to afford help. Volunteer and peer support can be very helpful and not too expensive.

Should Paul be allowed to stop dialysis?

There should be at least two psychiatrists to determine whether he is in the right mental state to make such a decision, and the determinations should be made over a period of time. And he should be offered psychotherapy and family therapy as mentioned above.

3.9.1.3 Andreas Heinz, Sabine Müller und Assina Seitz

Again, there is no mention of psychotherapeutic or psychosocial support provided to Paul after he decided to stop dialysis or as a matter of fact throughout his whole treatment. Bipolar disorders are not simply treated with lithium or other medications; any therapeutic offer should include psychosocial and as far as accepted by the patient also psychotherapeutic support.

The first transfer to a locked ward would not be possible in Germany without the decision of a judge based on an independent medical consultant's expertise. In cases of chronic mental disorders that impair a person's ability to take care of their severe somatic problems, a legal guardian would most likely be established, who in interaction with an independent medical counsellor and legal procedures presided by a judge could decide in Paul's best interest against his currently articulated will. However, this would only be possible in cases in which Paul would lack insight into the consequences of his actions due to the mental disorder. Electroconvulsive therapy would most likely not be applied but instead, medication could be applied in such cases. Also, in Germany, a legal consultant is always present who should inform the patient independently about their rights in the legal procedures.

The case report does not suggest that the mental disorder impairs Paul's insight in his situation and his capacity to consent, and the second psychiatrist voiced the opinion that Paul indeed had the capacity to consent. So Paul's will to stop treatment should be respected. Nevertheless, he should be provided with all possible support, including psychosocial counselling and psychotherapy, of course on a voluntary basis. Such support may help to motivate Paul to continue to live, but if Paul is able to consent, he should not be forced into treatment and has a right to stop treatment of his somatic disease.

Some authors suggest that judging the capacity to consent would be a violation of CRPD Article 14, because it states that "the existence of a disability shall in no case justify a deprivation of liberty." However, the Federal Court of Germany did not support such an interpretation of the CRPD. In fact, it would be severely inhumane if a person who under the impact of an acute drug intoxication decides that they can fly would be allowed to jump out of a window, because of an extreme interpretation of the CRPD stating that no disability should ever justify hindering a patient to do what they want to do. So common sense shows that there are cases in which a person acts without the capacity to consent and therefore without insight. However, Germany and many other countries lack supported decision-making, i.e., not a simple yes/no way of deciding if a patient has the capacity to consent, but rather an approach that takes every articulation of the patient seriously and tries to provide support and information on all levels of understanding, aiming at providing necessary support for regaining insight, and enhancing the capacity to consent. This being said, there will still be situations in which a patient has no insight and may require coercive treatment, however, all such cases should be decided by a judge based on psychiatric or neurological expertise, not by a medical doctor alone, and there should always be a second independent medical expert statement as well as all possible support to change such a situation into one in which the patient has insight and the capacity to consent.

3.9.1.4 Michaela Amering

At the center here I see the need for second opinions and procedures that involve other people and expertise. For the supported decision-making clearly necessary to facilitate for Paul, especially for his second time decision about ending dialysis, a team to support Paul in his decision-making would need to consist of not only mental health experts and community facilitators and friends and family, but also somatic medicine experts including renal medicine and palliative care experts. Information needs to come in a form that is understandable and time needs to be provided to work through the different sets of information and interactions between the members of the supported decision team, probably several meetings will be necessary. Some health systems have clinical ethics consultants, which could probably help. Another CRPD positive right comes to mind here, namely Article 31 on the right to participate in cultural life, recreation, leisure, and sport. Following this legal obligation might possibly have resulted in more meaningful re-engagement with his sporting life. And of course, while the past cannot be changed at this point, one cannot resist the question whether he did have/might have needed to make more use of his right to the monitoring of his somatic health while on lithium with enough controls and expertise to react to somatic problems early as well as access to other supports that can make life meaningful under special conditions, such as self-help from the renal as well as from the mental health community, peer help, enough financial resources to compensate for need for support, etc.

3.9.1.5 Oye Gureje

It would appear that Paul received appropriate medical care. The decision to put him on lithium appeared to have been made in consideration of the best possible way to stabilize his mental state. While lithium is an effective medication for bipolar disorder, it is not without side effects, some of which could be potentially serious and life threatening. Good clinical practice dictates that any patient being treated with lithium is routinely monitored for those side effects. It is plausible to suspect that this was done in Paul's case and the emergence of renal insufficiency was not otherwise preventable. Once renal insufficiency set in, the appropriate step to take was to stop the lithium and treat the side effect. This was apparently done in this instance. Unfortunately, Paul's renal problem deteriorated and ultimately required him to be on regular renal dialysis, a procedure that is commonly associated with great inconvenience and impairment of quality of life.

The decision to admit and treat Paul involuntarily with ECT when he was assessed to be clinically depressed and expressing suicidal intent seems justified. If not treated, Paul would have died and the psychiatrist's failure to act would have been partly responsible for that outcome.

The decision by Paul to stop his dialysis again and the assessment by another psychiatrist that he was no longer clinically depressed present a different consideration. At 40 years of age and with no mental disorder impairing his judgment, Paul was capable of making the decision about his treatment, including not to be treated with dialysis. The appropriate thing for the clinicians to do in the circumstance would be to offer him as much information, support, and guidance. This could include presenting him with information about the prospect of his condition and what he might still be able to do to improve his quality of life. This would require expertise and time of appropriately qualified staff. However, the final decision of whether to resume dialysis or not should be Paul's, perhaps with the active support of his parents.

There is right to live. That right is to be protected by the state but the assertion of it is for the adult individual. Protecting that right by the state should include actions to ensure that the individual in not encumbered by decisional incapacity to assert the right or decline it. That seems to me for a justification in ensuring that persons with mental illness of sufficient severity as to impair their decisional capacity are availed the required treatment so that they do not make the decision of life or death when they may be incapable of weighing all issues related to the decision. Paul's involuntary treatment was an effort by the state to offer appropriate protection to Paul so that he could exercise the right in full capacity.

Paul received a range of treatments that might not be readily accessible in settings with severe resource constraints. For example, even though lithium is a relatively cheap medication, it might not be readily accessible where the regular laboratory monitoring required for it use is unavailable. This might mean that the long period of clinical remission that Paul enjoyed might not have been possible. Of course, it might also mean that the renal complications might have been avoided.

Perhaps, the CRPD prescriptions might have been interpreted to suggest that Paul's involuntary admission and treatment with ECT was a violation of his right to freedom and dignity. Some would also suggest that the ECT amounted to cruel treatment. However, neither of these positions would be tenable. First, the right to life should be paramount and the decision to treat Paul such that he could make a decision when not impaired by mental illness would be a reasonable justification for the involuntary admission and treatment. Second, ECT is a safe and effective treatment. When administered under appropriate medical specifications, it is neither cruel nor crude.

3.9.1.6 Cecile Hanon

What should be done in this case? Are there any other options to act and if so in which order? Very complex situation, to which a univocal answer is impossible! In terms of autonomy, Paul does indeed have decision-making capacity, but it has already been shown that this capacity was impaired by depression, which was treatable, and he may have had a different opinion during a period of euthymia.

From a beneficence-non-maleficence perspective, it is not desirable to deprive Paul of dialysis as there is an almost immediate lethal risk. Forcing him to undergo antidepressant treatment or ECT may seem harmful in the first instance, but he has already experienced therapeutic success with improvement in his mood.

In terms of justice, the benefit-risk balance is in favor of continuing dialysis.

- There is a right to life. Is there a right to death?

  No, the right to death does not exist as a negative aspect of the right to life and it is up to each country to legally regulate the end of life.

  In France, the right to refuse care is a natural and legal counterpart to the right to care. "No one can force me to receive care, except if my refusal could endanger the life of others" (dangerousness underpinned by a psychiatric illness with the necessary psychiatric care to be provided under duress, but also, for example, the compulsory vaccination for tuberculosis). This is usually done in underage children. During the epidemic crisis of COVID 19, compulsory vaccination was imposed for vulnerable people, to protect them, but this was debated because many people were against it and had no choice. For example, carers who refused to be vaccinated were forbidden to go to work, or even dismissed.

- Should Paul be allowed to stop dialysis?

  In France, there is no legislation allowing for "somatic" forced care in the same way as "psychiatric" care. Paul cannot be forced to continue dialysis, i.e., physically forced to do so (by tying his arms, for example). However, the clinical vignette tells us that this has been done before when he was admitted to the psychiatric hospital for ECT, as he was sedated, which would not have been possible in France.

On the other hand, we can inform him, reiterate advice so that he makes an informed decision. If his mental state is too altered by intense depression, or even melancholy, we can then start forced psychiatric care again to give him a chance to get better and to have a mind more inclined to make an informed choice. If, despite everything, he persists in his choice, it is necessary to be able to accompany him in this direction and to offer him palliative care. In France, medical aid in dying is illegal. There can only be assistance with deep and continuous sedation in the case of an illness leading to death in the short term, so it would be necessary to wait until Paul is in terminal renal failure before accompanying him in this way. This is quite terrible in terms of dignity, suffering, and pain. But there is also a "right not to suffer," governed by a law of 9 June 1999 on palliative care, which allows me to set up so-called supportive care (analgesics, anxiolytics, body care, etc.).

3.9.1.7 Nicolás Martínez-López

The existence of a disease such as the bipolar disorder that Paul suffers, is not an indicator of permanent alteration of cognitive capacity, therefore his decisions will not always be biased by depression or mania. In addition, the fact of suffering from this disorder does not prevent him from freely exercising his legal capacity.

It is likely that, to a large extent, the propensity to become depressed due to bipolar disorder is greater than that of the average person with chronic renal failure who is on dialysis. However, Paul has a life experience that makes him visualize his life before and after dialysis, so bipolar disorder in this context does not seem to play a fundamental role in making the decision to leave treatment and have a dignified death.

His decision must be respected since it is not feasible in modern medicine to carry out forced treatments even if the patient has a fatal outcome. Therefore, regardless of the mental health diagnosis that a person has, their desire for a dignified death must be respected.

3.9.1.8 Soumitra Pathare

I do not think this can be equated with a right to death. It is about the right to make choices. If the psychiatrist has assessed the person as being capable of making decisions, then those decisions should be respected, however painful the outcome maybe. Paul is a person with a physical health condition (dialysis) and is judged to have capacity to make decisions. His mental health history is relevant and was presumably taken into account by the second psychiatrist. However, it cannot be presumed that all decisions made by Paul are invalid because of his past history of mental illness. The validity or invalidity of a decision cannot be based on its potential outcome (in this case potential death) or the past history of mental illness.

I would support the opinion of the second psychiatrist. I think the CRPD also supports this position.

3.9.1.9 Mohan Isaac

Since the decision about Paul's continuing or stopping dialysis is a "life and death" question, Paul's capacity to make such decisions should be reviewed/reassessed by another psychiatrist (a second opinion) or a board/panel of psychiatrists. Paul has been suffering for more than 10 years from bipolar affective disorder with history of multiple manic and depressive episodes, with the most recent successfully treated depressive episode occurring as recent as 6 months back. It is important to clearly rule out that Paul's decision to stop dialysis again is not the consequence of a new depressive episode. If the second opinion/review shows that his capacity to make treatment decisions is questionable, appropriate provisions of the Mental Health Act could be invoked, which will affect his human rights.

If, in fact Paul has capacity to make treatment choices and decisions, he should be appropriately educated about the consequences of his stopping dialysis—slowly progressive kidney failure, resulting in uremia and perhaps not a dignified death. Paul should be fully informed about what can happen if he actually stops dialysis.

There is a growing debate in many countries about the "right to die" and bringing appropriate legislation for the right to die. Already many countries and several states of Australia have legislations for "voluntary assisted dying."

3.9.2 Concluding Remarks on Case History 8

3.9.2.1 Neeraj Gill and Norman Sartorius

This clinical scenario invites a reflection on the right to autonomy, exercise of legal capacity, and the complex interplay between physical and mental health in the cessation of treatment for life threatening chronic disease; specifically, the withdrawal of dialysis for chronic renal failure. Such discussions will become increasingly relevant as voluntary assisted dying and euthanasia become legalized in more regions of the world.

A number of commentators lament that further efforts in this case should have been made to provide psychosocial treatment to motivate this young man to continue living with the prospect of an eventual kidney transplant. They reflect on the attempts at biological treatment including medication and ECT but suggest that more intense psychosocial support may have changed the choice of this man to cease dialysis.

Multiple commentators point out the complex nature of capacity assessment to make decisions regarding physical healthcare in the setting of a mental health condition. The presence of suicidality in the setting of a mood disorder indeed complicates the assessment of an individual's ability to refuse treatment. However, the majority feel that in the setting of well-controlled bipolar disorder, this patient was exercising his right to self-determination and had the right to withdraw from dialysis. The consensus held that if psychiatric assessment from at least two psychiatrists deemed the patient to have capacity, then his wishes ought to be respected.

3.10 Case History 9: Goonga Paagal—A Homeless Man with Intellectual Disability

He was a nameless homeless man in his twenties, in a small town in Pakistan. People called him "Goonga Paagal," which in Punjabi language means—"Dumb/Mute Madman." He could only make incomprehensible noises but could not use language. He would constantly gesture and mutter as if talking to himself or someone else, without using any words. He probably had an undiagnosed intellectual disability. Nobody knew where he came from. He wandered in the town aimlessly, begged for food from people, and slept in a park. Children feared him, and young boys often pelted him with stones.

Gradually, people realized that he was harmless and warmed up to him. The local mosque allowed him to stay overnight on its premises. He continued to wander around the town during the day and came to sleep in the mosque at night. However, gradually, his muttering and gesturing increased and he started to shout incomprehensibly. One day, he shouted at children in a park, upon which he was beaten up by people there. He was then taken to a local hospital where he was tied to the bed and treated for his injuries.

It was then that an NGO from a nearby city got involved. He was admitted to a mental asylum—run by an NGO—in which dozens of people with mental disorders were tied to pillars or beds, and fed. There was a mental hospital in a nearby town but knowing the over-crowded and under-resourced conditions of that mental hospital, this NGO believed that they did a better job of caring for people with mental disorders than the mental hospital. There were private psychiatrists in the nearby metropolitan areas but again, the NGO did not trust those Western medicine trained psychiatrists and also could not afford to pay for the private psychiatrist fee.

The "Goonga Paagal" now cannot wander around as he is tied to a tree during the day, and to his bed at night.

3.10.1 Commentary

3.10.1.1 Charlene Sunkel

First of all, the fact that the children behaved in an abusive manner toward him, raise the importance of starting to sensitize children from a young age about psychosocial and intellectual disabilities. Parents also have the responsibility to do the same.

Being considered harmless, the were no grounds for tying him up nor is it necessary or aligned with human rights to tie anyone up (as those in the asylum were). This man probably lived a much happier life on the street with the community accepting him (apart from the children's poor behavior toward him) and mosque providing him with shelter at night.

Asylums or institutions have a long-documented history of coercive and abusive practices in the name of "caring and providing shelter and food." Sadly, some countries are slow or even stagnant in progressing and acknowledging that these practices inflict great harm on those detained under those conditions, which are considered as torture, degrading and inhumane treatment and a gross violation of human rights. Governments and politicians of such countries fail to uphold their international commitments to protecting the human rights of all citizens. Another issue is the lack of proper regulatory mechanisms to ensure that all government and non-government organizations (NGOs) working with or providing or housing persons with disabilities align their practices with local and international human rights instruments (e.g., the CRPD).

3.10.1.2 Martha Savage

(a) As this man was harmless, the mosque was right to take him in. It would have been good if there had been a community housing place where he could have gone voluntarily. There should be more attempts to find out where he was from so that family or friends could be found, or at least a familiar place. When he started shouting more, there should have been more attempts to communicate with him and find out what was wrong and to find out his background.
(b) Once he was in the hospital, again it would be better for him to go voluntarily to community housing with counselling, perhaps through volunteers, or to the mosque, to try to understand him.
(c) Now he should be taken out of the NGO asylum and invited to go to community housing and to get help. If there is no community housing, perhaps the mosque could be asked to help him again. Again, more attempts should be made to find his family.

Tying people up is a form of torture and is a violation of the CRPD. He needs to be untied immediately. The NGO should be educated in the problems that can happen to people who are tied up, such as deep vein thrombosis and suffocation, and they should be encouraged to change the way they operate to find more creative solutions. As stated above, community housing to give him a place to sleep at night and food would be the best thing. The country is indeed poor, and there seems to be not enough staff in public hospitals. But wealthy countries such as Japan also tie psychiatric patients to their beds for long periods, sometimes until they die. So the use of torture on psychiatric patients and the violation of their right to life is not only a problem of the wealth of the country, but also of its values and culture.

Psychiatrists should try to work more closely with NGOs to try to listen to their concerns and try to reconcile with them at least to get them to abide by the CRPD. They should point out that if people are treated poorly in the hospital, it will make them try to avoid getting any care in the future. The psychiatrists and NGOs should work together to try to get more money for psychiatric, psychological, and/or social worker care. Alternatively, they could help set up programs with peer supporters or volunteers to help.

3.10.1.3 Andreas Heinz, Sabine Müller und Assina Seitz

The nameless person in this case vignette did not display any violent behavior that could justify any restraint on his freedom to move, particularly there was no reason to tie him to a bed. Treatment for his injuries has to occur in accordance with Article 25 of the UN CRPD, one could argue that based on this article, this person should have been provided with shelter and food in order to avoid harmful impact of his life conditions on his health.

There was also absolutely no justification for transferring this nameless person to a faith-based NGO and again, there was no reason for restricting the freedom of this person by physical means. Additionally, again, in violation of Article 25 of the CRPD, no adequate medical treatment was provided. As far as this case vignette shows that there was not only a lack of mental health care but also no somatic health care. The physical restriction with chains in this faith-based organization is in violation of Article 14 of the CRPD, also there appears to never have been any access to justice provided (Article 13 of the CRPD). Article 10 was violated throughout the whole procedure, as there were no attempts made to provide this nameless person with shelter and food without coercion.

3.10.1.4 Oye Gureje

This young man with presumed intellectual disability was probably dumped in the street by his family who, either because of social stigma and shame or poverty, were unable to care for his long-term needs and had no access to formal support. Lacking in family support and any form of formal care provided by government, he has become a homeless vagrant with severe disability. None of his human rights to health, dignity, and respect are protected or assured. The care that he has been offered by the NGO is hardly more humane than what he received as a severely disabled person living in the street.

We do not know the cause of his intellectual disability. However, preventing its emergence would have been the first course of action. This could have been through appropriate perinatal care for his mother, adequately supervised delivery, ensuring that he received all required childhood vaccinations, adequate nutrition, and attention to any childhood illness to which he might have been exposed. Perhaps, these actions could have prevented the emergence of intellectual disability. Should intellectual disability still occur, he should have received appropriate professional care that would improve his functioning and perhaps be able to receive some form of special education.

If all of this did not happen and he ended up in the street, the social services of the jurisdiction should have promptly identified him and taken him up for supervised care with appropriate professionals overseeing the care. Such care might still be provided by a well-supported NGO who have the resources to deliver good quality care to persons in need.

While it is unclear whether the original cause of his disability was due to inability to access health care, it is certainly the case that ending up in the street is an indication that he has been denied his right to adequate health care. His experience in the street and in the NGO facility is characterized by denial of several human rights, including to be treated with dignity and respect, to have adequate housing and to have freedom and choice, all of which are specified CRPD prescriptions as in need of protection. The young man's experience is not uncommon in low- and middle-income country settings and probably much less likely to occur in a high-income country setting.

3.10.1.5 Nicolás Martínez-López

The presence of an intellectual and auditory disability generates a greater complication for treatment and support from the community; however, the action of this NGO is clearly a violation of human rights, by holding this person day and night, and also violates his right to health (Article 25 of the CRPD) by not allowing or providing quality care that could lead to rehabilitation and a better quality of life.

Unfortunately, these types of actions prevail in our days throughout the world and generate a greater violation of human rights than the actions of psychiatry in the nineteenth century. In my country, Mexico, it happens not only with people with intellectual disabilities, but also with people with disorders due to the use of substances and addictive behaviors, through isolation and deprivation of liberty for months without psychiatric and psychotherapeutic treatment.

This case reflects the impotence that mental health professionals have in the face of the uses and customs of certain regions of the world. The continuous mechanical restraint and the non-administration of medication generate a violation of the human right to health and is torture.

3.10.1.6 Soumitra Pathare

Keeping this person confined and tied to a tree during the day and the bed at night are human rights violations and irrespective of the good intentions of the NGO, they should be prosecuted for the same. The CRPD requires State Parties (governments) to protect people from rights violations by third parties too.

The government and public health authorities need to be held responsible for this state of affairs. It is an abdication of their responsibility under Articles 25 and 26 of the CRPD that has led to this unfortunate situation. If the country has ratified the CRPD, they have a duty to respect the provisions of the CRPD. Countries cannot use lack of resources as an excuse to permit third party violations of human rights of persons with mental illness.

The government of the country has a legally binding duty under the CRPD to make provisions for long-term rehabilitation of persons with disabilities including persons with mental illness and/or intellectual disability. Such rehabilitation services must be affordable (or free), accessible, available, and of good quality.

3.10.1.7 Mohan Isaac

The arrangement of Goonga Paagal (GP) being under the care of an NGO which ties him to a pillar, 24 × 7, violates his rights. The assertion of the NGO that they do a better job of caring for people with mental disabilities than the mental hospital is debatable. GP should be sent for assessment by a mental health professional to the mental hospital in the nearby town or a general hospital with psychiatry department and appropriate action taken based on the outcome of the assessment. GP could be admitted to this hospital and treated as per the provisions of the mental health care legislation of the country. Efforts could be made to locate the person's family, and if found, this individual could go back to stay with his family.

3.10.2 Concluding Remarks on Case History 9

3.10.2.1 Neeraj Gill and Norman Sartorius

This vignette sheds light on the fact that the main abuse of human rights in the field of mental health is not that some of them are mistreated (although this should clearly be avoided) but the behavior of governments which do not provide resources to provide treatment and care for people with mentally illness. This case history further explores how the violation of positive (economic, social, and cultural) rights leads to violation of negative (civil and political) rights. The Goonga Paagal lived in perpetual violation of his positive rights as evidenced by the impact of homelessness, lack of community supports, and lack of access to mental health services. Ultimately, he ended up mechanically restrained in a so-called asylum. The abhorrent disregard for personal liberty through prolonged mechanical restraint performed by this NGO was unanimously chastised by the commentators.

The consensus from all reviewers was that this individual had a right to a psychiatric assessment and treatment plan. Most comments suggest that he would also benefit from community housing and social supports rather than restrictive treatment in the NGO asylum.

Respect for inherent dignity, autonomy, liberty, and right to social inclusion and right to access to health services are key pillars of the CRPD. Neglect by the community/State to begin with, and then disregard for this man's rights by this NGO are in direct violation of the CRPD. Consideration to the economic status of the country was given but noted by most reviewers to only be a small, if at all, mitigating circumstance. One commentator appropriately points out that the values and cultural priorities of a nation are the primary driving factor in the prevention of human rights violations rather than their economic status.

3.11 Case History 10: A Man on Long-Term Community Treatment Order (CTO)

Jim is a 46-year-old man in Australia, with more than 20 years' history of paranoid schizophrenia. In his 20s and 30s, he had several admissions to psychiatric institutions with relapses of his psychosis, because of non-adherence to treatment with medications. During his previous relapse 2 years ago, he was admitted to the acute psychiatric inpatient unit after the police apprehended him for erratic driving and bizarre behavior.

Many years before that he had been charged with a stalking offence and assault for which he served a 3 months' sentence in prison.

The examination in the hospital showed that they had psychosis, characterized by persecutory delusions, auditory hallucinations, and aggressive behavior. He was discharged from the hospital after 3 weeks and placed on a Community Treatment Order (CTO) upon discharge.

Jim has been maintained on monthly paliperidone long-acting antipsychotic injection under the CTO now, and his psychotic illness has been in remission for almost 2 years. There are no acute risk issues currently. However, Jim does not accept that he has a major mental illness. He believes that his admissions were caused by nervous breakdown due to stress and claims that cigarette smoking calms his nerves. Therefore, he continues to smoke about 20 cigarettes daily. He reports ongoing stiffness in his body and restlessness due to the depot injections.

Jim wants to come off the compulsory treatment and wants oral medications rather than depot injection. The treating psychiatrist is reluctant to take him off compulsory treatment in the community because of history of non-compliance with oral medication which led to relapses of florid psychotic episodes in the past and the risk of relapse due to non-adherence. The current period of stability for 2 years with CTO is the longest that he has ever had.

Specific questions:

- Under the human rights framework adopted by the CRPD, is it justified to keep Jim under the CTO and treat him with depot antipsychotic injections against his wish?

3.11.1 Commentary

3.11.1.1 Charlene Sunkel

Despite someone's history of non-compliance to treatment, a Community Treatment Order is a form of coercion and alternatives should be made available in the community, such as peer support, psychoeducation, psychosocial rehabilitation, and recovery programs, that could have a far more effective outcome in that it can support and provide the person with the necessary tools to navigate through crises, manage side effects of medications (unless it has a significant negative impact), and find ways that enhances opportunities for the person to thrive despite their mental health condition.

The question is always, why a person fails to be compliant on treatment and if this question is asked to the person to understand their choice instead of forcing a choice onto them, which will only end up in non-compliance. For example, if a person's reasons are based on intolerable side effects (that can be debilitating and reduce quality of life), it can be perceived the same as torture to force the person to continue with the same treatment. Choice of treatment must always be what the person feels comfortable with and considers beneficial to their overall well-being and recovery.

In Jim's case, he is not refusing treatment, he is merely expressing his choice about the medication and why he prefers the option for oral medication—he has a right to make this choice and his choice should have been respected.

3.11.1.2 Martha Savage

What should have been done in this case? Were there any other options to act and if so in which order?

(a) Compulsory treatment for 2 years despite being symptom-free is wrong. The treatment should have been voluntary.
(b) Jim should be offered help to try different medications or to slowly reduce his medication and see whether he can use behavioral techniques or other types of therapies to keep from a relapse.
(c) They should attempt to contact Jim's family and see if they need support to help him.

Breaches of human rights:

The long requirement for community treatment breaches Article 12(4) of the CRPD—Any measures relating to exercise of the legal capacity must be proportional and tailored to the person's circumstances and apply for the shortest possible time.

There need to be more resources put into talking to people and helping them use non-medical methods. In the long run providing the resources might save the country money by keeping people out of the criminal justice system.

3.11.1.3 Andreas Heinz, Sabine Müller und Assina Seitz

There are no community treatment orders allowed in Germany, which are seen as a severe infringement on the human rights of any person who does not acutely pose a danger to themselves or others. Acute medication against the will of a person would only be allowed if there is acute harm to the person themselves, for example, if they threaten to kill themselves out of a lack of insight in the current situation due to mental disorder, or harm themselves, or when the afflicted person is supposed to have a right to regain insight in the momentary psychotic or delirious state.

The clinical vignette does not include any description of any alternative treatment offers provided to Jim. Social support, psychotherapeutic interventions, self-help groups, and information regarding his illness could all help to stabilize him. In case hospital treatment is required, open (instead of locked) wards for acute patients help to motivate patients to seek treatment and can reduce violence without generally increasing suicides or absconding (Huber et al. 2016; Cibis et al. 2016; Schneeberger et al. 2017). Furthermore, long-term neuroleptic medication is of dubious advantage in patients with mental disorders (Samaha et al. 2007; Wunderink et al. 2013). Moreover, Jim is overdosed (Heinz et al. 1996), so he displays stiffness in his body and restlessness, symptoms of akathisia and Parkinsonism. Many patients smoke in order to reduce such side effects, so overdosing this patient is potentially at least partially responsible for this harmful habit.

From a medical point of view, low doses of neuroleptic medication in combination with psychosocial support and psychotherapeutic help may be the best treatment option, but ultimately Jim must decide himself about his own life. In Germany, judges may check for patients with chronic limitations of insight due to a severe mental disorder whether the patients require a legal guardian for certain areas, namely for housing, spending one's own money, and/or medical treatment. In the latter case, judges might allow compulsory treatments demanded by the legal guardian, but only if they are necessary to avert severe physical harm or death, or to restore the capability of insight. Therefore, to stabilize a patient in good condition would be absolutely no reason for allowing a legal guardian to order compulsory medication. In case, Jim would stop eating and drinking because he feels poisoned and in case that this belief is due to his mental disorder (and not some environmental hazard in his environment), compulsory treatment would be legal in Germany in order to avert severe physical harm.

In Germany, it is criticized that legal guardians too often decide in place of patients without previously trying to come to a helpful decision by providing support in decision-making that includes friends or relatives. In Germany, any person confronted with legal procedures to install a legal guardian must have legal counselling by a third person, usually not a lawyer but a person experienced in legal proceedings. It is criticized that such persons too often do not really act as independent counsellors but are too passive or silent during such procedures. In summary, strengthening the role of legal counsellors and training guardians in supported decision-making appear to be urgently necessary to reduce supported decision-making to a minimum, which is defined by situations in which severe harm to the afflicted person cannot be averted otherwise.

3.11.1.4 Michaela Amering

Jim had the right to access to a mental health specialist able to inform and support him on risks of coming off antipsychotics the wrong way (e.g., about possible dopamine supersensitivity, which will affect him and his efforts to reduce or come off medication independent of his or anyone's assessment of the reason for the treatment in the first place and options of changing and reducing and coming off antipsychotic medication, which needs a lot of expertise, support, and patience. Also, there is certainly a need to optimize the quality of assessment and treatment of akathisia and other major unwanted side effects of AP. In general, as we know that support for everyday life is the essential cornerstone for the health of persons with Jim's disorder and disability. We must of course question whether there was too much focus on medication and too little support for day-to-day living, which he should have been entitled to as spelled out in different articles of the CRPD, but certainly in Article 25—the right to the highest attainable standards of health. But of course, we cannot change the past and need to discuss what can be done for him now. Considering the data that seem to indicate that the effects of CTOs can be explained by the intensity of the support rather than its coercive nature assertive community treatment is clearly indicated. If the necessary resources are tied to the coercive nature as seems to be the case in some mental health systems, a terrible trap results for psychiatrist in responsibility such as Jim's leading him toward violating Jim's human rights out of worry and inability to offer him assertive support in another form. Such a situation seems to violate ethical as well as legal standards.

3.11.1.5 Oye Gureje

Jim received appropriate medical treatment for his illness, both the admission and medication seemed to have been indicated. On the other hand, it is not clear whether the incarceration for stalking and assault many years ago was justified or whether a committal to treatment rather than to prison would have been more appropriate. While it is appropriate for any adult who commits an office to receive the appropriate prison sentence when that is the dictate of the law, this is unlikely to be appropriate if mental illness is determined to be a major reason for committing the offence. In this instance, we are not sure whether Jim's illness was in any way instrumental for his criminal behavior.

What seems to be a major issue in regard to the human rights of Jim is his placement on community treatment order (CTO). Based on his poor adherence to medication, the initial decision to place Jim on CTO is justified as this would allow for a rapid response to any sign of relapse, thus helping to ward off any major crisis such as the one that led to his incarceration many years earlier. That decision, even though constituting a restriction on his freedom and therefore an abridgement of his human rights, seems a reasonable trade-off in order to provide him with an equally important right: that of quick access to treatment and protection against the negative consequences of a relapse during which he might not have full capacity for rational decision-making and could therefore become a risk to himself or to others.

His continued placement on CTO after 2 years of clinical stability presents a different consideration. Even though Jim rationalizes his illness, ascribing his symptoms not to a major mental disorder but to "stress" is not an uncommon phenomenon among persons who have experienced mental illness. That is probably not a sufficient reason to doubt the possibility that he might be more compliant with a medication with which he is more comfortable. It could be that paliperidone would not have been such a medication as it caused him some side effects. I think the doctor should differ more to a consideration of respecting Jim's demand for his freedom by taking him off the CTO rather than the clinician's continued concern about the possibility of treatment noncompliance and therefore a likelihood of relapse. Jim's request should be respected given that he seems to have full capacity to make decisions about what is best for him. The same applies to his request to be taken off depot medication. There is a balance to be struck here but it seems reasonable that the balance should be weighed in Jim's favor, thus respecting his need for autonomy in decision-making. His stable clinical condition, now for 2 years, is a sufficient ground for the psychiatrist to take that decision.

3.11.1.6 Cecile Hanon

What should have been done in this case? Were there any other options to act and if so in which order?

It is possible to retry the oral treatment after all, and to set up a close follow-up to be sure that it remains effective, and that Jim remains stable.

Whether any of the actions taken affected human rights, and if so, what else could have been done?

Care in the community is not the same in all countries. In France, it is possible to come and take your medication in the local dispensaries, for example, once a month, once a week, or even every day. It is also possible to receive delayed treatment injections. This helps to maintain a link with the patients, and to avoid relapses with hospital care obligations.

- Under the human rights framework adopted by the CRPD, is it justified to keep Jim under the CTO and treat him with depot antipsychotic injections against his wish?

  Beyond human rights, this is a discussion of biomedical ethics principles. We must think in terms of the benefit/risk balance for Jim. If granting his wishes, and he will stop quickly, is taking the risk of putting him in a psychotic relapse situation, with more difficulty in treating him again, and possibly a forced hospitalization, it is therefore harmful. If giving access to his will, giving him oral medication, that he does not stop it and that it is effective, and that it gives him better autonomy and a better quality of life, then it is beneficial.

3.11.1.7 Nicolás Martínez-López

On several occasions, prolonging the depot treatment not only obeys the treatment guidelines, but it is also done because of the doctor's fear of relapse due to a history of serious episodes or poor adherence to treatment.

However, in this case, the stability of 2 years in the treatment can reveal the erroneous consideration of disability in decision-making, since by adapting the treatment model to the standards of the convention. It is feasible to establish an advance directive in psychiatry, for hospitalization if necessary and to start interspersing lower doses of other depot antipsychotics with oral ones. In addition, the side effects that he refers to should be addressed so that before his decrease, he will probably accept the depot antipsychotic more easily.

3.11.1.8 Soumitra Pathare

Community Treatment Orders (CTOs) are not compliant with CRPD requirements. The evidence for CTOs is equivocal; they need substantial and good quality community mental health services to provide necessary support. User groups have frequently argued that if good quality community mental health services are available, there is possibly no need for CTOs. Involuntary treatment in the community is not a substitute for necessary investment that countries need to make in setting up good community mental health services.

Jim is based in Australia, a high-income country and therefore lack of resources is a relatively poor justification for using CTOs.

Jim's desire to take oral medications should be respected, while concerns about non-compliance can be addressed by putting in the place the necessary community support.

3.11.1.9 Mohan Isaac

Use of Community Treatment Orders (CTOs) is one of the most contentious issues in mental health care, particularly in the management of persons with chronic, severe and recurring mental illnesses where recurrence of symptoms, relapse, and rehospitalizations occur mainly due to non-adherence to medications.

Jim is a good example of such a person with a chronic illness requiring regular medications but with proven non-adherence to oral medications which result in relapse and rehospitalization. The longest period of stability of 2 years that he has had during the 20 years of his illness is only when he was under a CTO and a long-acting antipsychotic injection (LAI). Jim has no insight about the nature of his illness, he does not accept that he has a major mental illness and he does not want to continue on LAI. Under these circumstances, the reluctance of his treating psychiatrist to take Jim off his CTO is understandable. The psychiatrist may rightly be apprehensive of repeated major relapses contributing to deteriorating course of the illness (poorer outcome after each relapse), brain tissue loss, and treatment resistance.

However, under the human rights framework adopted by the CRPD, it may not be justifiable to keep Jim under a CTO for long periods of time. Data shows that CTOs are used to a disproportionately higher level in Australia as compared to many other countries. Different jurisdictions in Australian states have different guidelines for the use and length of use of CTOs. For example, in the state of Western Australia, the life of a CTO is 3 months. Following the expiry of the CTO after 3 months, it can be extended for a further period of 3 months, with subsequent extensions for as long as it is deemed necessary. During each 3 months life of CTO, it is reviewed by a Mental Health Tribunal where the person on the CTO can appeal for its withdrawal.

3.11.2 Concluding Remarks on Case History 10

3.11.2.1 Neeraj Gill and Norman Sartorius

This case highlights the ethical dilemmas surrounding community treatment orders and involuntary treatment with long-term long-acting injectable antipsychotic medications.

There was a degree of disagreement among the commentators, regarding the utility of compulsory community treatment for psychotic illness. Some reviewers suggested that such an order was an unacceptable form of coercion which could not co-exist with the values of the CRPD. As an alternative, the necessity of robust community support programs with peer involvement and a focus on psychosocial rehabilitation and recovery was emphasized. To assist with medication compliance, the priority must be to manage side effects and provide individual skills to minimize the risk of premature treatment cessation.

Alternatively, some commentators reflected on the exceptionally detrimental consequences of a psychotic relapse in the setting of treatment cessation. The risk of progressive brain damage and risk to individual well-being following psychosis are very real harms that may be prevented through the administration of a community treatment order. A significant concern was raised in the setting of impaired insight as to whether this individual is truly making an informed choice in regard to changing to oral medications.

Ultimately, the opinion from most reviewers was that this patient had the right to self-determination, and it may be unethical to continue compulsory treatment against his wishes. The suggestion raised was that of a trial of oral medication with significant peer support and community support to aid in ensuring the patient was able to access and reliably take his medication.

3.12 Case History 11: A Man with Mental Illness on Death Row

Vinod, a 30-year-old man, lived with his mother and younger brother, Pramod (and his wife, Asha) in a small town in India. His father became a saint and went to the Himalayas to meditate almost 20 years ago and never returned. His mother raised him, and his brother earning her livelihood by sewing clothes in her home business.

Vinod was always a loner and did not do any work. He often talked to himself. People in the locality knew him be a bit "crazy." Pramod worked in a shop and had an arranged marriage with Asha. They had no children.

Vinod was often abusive toward his sister-in-law, Asha, calling her a "witch." Gradually, Vinod's preoccupation with Asha being a "witch" increased and he started saying that she drank his mother's blood. This strange idea was brushed aside by the family as one of his crazy thoughts.

One day, while Pramod and his mother were out of home, Vinod murdered Asha using an axe. When Pramod and his mother came home, Vinod was sitting next to Asha's body in a pool of blood, and he insisted that he had saved his mother's life by killing Asha.

Both the brothers and their mother were arrested by the Indian police. After many weeks, Pramod and his mother were released, but faced serious stigma and discrimination in society. In jail, Vinod was almost beaten to death by other prisoners because he murdered his sister-in-law. Vinod was sentenced to death by hanging. He was evidently psychotic and under the law, a psychotic person could not be executed. Therefore, Vinod was treated by a visiting psychiatrist in jail, with oral antipsychotic medication. The psychiatrist tried to get the patient an insanity plea, but he was told that this case had been very sensational in media, and it would not be easy to save Vinod. When his mental state improved with treatment, Vinod was hanged to death.

3.12.1 Commentary

3.12.1.1 Charlene Sunkel

Vinod's family's poor mental health literacy prevented them from picking up on behavior that could have been caused by a serious mental health condition that required assessment and treatment. His delusions related to his sister in-law that led to her death, was not of malicious intent. However, a crime has been committed, but his mental health status should have been taken into consideration on whether, at that moment, could be deemed as responsible. The CRPD states that everyone is equal before the law, yet Vinod's sentence to death was based on public (mis)perceptions and not on his circumstances where he had diminished capacity to make choices due to a mental health condition. The death sentence was unfair as it based its verdict on his mental health status after receiving treatment, and treatment should have been available to prevent such an incident. All role players in this scenario should have exposed to anti-stigma programs, awareness, and educational information about mental health and mental health conditions, including his family, community, and the justice system. Both in the community and in prison, his rights should have been protected and respected to avoid abusive treatment, irrespective of the crime that was committed.

3.12.1.2 Martha Savage

The CRPD was definitely violated. The important thing for a "not guilty by reason of insanity" plea, or for a law making it illegal to give the death penalty to a person with disabilities, should be the state of mind of the person when the crime was committed. The right to life section of the CRPD forbids the death penalty for a person with a psychosocial disability.

1. The family should have sought help for Vinod when it became clear that he was talking to himself, and people considered him “a bit crazy.”
2. When he became abusive to his sister-in-law, they should have been even more insistent that he get help. If he made explicit threats to her safety, they might have had more ability to get help for him. At that point they should also have tried to keep Vinod away from his sister-in-law.
3. When Vinod was arrested, he should have been taken to secure unit for forensic psychiatric patients, rather than being put into a regular prison. To satisfy the desire of society for justice, he could be kept in the secure facility for the length of time that he would be in prison for the crime he committed. In this case, probably for life, but he should be eligible for parole if his treatment makes him better.
4. Lack of resources may have been part of the reason the family didn’t ask for help, and part of the reason that Vinod was not put into a secure forensic psychiatric unit after he was arrested. But such tragedies can happen even in wealthy countries if people don’t realize the extent to which their loved ones need help. And people don’t want to believe that their loved ones are capable of such horrible acts.

3.12.1.3 Andreas Heinz, Sabine Müller, Assina Seitz

1. There appears to be a complete lack of psychosocial counselling, medical diagnosis, psychotherapeutic treatment offers as well as medical treatment with neuroleptics or other adequate drugs. Given that the case most likely (depending on evaluation) was committed under the influence of a psychotic distortion of perception and systematic delusions, with complete lack of insight in his condition, the afflicted person, Vinod, should have never been sentenced to death. Instead, he should have been diagnosed before the trial by a trained psychiatrist. It is not clear whether Vinod consented to treatment with oral antipsychotic medication in jail.
2. The CRPD demands that adequate medical, psychotherapeutic, and psychosocial training is provided to any person, which was not done in this case. In addition, a person should be protected from being executed or sentenced when the crime was carried out under the influence of a serious mental illness that impairs insight into the action carried out. This is true for all countries, independent whether they are low-, middle-, or high-income countries. Punishing a crime by execution is also a human rights violation that should not be implemented at all, irrespective of diagnostic and treatment options for mentally ill persons. It is not clear whether oral medication in jail was consensual or not; if not, this would also amount to a violation of the CRPD.
3. The CRPD claims that all persons irrespective of mental disability should be treated equally under law. This can be read and is read by some institutions in the WHO to promote an approach as described in this example, i.e., to treat a person with mental illness like any other person in society. Consequently, persons with severe mental impairment may then be violated with respect to human rights and executed while denying that the mental illness can cause severe impairment of the decision-making and insight in the current situation, which would instead render a person legally innocent.

Treating a person with neuroleptics just to declare her or him non-psychotic is a severe violation of good clinical practice and CRPD-protected human rights and it is absolutely inappropriate for any medical doctor to participate.

3.12.1.4 Michaela Amering

What a tragedy! From the lack of awareness to the failure of offering support much earlier to the obvious lack of forensic psychiatric authority and lack of necessary support and protection during the trial and lack of protection of his rights as a prisoner, there is ample evidence for serious current neglect as well as significant requirements under human rights obligations including the CRPD. Certainly, the trial and sentencing should not have happened in the described way, because his human rights would have needed protection. Vinod clearly is a "person with a psychosocial disability" and suffers from a severe mental illness. Once sentenced, it is a question of some legal dispute whether psychosocial disability or any disability in every case has the legal power to be hindering such cruel, pointless, and anachronistic measure as the irreversible death penalty. While the fight for abolition of the death penalty in general must continue, I also join many calls for an immediate moratorium on the death penalty for persons with disabilities specifically.

3.12.1.5 Oye Gureje

Seems possible that an early assessment and treatment of Vinod could have averted the series of negative events that resulted from his illness. It is likely that a combination of poor knowledge and a fear of stigmatizing reaction by neighbors might have prevented Vinod's mother and brother from seeking an early treatment for him since the features of a mental illness were obvious to them and to others. However, it is unclear what mental health service would have been accessible to Vinod. It is plausible to speculate that, given the known limitations and constraints in mental health system in India, there might have been poor access to appropriate mental health service in a small town in the country.

The arrest of Pramod and his mother was a clear violation of their rights to liberty and a particularly painful infringement given that Pramod had just lost his wife under very gruesome circumstances. Vinod's arrest was justified but a mental health assessment should have been sought during trial as a way of determining an appropriate course of action. Perhaps, if that had been done, he would have been sent for treatment rather than to a prison where he suffered abuse from other inmates. It is striking that, even after a diagnosis was made by a psychiatrist while Vinod was already in jail awaiting execution, a stay of execution could not be obtained as recommended by the psychiatrist because the case had generated a sensation in the media.

Overall, a system that facilitates early help-seeking, easily accessible quality care, and knowledge and adherence to the CRPD guidelines about the appropriate ways to provide care for persons with severe mental illness would most likely have resulted in a different set of outcomes. In such a system, Asha would not have suffered a gruesome death, Vinod would have received appropriate treatment, and the family would have experienced less trauma occasioned by his illness.

3.12.1.6 Cecile Hanon

The framework of homicide by patients suffering from psychiatric disorders is legislated in different ways in different countries. In France, criminal irresponsibility in case of psychiatric illness is possible after an extensive psychiatric input and is not subject to a trial, but to constrained care (Article 122.1 of the public health code). The death penalty no longer exists in France.

In Vinod's case, it is terrible to imagine the conditions of his detention and the fundamental injustice of which he was a victim, without any respect for human rights.

3.12.1.7 Soumitra Pathare

This is a particularly unfortunate case and it does happen in some countries in the world.

There is a need for the World Psychiatric Association (WPA) to have a clear position statement on the death penalty (for example, advocating for abolishing the imposition of death penalty for persons with mental illness) and for the profession to be clear on its opposition to the death penalty. The involvement of psychiatrists in treating people only to get them well enough to be executed goes against all principles of medical ethics and the WPA should take a lead in advocating with international organizations and governments to ensure that no psychiatrist is placed in this unenviable situation.

There are many errors of omission in this case. For example, did his defence raise the issue of mental illness at his trial and/or at the sentencing stage of the trial? Was a mental health report presented to the trial court, so that the court could be aware of his significant mental health issues?

A number of CRPD rights are violated in this case—in particular Article 10 (Right to Life), Article 12 (Equality before the law, in particular sub-sections 3 and 4), Article 13 (Access to Justice), Article 14 (Liberty and security of person—not providing reasonable accommodation), Article 17 (Protecting the integrity of the person), and Article 25 (Access to Health services).

3.12.1.8 Mohan Isaac

Vinod's talking to himself, abusiveness, and abnormal belief that his sister-in-law was a witch who drank his mother's blood were not recognized by his family members as the symptoms of a mental disorder that he was suffering from, until it was too late. Vinod should have been shown to a mental health care doctor (psychiatrist) who could have treated Vinod and thus could have prevented the death by murder of Vinod's sister-in-law, Asha. The context of the country, namely inadequate resources and personnel for managing mental illnesses, lack of services close to people's homes, may have contributed to Vinod continuing untreated and going on to commit a murder responding to his abnormal, false belief.

After the bizarre murder committed by Vinod due to his mental illness resulting in his arrest by the police, he should have been sent to a mental health clinic for assessment and management. Instead, he was sent to jail where Vinod had to undergo maltreatment (stigma, discrimination, and almost beaten to death by other prisoners). He did not get the benefit of "insanity plea" (crime committed due to symptoms of a serious mental illness). Instead, he was sentenced to death by hanging. The law was violated as Vinod, a person suffering from psychosis, was executed for a crime committed under the influence of mental illness. The authorities who should have protected him were apprehensive of the media reaction if Vinod was given the benefit of insanity plea. The order of actions was certainly influenced by the context of the situation existing in India.

3.12.2 Concluding Remarks on Case History 11

3.12.2.1 Neeraj Gill and Norman Sartorius

This case history demonstrates the essential need to safeguard human rights and prevent discrimination at the interface between mental health and the justice system. This tragic story describes several UN CRPD article violations including the right to access to healthcare, the right to life, equal recognition before the law, and access to justice in the setting of an undiagnosed and untreated psychotic illness. The importance of early intervention, address of stigma, and appropriate psychiatric care were unanimously endorsed by the case commentators.

All the reviewers emphasized that this individual was entitled to a timely and culturally appropriate psychiatric review at the time of the alleged offence. He ought to have been offered a biological, psychological, and social supportive treatment This patient should have been protected from assault by other prisoners. Furthermore, even with varying legislation around the world, the commentators agreed that criminal responsibility should have been absolved in the setting of active mental illness with impaired judgment and insight.

This case highlights the potential for atrocity in countries using death penalty. The commentators also stress the right to life under the UN CRPD which should lead to a moratorium on the death penalty for persons with disabilities. Of note, as recommended by one of the commentators (Pathare), the WPA has now developed a position statement resolving that individuals with mental illness or intellectual and developmental disabilities should not be subjected to the death penalty (Misra et al. 2024).

3.13 Case History 12: A Pacific Island Country Overcoming the Past

A Pacific Island country is spread over 30 islands and has a population of 500,000. The only mental health facility is a 90 years' old stand-alone mental hospital with 100 beds. It has one psychiatrist who spends most of his time in the busy outpatient department of the hospital and takes the rounds of the "acute ward" twice a week. There are two other doctors who look after the patients in four "chronic wards" and consult the psychiatrist as needed.

The country has signed and ratified the UN CRPD and is embarking on a reform agenda for mental health service delivery. A Task Force has been set up to plan a contemporary recovery-oriented system which aligns with the principles of the CRPD. A consultation forum organized by the regional WHO collaborating center noted suggestions of:

- Setting up acute psychiatric wards in the general hospitals on five islands
- Establish outpatient clinics attached to those hospitals
- Enact mental health legislation to regulate involuntary psychiatric treatment
- Address social determinants of mental health

The ground reality is that the country has very low Gross Domestic Product (GDP). Barely 1% of that GDP is spent on health. There is no budget for mental health facilities outside of the mental hospital. Mental health literacy is poor, there is widespread stigma against mental disorders. The government and public health department have other pressing priorities, e.g., provide treatment to people with malaria and viral encephalitis.

Questions:
- How can the principles of the UN CRPD be realized in this scenario?
- Who should be members of the Task force, which will produce the plans for the reform?
- What should be the priorities of the Task Force?

3.13.1 Commentary

3.13.1.1 Charlene Sunkel

The most important aspect would be to involve people with lived experience and family/carer representation in the Task Force and throughout and beyond the processes of domestication. Before this process starts, participating individuals should be empowered to ensure meaningful contributions. A lived experience and family/carer council could be established that promotes diversity and adopts the principles of meaningful and authentic engagement (mutual respect and trust, transparency, diversity and equality, non-discrimination, safe space, enhance wellness, valued contributions, and non-tokenism). The dignity and worth of service users must be prioritized and services that are developed should reflect that, therefore any existing practices that do not align with this or any human rights, should be addressed first. Access to services need to be improved, hence the development of community-based services that includes peer support services, which could be financed from reducing inpatient care and promoting mental health in the community. Mainstreaming mental health across sectors could provide additional sustainability of the mental health system, while helping to address stigma and discrimination and promote inclusion of people with lived experience and ensure access to life opportunities.

3.13.1.2 Martha Savage

The first thing the Task Force should do is to consult directly with the Pacific Island community rather than to try to impose a solution from the outside. They need to discuss the problem with the community leaders, the people who have been treated and are still treated in the hospitals, and their family members and the mental health professionals currently providing treatment. They need to speak to everyone with respect and listen to everybody's ideas to try to come up with some creative solutions that will provide culturally appropriate treatment that is practical. Traditional methods of dealing with mental health needs should be considered as possibly working alongside more modern methods.

It may not be as difficult as assumed to decentralize the hospital if they can get training, use volunteers, and use online consultation with the three doctors and a program of visits by the psychiatrist to the larger islands.

A concerted program to reduce the stigma of mental illness and train the locals should begin as soon as possible. Alongside that, a trial of a small mental health ward in one of the hospitals should be started, and expanded to other hospitals as people get trained, to the point that they do not need the large facility.

The people in the chronic wards should be evaluated as soon as possible to try to find community care and other options for them that could help them to return to normal life.

3.13.1.3 Andreas Heinz, Sabine Müller, Assina Seitz

1. In situations of dire need for medical or psychological staff, basic psychosocial interventions can be provided to help resolve a substantial number of mental health problems on a community level. For example, in Afghanistan, a basic package of healthcare services was developed that places a nurse or related healthcare professionals (not a medical doctor) in every district. Such nurses or other health practitioners can be taught basic psychosocial interventions including accepting different perspectives on a patient's situation, voicing empathetic support for a patient, encouraging and empowering the patient and their family to explore new ways of dealing with the situation, and referring a patient in case of absolute need to a regional hospital (if any exists) or to a central facility (regional hospitals are preferred as they facilitate contact with relatives and the community).
2. The Task Force should focus on providing psychosocial interventions by non-medical personnel. A focus—unfortunately also promoted by the WHO—on medical doctors is inadequate as there is a huge gap between personnel required to supervise medical interventions on the one hand and the available number of medical doctors in many low-income countries on the other. The priority should be—different from the approach suggested in this case vignette— on promoting primary healthcare services including psychosocial interventions and teaching such psychosocial interventions to nurses, social workers, and (general) medical doctors, who are usually inexperienced in even basic techniques of understanding a person's mental illness. A focus on specialized psychiatrists is hopeless, as there is an absolute lack of such specialists in low- and middle-income countries, and if any are present, they need to coordinate the system rather than providing high level care to an absolute minority (usually a rich elite).

   Within a basic package of healthcare services, decentralization of the existing, standalone mental hospital should be promoted by setting up mainly outpatient and some small day care or inpatient wards in the general hospitals on the five islands. Inpatient treatment is often avoidable and not a priority.

   Mental health legislation is necessary but should go hand in hand with developing a basic package of healthcare services. Addressing social determinants of mental health is usually an absolute priority, however, given the limited resources in low-income countries, a preferable first step would be to develop a healthcare plan for the entire population including mental health as well as somatic health approaches.

This is even more necessary given the fact that there can be viral encephalitis or brain problems related to malaria and other transmittable diseases that primarily manifest as mental disorders (Berkowitz et al. 2015). So, teaching general/somatic doctors basic knowledge of mental disorders and interaction skills is the way to go.

3.13.1.4 Michaela Amering

The CRPD can certainly guide such a process, with its general principles such as accessibility, non-discrimination, and community-based rehabilitation as well as the formulated rights of persons with disabilities and its focus on mainstreaming disability rights and awareness raising, international cooperation, data collection, and implementation monitoring bodies. Of course, such guidance is most valuable in the hands of motivated and resourceful citizens and civil servants. People with a lived experience with mental health conditions and as family members of somebody with a mental health condition have often played a central role in reform processes. This is true for lobbying organizations and especially also for their cooperation with such experienced and motivated persons, who have a position in regional and national governments as has been shown to be very effective, time and again in different situations. The constant support of such organizations and processes needs to be accommodated by making sure that different development initiatives and strategies stay not only disability-inclusive but also always include the needs and rights of persons with psychosocial disabilities with extra attention as this is a "new" group within the disability community and its legal frameworks. The necessary awareness campaigns in a situation as described here must go hand in hand with finding the vast number of people with a lived experience of mental health conditions in the community and their families and friends and supporting their efforts and organizations in order to use their experience at every step. Regarding the specific plans here, I want to make a point about not hindering progress by risking losing any of the already low allocated resources when making probably worthwhile steps such as freeing beds on the "chronic wards" by moving people living there to the community as has unfortunately happened historically in some high-income countries. Of course, digital mental health will have to play a significant role. It seems of utmost importance to make sure that mental health is part of all health, social, and technical development processes.

3.13.1.5 Oye Gureje

Realizing all the principles of the UN CRPD as they relate to humane treatment of persons with disability will be very difficult in this scenario. The human and material resources for implementing person-centered care, which is required for a contemporary recovery-oriented system and that fully respects the rights of persons with mental disorders, are not available. However, with sensitization and training, some improvement that is informed by some of the principles could still be brought to the delivery of care.

The suggestions of the consultation forum are appropriate to inform the components of a revision of the mental health system of the country. The priorities to be developed should provide a practical approach to implementing the suggestions. In this regard, the first priority would be to address the challenges of limitation of human resources by mapping the available health care resources on the island. Specifically, it is necessary to know the number and distribution of health care providers, especially those available at primary and general health care settings some of whom may be non-physician frontline health care providers. The Task Force could then design a program of task-sharing in which these general health care providers are provided with short training to empower them with the skills to diagnose and treat persons with mental disorders. The training should include an emphasis on awareness of and respect of human rights in the process of delivering mental health service. Task sharing would mean that the only psychiatrist will have their schedule of work revised such that they provide less of direct care to patients and more of support and supervision to the lower-cadre providers, including attending to referrals.

The second priority of the task force should be to develop a mental health policy that lays out the necessary activities for improving the mental health system of the country. Along with the task-shifting plan, the policy will also describe the steps to be taken in mainstreaming mental health into general health care, including the gradual decentralization of the stand-alone psychiatric hospital and the development of the mental health manpower. This would entail a process of developing community service as well as building capacity to increase the number of persons trained to deliver evidence-based mental health care, especially the training of mental health nurses.

An important priority would be to develop a set of advocacy activities targeting decision makers at various levels of the health system. The aim would be to create an enabling environment for the implementation of the policy and raising the level of attention that mental health service receives. This will include activities to inform and educate both the general public and policy makers about the importance of mental health, the need to provide for the care of persons with mental health conditions, the importance of protecting the human rights of such persons, and the feasible ways of improving the service incrementally. The latter can be achieved through the provision of funds and the use of such funds to develop an integrated service in which mental health care is mainstreamed into general health care. All training and enlightenment programs should include sensitization to CRPD guidelines as appropriate, including the most feasible ways to implement the specifications within available resources.

3.13.1.6 Cecile Hanon

It is clear that the resources a country can allocate to mental health are crucial to ensure a high standard of care and training of professionals. These are extremely complex political issues. Ratification of the convention should help states to make decisions that respect human rights but that is easier said than done!

3.13.1.7 Nicolás Martínez-López

This case, even if it seems extreme, depicts the great difficulty that many countries face in the implementation of what the convention dictates, the observations to which we are subject and the need for political will for this purpose.

Having such a low budget is not far from what happens in Mexico; the stigma on those of us who suffer from a mental disorder is continuous and generates psychosocial disability in many areas. In addition, the budget for mental health is centralized in psychiatric hospitals that by far are not enough to cover the needs of 145 million inhabitants that we are. That is why this case is very familiar to me and Mexico finds itself in this question, as it needs to modify its mental health system.

Currently, what the health authorities have carried out in my country is a series of reforms that guide the prohibition of new psychiatric hospitals, the creation of psychiatric wards in general hospitals, the regulation of involuntary hospitalization, the creation of advance directives, conducting awareness campaigns for the population, and creating a first level of care for mental health conditions including addictions. However, the budget remains the same and psychiatric hospitals cannot close since even with the laws in force this year, if mental hospitals are closed, there is no necessary infrastructure to care for patients.

3.13.1.8 Soumitra Pathare

When countries ratify the CRPD, they are obliged to ensure that they comply with the provisions of the CRPD. There is also the principle of equity—mental health services should get adequate funding from the health budget commensurate with the burden of mental health problems.

International organizations and donor agencies also have a responsibility to ensure that any international development aid is also directed toward the mental health sector to help the government carry out actions required for them to comply with the provisions of the CRPD.

The priorities identified in the vignette above are reasonable and if implemented will allow the government to make significant progress toward fulfilling the CRPD-based rights of its citizens.

3.13.1.9 Mohan Isaac

The situation of mental health care services described in this Pacific Island country—archaic, stand alone, asylum-like institutions, long-stay patients, severe shortage of trained mental health professionals, competing priorities such as communicable diseases and grossly inadequate financial resources for improving services—is not very different from that exists in many small and big countries of Asia, Africa, and Latin America. The suggestions made by the WHO collaborating center supported consultation forum are appropriate and in the right direction.

The principles of the UN CRPD can be realized only by restructuring and improving mental health services in the country. Mental health care should be decentralized from the stand-alone mental hospital. Basic mental health care should be integrated with the existing primary health care system by training all levels of the existing health care staff in aspects of mental health care.

The Task Force should work with the government to prioritize mental health within the health department as well as in other related government departments such as social welfare, housing, and employment and enhance financial allocation for mental health. Efforts should be made to create a budget for community-based mental health care and training in mental health for different categories of health care personnel.

Since the country has very low Gross Domestic Product (GDP) and must deal with priorities such as communicable diseases, international assistance could be sought for improvement of mental health care. Task Force should recommend for mental health legislation to guide and regulate treatment for mentally ill persons unable to or unwilling to consent for treatment.

3.13.2 Concluding Remarks on Case History 12

3.13.2.1 Neeraj Gill and Norman Sartorius

This vignette explores the need, and ways, to make the mental health system in low- and middle-income countries more contemporary. Practical infrastructure and budgetary constraints are tangible roadblocks to CRPD realization. In the setting of mental health stigma, it can be difficult to achieve government support to fund projects relating to human rights and mental health.

Unanimously, the commentary on this vignette supports the role of lived experience of people in the creation of any policy or decision-making. A priority must be made to ensure changes are focused on solutions from within the community rather than those externally applied. Capacity building is an essential component and includes upskilling of general practitioner as well as non-medical health professionals to address gaps in the provision of care for people with mental health conditions.

To assist with compliance with the CRPD articles, the commentators support the idea of decentralization and formation of mental health units within local hospitals and community-based services. It is recommended to review and consider the "chronic" patients to assess suitability for treatment within the community. However, note is made to ensure that this process would not hinder current treatment capacity/funding as has happened in other nations—specifically, any downsizing of stand-alone psychiatric institution must be accompanied by adequate resourcing of the community mental health sector. A key point discussed is the importance of mental health psychoeducation and a targeted breakdown of stigma against people living with a mental health condition.

Finally, the commentary supports the establishment of mental health legislation to legally guide the treatment and support of individuals with mental illness. Such legislation should be formed with the principles of the CRPD at its core with a key focus on accountability, reporting, consumer involvement, and a focus on least restrictive practices and respect for advanced decision-making. The creation of this legislation could create formal accountability in terms of budgetary allocation by setting minimum standards that must be achieved in terms of reviews and tribunal processes.

Ultimately, there are significant barriers to the implementation of CRPD articles in nations with low Gross Domestic Product (GDP) but the public health benefits in terms of mental health treatment are a necessary pursuit.

3.14 Case History 13: An Elderly Woman with Dementia Refusing to Go to a Retirement Village

Valda is an 80-year-old lady who lives with her 85-year-old husband, Andre in a small town in Austria. She retired having worked as a teacher until some 15 years ago. She has four grown-up children, three of whom live in different cities in Austria with their families. One of her sons lives in England.

Valda has been getting very forgetful lately. She misplaces things, e.g., glasses, walking stick, etc. and then keeps looking for them. She often gets confused while making payment at the groceries. She has had difficulty finding her way on familiar routes. She had a couple of minor accidents while driving her car almost a year ago and Andre insists that she should not drive. She likes to drive to the shops to meet a friend for coffee and continues to drive for a short distance.

Valda used to do most of the cooking, but she left the gas knob open a few times. Andre was horrified when the whole house was smelling of cooking gas and Valda appeared totally unconcerned. Consequently, Andre has taken over the responsibility for their meals which involves a basic level of cooking. He had a heart attack a few years ago, and his own health has been very fragile. He is showing signs of carer burn-out and depression. Their GP has arranged for an aged care package, which includes a support worker making a home visit every day for an hour, to help with the activities of daily living. Despite that, Andre remains concerned about Valda's welfare and safety.

Andre calls one of his daughters to advise her of all these difficulties, especially the risk issues with Valda's driving and cooking. This daughter speaks to the other two siblings in the country and all three of them visit their parents in their hometown. Andre says he is at the end of his tether and cannot look after Valda anymore. The children can't take her with them as they are busy with their families and work. Two daughters are very worried about the risk-issues and would like to consider options like an old-age home for both parents, especially as Valda's condition deteriorates further. The son asks the parents what they want—Andre wants to continue living in their family home, and so does Valda, who is very distressed and angry as she thinks the problem is being blown out of proportion.

3.14.1 Commentary

3.14.1.1 Charlene Sunkel

Valda should draw up an Advance Directive to stipulate her will and preferences in the event that her condition further deteriorates and her decision-making capacity diminishes, and where she is able to appoint a support person of her choice to help her make decisions. Her family appears to have been supportive, respectful of her wishes despite the difficulties in their own lives and they have explored options that would be good for her. It would have been helpful for Andre to join a family/carer support group so his own mental health is validated and where he can receive support. Based on financial resources, a full-time caregiver could be a solution that would allow the couple to remain living in their home.

3.14.1.2 Martha Savage

It doesn't appear that human rights have been violated yet. The family and the government are mostly doing the right thing, to try to come up with a good solution that will be acceptable to all. It is good that the government can offer some help to Andre. But Andre needs more support.

Peer support groups for both Andre and Valda should be considered.

Valda should not drive. Her friend could pick her up to take her to the coffee shop and to the stores so that she can keep up important relationships outside the family. Andre and Valda could cook dinner together and do other activities that Valda can do safely to feel that she is contributing to the family and the community.

The children could also consider pooling their money to help pay for more help for Andre, and they could take turns visiting on weekends to be with their mother and give their father a break. It might be good for the grandchildren to help out a little with their grandparents as well, even just playing games with them or reading books together.

Dementia usually gets worse over time. The children should start now to try to find acceptable alternatives to the present state. There might be elder day care centers to take Valda for short periods to give their father a break. They could visit the center together to see if there is one that is appealing to Andre and Valda. They might also find a center that would allow gradually increasing levels of services. The important thing is to try to get to a solution that both Andre and Valda can agree to and that will keep them both safe.

Gradually introducing them to the idea of changing their lifestyle would help.

3.14.1.3 Andreas Heinz, Sabine Müller, Assina Seitz

1. The case describes a typical dilemma regarding the initial stage of dementia in elderly persons. Driving a car after a couple of what are described as "minor accidents" is dangerous and the driving license could be revoked depending on a test of psychomotor reactions, as any of such minor incidents could cause major damage to other persons and to the persons themselves. However, minor incidents or accidents can occur with any driver, so automatically revoking a driver's license is not justified, it should be based on a psychometric assessment. As both persons do not want to leave their flat and the husband of the afflicted person, Andre, complains that he cannot bear the responsibility anymore, there is a real dilemma of how to proceed.

   There is outpatient-nursing care in Germany, which is financed by an insurance that every person pays into during their lifetime. In Germany, more than one visit per day by such outpatient services is possible; however, continuous surveillance by a nurse at home is not within the scope of this treatment. Therefore, in many high-income countries, the problem is solved by paying a person (often from low- or middle-income countries) to spend part or most of the day with the elderly people; this, however, takes advantage of large income differences and compensation for persons helping elderly people, and hence is often socially inadequate.
2. In Germany and many other countries, a severely demented patient can be placed under legal guardianship. In the current case, this does not appear to be justified and should not be considered. Legal guardianship has been attacked by some but not all institutions of the United Nations as being in violation of the CRPD, and in this specific reading of the CRPD, any person (irrespective of mild, moderate, or severe dementia or no impairment at all) has a full right of not being under any kind of legal guardianship. In our view, this can violate human rights, for example, for adequate treatment or protection of the afflicted person's health, such as, when hygiene suffers severely in demented persons who live alone.

   Currently, the case appears to be handled correctly with a focus on the wishes of elderly persons. In Germany, legal guardianship is avoidable if you decide beforehand that a certain person of your trust can act in place of a legal guardian (*Vorsorgevollmacht*). In any case, this person of trust or a legal guardian should always ask the patient first about their personal preferences, and only override their current (actual) will when these preferences would result in severe physical harm to the person themselves or to others, for example, due to malnutrition.
3. Inquiring about the preferences of the afflicted person, as in the current situation, is always adequate. As discussed under point two, the CRPD or at least some of its interpretations prohibit any kind of legal guardianship in case of severe dementia, even if it causes severe harm to the afflicted person (which, however, does not apply to the current case). Leaving a person alone (due to the above-named specific reading of the CRPD), in spite of severe dementia and lack of insight, can severely hurt the patients and can violate other protections listed in the CRPD.

3.14.1.4 Michaela Amering

I would consider the CRPD in support of the described process. More and growing assistance for Valda certainly is in line with the CRPD. A central aspect from now on must be the support and expansion of a supported decision-making network. In this context, as well as independently from that, the family carers, relatives, and friends do need support now and ongoing.

3.14.1.5 Oye Gureje

The main issues here are how to provide for the care of Valda while respecting her wish to remain in her home and how to take account of the welfare of Andre, the sole caregiver who is himself in less than robust health. Given that the children who are physically able are not able to take care of Valda, there seems to be only two options open to addressing the issues: taking advantage of the home care as suggested and arranged by the GP or moving Valda to a nursing home. Since she objects to the latter, the former is the only option that meets the need of providing for her care while protecting the health of Andre. Even though supported home care does not fully address Andre's concern, there is nevertheless sufficient ground to give this a try and to see how it might work out. A period to try the home care arrangement should be set, and Andre should be persuaded to allow for this trial. If the arrangement does not fully provide for the care of Valda, including persisting concerns for her safety and that of Andre, the option of a nursing home would then become necessary. Valda should be encouraged to provide consent for this arrangement, especially at a time when she still has decisional capacity. If the situation does deteriorate and nursing care becomes necessary, the step might still meet with Valda's reluctance. But it would nevertheless become justified given that her safety and that of Andre would be enough reason to implement the arrangement to which she would have previously consented.

3.14.1.6 Cecile Hanon

The situation of this couple is unfortunately frequent. The issue of freedom of choice of where to live is paramount, but so is the issue of maintaining safety. So, there is always a tension between these two fundamental principles of human rights: freedom and safety.

Valda and her husband obviously prefer their freedom, while the children prefer safety. It is therefore necessary to balance the reflection with the notion of risk, and of what risk the couple and their children are able to take in a given situation.

That being said, it is obvious that no one can be forced to enter a retirement home, at least not physically. The question of "moral compulsion" is another matter—"if you don't go into a nursing home, we won't come to see you anymore" the children might say to influence the decision.

3.14.1.7 Nicolás Martínez-López

The issue of mental and physical health of older adults is increasingly worrying, given that the stigma that weighs on age and decision-making generates excessive action and planned isolation.

Consequently, this case is the reality of many older adults who little by little present with alterations due to deterioration, either due to vascular diseases or various causes, and who finally, before the departure of their children, end up being cared for by their partner, leading to a burnout syndrome of the caregiver and a risk for both, therefore, and at the request of both older adults, it would be best to respect their decision and place nursing staff, ideally 24 hrs a day, so that they can provide necessary care at home and avoid hospitalization.

With regard to an analysis of the human rights of this case, it is necessary to understand that the presence of cognitive impairment and depression on the part of the caregiver are not indicators of the loss of autonomy, or of the loss of legal capacity; therefore, everything must be done that is feasible for the respect of his will.

3.14.1.8 Soumitra Pathare

It is the responsibility of the public health services to provide support and domiciliary assistance to Andre and Valda to be able to continue living safely in their home. This requires that the public health services and social services provide home-based mental health care, physical health care, and practical support services to the couple.

In this particular case, it's a high-income country and there is really little excuse for the Government and public health services to not provide these services. In fact, domiciliary support is likely to be less expensive and more sustainable in the long term rather than moving the couple into a residential home.

CRPD supports community living (Article 19), and people should be enabled to live in their own homes with adequate support.

3.14.1.9 Mohan Isaac

Due to progressive cognitive decline, Valda has lost capacity to carry out routine household chores, drive, and independently manage her affairs. Her husband, Andre has physical disabilities which interfere with his ability to take care of Valda.

Their children should spend adequate time and speak with them to convince them to willingly move to a nursing home where they both could be taken care of. They, particularly Andre, should be made to understand that while they may want to continue living in their family home, it would not be feasible. Valda may not have the capacity to understand but Andre can understand that continuing to live in their family home even with the aged care package and assistance of a support worker could be detrimental for the continued health and welfare of both Valda and Andre.

3.14.2 Concluding Remarks on Case History 13

3.14.2.1 Neeraj Gill and Norman Sartorius

The case history exemplifies the importance of the correct interpretation of the CRPD (which includes support to persons living in the community) and the need to include training about existing legal documents and procedures in the curricula of health staff. It calls for reflection on the role of guardianship and substitute decision-making in the setting of neurodegenerative diseases with impaired capacity to make decisions regarding health and accommodation. The provision of substitute decision-makers from family, relatives, or appointed members from the state is a process upheld in the legal tradition of multiple nations. This process is typically legislated to allow decisions regarding health, accommodation, and finances to be made when individuals are unable to appropriately make such decisions due to a sustained cognitive disorder impairing their judgment.

There was some disagreement in the commentary in this case. Some commentators expressed that with increased levels of psychosocial support from family, an effort should be made to support the individual to continue life in their own home. This, it was argued, would be most in keeping the CRPD principles of right to exercise legal capacity, supported decision-making, and the right to community living (Article 19).

On the other hand, some commentators pointed to significant health risks associated with living at home in the setting of a neurocognitive disorder. They recognized that personal liberty and the ideal of community living may sometimes require overriding if they pose a significant risk to their own life as a consequence of impaired judgment secondary to dementia.

Overall, there was agreement that community living with additional support must be continued as long as safely possible until the risks increase to a level where they cannot be mitigated by additional support.

3.15 Case History 14: A Teenage Boy with Gender Identity Issues

Juan is a 14-year-old boy who identifies as a girl. He lives in South Africa with his parents and 17-year-old sister.

At the age of 12, Juan started feeling that he was a girl stuck in a boy's body. He started to secretly wear his sister's clothes whenever he could. Over the next few months, his dysphoria with having to act as a boy increased. He attempted suicide by cutting his wrists, which came as a shock to his parents who knew nothing about his problems. Juan was taken to a hospital where he disclosed his identity issues to the psychiatrist. His parents were very distressed when they came to know about Juan's thoughts about being a girl. They started to take him to the Church regularly for pastoral care to help him accept his male gender. While Juan passively went to those sessions, his preoccupation of being a girl continued to grow.

At the age of 13, he discovered gender transformation treatments on the internet. He ordered drugs to delay puberty, from internet, using his parents' credit card. His parents found this from a credit card statement a month later and confronted Juan. They threw the drugs away and started to closely monitor Juan's internet use.

At the age of 14, while in grade nine, Juan got into serious trouble at school, as he was caught in the ladies' toilet. He had to appear at the school principal's office along with his parents. There he declared that he identified himself as a girl and wanted gender transformation surgery to convert from male to female. The school principal advised Juan's parents to see a psychiatrist. The psychiatrist diagnosed gender identity disorder along with major depression and suicidal ideation and prescribed low dose fluoxetine. Juan's parents refused to let Juan have what they called "mind altering drugs." The psychiatrist then advised referral to the gender dysphoria clinic. The parents went for one session, but they are now refusing to bring him back to the clinic because they felt that the psychologist was supporting Juan's "weird ideas" rather than treating those ideas.

3.15.1 Commentary

3.15.1.1 Charlene Sunkel

Despite Juan's age, his disclosure of his gender preferences should have not been dismissed but rather he should have been provided with the opportunity to explore what he felt was right for him, irrespective of what others felt was in his best interest. He should have been supported in his decision to transform from male to female and claim his own identity, instead of exposing him to prejudice by the church and school. A LGBTQ peer support group could have helped him through the emotions of disclosure and acceptance of who he was and dealing with stigma and discrimination. His parents could have benefitted from a parent support group for LGBTQ children. In regard to the psychologist who considered his views and identity, Juan should have been given the choice whether to continue therapy or not. The CRPD is clear about freedom to make one's own choices, and there is no difference for a young person. As parents, their focus should have been on protecting him from the outside world's judgments and the impact this could have on his mental health, and perhaps their own judgment could have changed should they had better insights themselves on the matter and should this have not been classified as a disorder (at the time).

3.15.1.2 Martha Savage

Juan is still quite young, so I think in most countries regardless of wealth, the parents would have the main say in what would happen to him. So, although for adults, the CRPD might be violated, I don't think that's necessarily the case here.

I think that it would have been difficult for the parents to do much differently until the suicide attempt, although if they had been more aware or accepting of their child, he might have confided in them rather than attempting suicide.

After the suicide attempt, the parents should be offered counselling as individuals and as a family, and peer support groups should be considered for both the parents and Juan and his sister.

For all their sakes, it would be best to try to get each person to accept others as they actually are, rather than to try to make them conform to some ideal. The parents should be gently brought to the realization that if they continue to reject Juan, they might end up losing him. Perhaps the sister can help to bridge the gap.

Juan should be encouraged to explore his feelings and consider trying out what life would be like as a girl via cross-dressing, but without going through the irrevocable step of surgery. He is still young and might not really know what he wants—part of his desire to change may just be a way to rebel against controlling parents.

3.15.1.3 Andreas Heinz, Sabine Müller, Assina Seitz

1. In this case, the afflicted person, Juan, should be provided with adequate psychosocial care

in order to clarify his identity and to address his depression. Juan and his parents should be provided with family sessions trying to help them to better understand his identity issue. It is up to Juan to define his personal gender identity and fortunately, ICD-11 will stop pathologizing transgender persons. Nevertheless, this right exists often only on paper, and in real life, transgender persons often face gruesome violence, discrimination, and harassment directed against them.

According to the CRPD and good clinical practice, Juan should be provided with all mental health care required by stress-related or any other mental condition, also in case any of these conditions or challenges interact with his gender identity.

2. The legal situation is difficult with parents prohibiting the use of a drug that may help against severe depression and suicidal ideation. It is not reported whether Juan himself wanted to take this drug, which would be of key importance when deciding on the ethics of both the psychiatrist intervention and the refusal of the parents to have Juan take these drugs. Even if Juan is legally a minor, his opinion should be of key importance in this case. That Juan was not provided with treatment in the gender dysphoria clinic could amount to a severe infraction of his human rights, however, only in the case he wanted to go there, which again is not reported. Since it is stated that the psychologist was accused of supporting his "weird ideas," it is, however, likely, that Juan profits from this treatment, so he should be provided with adequate treatment in this clinic or in other settings in accordance with the CRPD.
3. The CRPD demands that any person without discrimination should be provided with adequate medical and psychosocial as well as psychotherapeutic treatment, which in this case was not provided.

3.15.1.4 Michaela Amering

The trans health and human rights situation is in flux all over the world.

Regarding Juan's age-group, the CRPD in Article 7 proclaims states' obligation to secure "full enjoyment by children with disabilities of all human rights and fundamental freedoms on an equal basis with other children." In its preamble under paragraph (e), it recognizes *that disability is an evolving concept and that disability results from the interaction between persons with impairments and attitudinal and environmental barriers that hinders their full and effective participation in society on an equal basis with others.* Juan might be covered under the CRPD because of his problems including depression over some time. In any case, his right to access to health care as would be provided by the gender dysphoria clinic sure needs protection. The school might be able to engage in a process of securing his rights and at the same time offer assistance to his parents and maybe other members of the family in this situation.

3.15.1.5 Oye Gureje

The issue around transgender status in a child is almost always a difficult one for parents to handle. It is therefore not surprising that Juan's parents are having problems with accepting the situation presented by his wish to be a girl rather than the assigned male gender. Some of the actions taken by the parents (e.g., seeking pastoral care for Juan) might be seen as a violation of Juan's rights but parents also do have a duty of care for a child who is still a minor and they might have considered their actions to be within that duty.

Given the circumstance, it is appropriate to consider the first major step as the need to attend to the concerns of the parents through education about the nature of the issues as well as to provide them with support in negotiating the emotional challenge that the situation poses. The goal would be for them to achieve sufficient level of acceptance of Juan's status, so they become ready to work with the health care providers in designing an appropriate procedure to support Juan to achieve her desired goal of being a girl. Juan is a minor and will need parental consent to proceed on any indicative intervention. The support that the parents receive will enable them to be able to play this role effectively by gaining the trust of Juan who will then see that the parents do understand his wish and need. The plan of action would also need to recognize that, since Juan is still a minor, sufficient time should be allowed for the process to ensure that the eventual outcome of any intervention would be found acceptable to Juan as he attains adulthood.

3.15.1.6 Cecile Hanon

Juan is a minor, under the parental authority of his parents, there is nothing he cannot do until he reaches his majority. Whatever one thinks…

3.15.1.7 Nicolás Martínez-López

Given the need for care for trans people, the WHO has appropriately placed gender incongruence outside of mental disorders and conditions related to sexual health, to de-pathologize this condition within mental health, which favors a reduction of stigma.

This advance allows trans people through ICD-11 to access treatment from their health systems and public policies without the stigma that they suffer from a mental disorder. In fact, the definition of gender incongruity in ICD-11 as a condition is characterized by a marked and persistent incongruence between an individual's experienced gender and the assigned sex. Gender variant behavior and preferences alone are not a basis for assigning the diagnoses in this group and for this specific case, the classification provides a definition of gender incongruence of adolescence or adulthood.

This is of the utmost importance since what can happen to Juan is that, as has been shown in various investigations conducted by the ICD-11 group, stigma, rejection, and violence towards trans people leads to depression, post-traumatic stress, among other mental disorders. A trans person has the same human rights as any other person.

In fact, the convention would not apply to them since it would not be considered a psychosocial disability.

3.15.1.8 Mohan Isaac

Juan suffers from gender identity disorder with secondary depression both of which need to be appropriately managed by competent professionals. But his parents are ignorant about the nature of Juan's problems. They seem to believe that it may be a character deficit which probably can be corrected by pastoral care. They don't trust the mental health professionals and even believe that psychiatrists prescribe unnecessary "mind altering drugs." They do not want Juan to attend the gender dysphoria clinic.

Parents should be provided psychoeducation to understand the nature of their son's problem and the appropriate way of managing the problem. Juan should be allowed to continue proper management of his gender dysphoria and gender identity disorder.

It is good that the country (South Africa) has a gender dysphoria clinic. Such specialized clinics may not be available in many other countries.

3.15.2 Concluding Comments on Case History14

3.15.2.1 Neeraj Gill and Norman Sartorius

This case highlights the complex ethical dilemma related to gender incongruence in young people. It portrays psychological consequences of lack of holistic care and support for young people experiencing gender incongruence. This case history also illustrates the difficulty of drawing limits of the competence of the CRPD and the difficulty of following the rules in the instance of mental health issues which may not cause impairments or disability.

Commentators agreed that care should be taken to recognize the sociocultural milieu from which the individual's parents were raised and provide appropriate psychoeducation to empower them to support their child in the setting of rapid cultural evolution. With more education, the parents may realize the significant mental health issues that their child is experiencing and the role of biopsychosocial treatment as needed.

Most commentators reinforced the notion of parental guardianship and support parents as decision-makers. In addition, it was commented that this individual would have benefited from greater peer support and recognition from their parents. This young person does not have a disability, but every effort should be made to provide appropriate treatment and support, and to prevent stigma, rejection, and violence as per the principles of CRPD. Special mention is made of the new ICD-11 chapter of sexual health with the new condition gender incongruence—separated from the mental health chapter.

3.16 Concluding Remarks on Case Histories

3.16.1 Neeraj Gill and Norman Sartorius

These case histories portray a picture of several violations of human rights of people with mental illness, e.g., the right to access to health services, the right to social inclusion and social services, the right to exercise autonomy and liberty, and the right to physical and mental integrity, among others. The main problem in the field of mental health which leads to human rights violations is the behavior of governments which do not provide resources for treatment and care for people with mental illness (and their family).

Most of the people in the world do not get the care they need and that is a greater, more important infringement of human rights than the imposition of treatment on those who do not want it. The emphasis of the CRPD implementation is, therefore, equally on the obligation of government to provide care as on the obligations to prevent violations of the human rights of those not wanting to receive treatment.

The case histories and the commentary also highlighted the issue of interpretation of the CRPD. While in some cases, brief or long-stay involuntary hospitalization and long-term community treatment order were considered violations of individual human rights, in other cases short-term involuntary hospitalization and treatment were considered necessary to protect the right to health of the individual and the right of the community for safety. However, even when involuntary treatment is required, it can be administered in a way that respects the dignity and integrity of the person with mental illness.

In addition to the civil and political rights, some case vignettes highlighted the need to protect and promote economic, social, and cultural rights in the form of employment, housing, health, social inclusion, and participation.

In addition to the above inference regarding human rights protection and promotion, three important lessons were learnt from this exercise:

(a) The case history approach to discussing (and teaching about) the use of the CRPD is useful.
(b) There is remarkable agreement about most of the issues emerging through the study of case histories.
(c) The main problems in the implementation of the principles of the CRPD include the traditions prevailing in the provision of services, the lack of resources which are necessary to improve services and the need for training to all staff related to the use of the crpd in the protection of human rights.

References

Berkowitz AL, Raibagkar P, Pritt BS, Mateen FJ (2015) Neurological manifestations of neglected tropical diseases. J Neurol Sci 349:20–32

Cibis ML, Wackerhagen C, Müller S, Lang U, Schmidt Y. & Heinz A (2016) Vergleichende Betrachtung von Aggressivität, Zwangsmedikation und Entweichungsraten zwischen offener und geschlossener Türpolitik auf einer Akutstation. Psychiatrische Praxis 44(03):141–147. https://doi.org/10.1055/s-0042-105181

Heinz A, Knable MB, Weinberger DR (1996) Dopamine D2 receptor imaging and neuroleptic drug response. J Clin Psychiatry 57(Suppl 11):84–93

Huber CG, Schneeberger AR, Kowalinski E, Fröhlich D, von Felten S, Walter M, Zinkler M, Beine K, Heinz A, Borgwardt S. & Lang UE (2016) Suicide risk and absconding in psychiatric hospitals with and without open door policies: a 15 year, observational study. The Lancet Psychiatry 3(9):842–849. https://doi.org/10.1016/s2215-0366(16)30168-7

McCall-Smith K (2016) United Nations standard minimum rules for the treatment of prisoners (Nelson Mandela rules). Int Legal Mater 55(6):1180–1205

Missmahl I, Kluge U, Bromand Z, Heinz A (2012) Teaching psychiatry and establishing psychosocial services—lessons from Afghanistan. Eur Psychiatry 27(Suppl 2):S76–S80

Misra M, Sinha N, Pathare S. Gill N, Javed A. World Psychiatric Association position statement on mental health and the death penalty. Published online 5th Feb 2024. The Lancet Psychiatry. https://doi.org/10.1016/S2215-0366(23)00434-0

Nienaber A, Heinz A, Rapp MA, Bermpohl F, Schulz M, Behrens J. & Löhr M. (2018). Einfluss der Personalbesetzung auf Konflikte auf psychiatrischen Stationen. Der Nervenarzt 89(7):821–827. https://doi.org/10.1007/s00115-018-0521-5

Samaha AN, Seeman P, Stewart J, Rajabi H. & Kapur S. (2007) "Breakthrough" Dopamine Supersensitivity during Ongoing Antipsychotic Treatment Leads to Treatment Failure over Time. Journal of Neuroscience, 27(11):2979–2986. https://doi.org/10.1523/jneurosci.5416-06.2007

Schneeberger AR, Kowalinski E, Fröhlich D, Schröder K, von Felten S, Zinkler M, Beine KH, Heinz A, Borgwardt S, Lang UE, Bux DA. & Huber, CG (2017) Aggression and violence in psychiatric hospitals with and without open door policies: A 15-year naturalistic observational study. Journal of Psychiatric Research 95:189–195. https://doi.org/10.1016/j.jpsychires.2017.08.017

Siebenförcher M, Fritz FD, Irarrázaval M, Benavides Salcedo A, Dedik C, Fresán Orellana A, Herrera Ramos A, Martínez-López JNI, Molina C, Rivas Gomez FA, Rivera G, Sandia Saldivia I, Torales J, Trujillo Orrego N, Heinz A. & Mundt, A. P. (2020). Psychiatric beds and prison populations in 17 Latin American countries between 1991 and 2017: rates, trends and an inverse relationship between the two indicators. Psychological Medicine, 1–10. https://doi.org/10.1017/s003329172000269x

Silvestri S, Seeman MV, Negrete JC, Houle S, Shammi C, Remington GJ, Kapur S, Zipursky RB, Wilson A. A, Christensen BK. & Seeman, P (2000) Increased dopamine D 2 receptor binding after long-term treatment with antipsychotics in humans: a clinical PET study. Psychopharmacology 152(2):174–180. https://doi.org/10.1007/s002130000532

United Nations (2006) Convention on the Rights of Persons with Disabilities, adopted on 13 December 2006, GA Res 61/106, UN Doc A/Res/61/106 (entered into force 3 May 2008). https://www.un.org/development/desa/disabilities/convention-on-the-rights-of-persons-with-disabilities.html

Wunderink L, Nieboer RM, Wiersma D, Sytema S. & Nienhuis FJ (2013) Recovery in Remitted First-Episode Psychosis at 7 Years of Follow-up of an Early Dose Reduction/Discontinuation or Maintenance Treatment Strategy. JAMA Psychiatry, 70(9):913. https://doi.org/10.1001/jamapsychiatry.2013.19

Part III

Mental Health Legislation in Countries Influenced by Different Legal Traditions

4 China: The Implementation of the United Nations Convention on the Rights of Persons with Disabilities in Mental Health Services

Shaoling Zhong and Xiaoping Wang

Contents

4.1 Introduction

China acceded to the United Nations Convention on the Rights of Persons with Disabilities (CRPD) in 2008, following ratification in a regular session of the China's National People's Congress. The CRPD entered into force in China in the same year. Since then, China has followed the principles of the CRPD in formulating laws, regulations and policies relating to persons with disabilities, as well as when providing services to persons with disabilities.

Based on this context, this chapter will describe the legal rights and interests pertaining to individuals with mental disorders or disability

S. Zhong
The Affiliated Brain Hospital of Guangzhou Medical University, Guangzhou, China
e-mail: shaoling_zhong@gzhmu.edu.cn

X. Wang (✉)
The Second Xiangya Hospital of Central South University, Changsha, China

N. Gill, N. Sartorius (eds.), *Mental Health and Human Rights*, Sustainable Development Goals Series, https://doi.org/10.1007/978-3-031-52179-9_4

due to impairments caused by mental illness[1] and introduce the relevant legal provisions and interpretations. In order to better understand the background of current mental health laws and regulations in practice, the first section of this chapter describes the current mental health services for persons with disabilities related to mental illness in China over the past few decades. The second section discusses various fundamental rights for people with mental disorders, including guardianship, voluntary treatment, rehabilitation, and employment. The third section makes recommendations on how to meet the criteria of the CRPD and improve the situation of people with mental disorders and disabilities resulting from impairments caused by mental disorders in China, based on the existing state of needs and legal safeguards. The main laws discussed in this chapter are China's *Mental Health Act 2013*, the *General Rules of the Civil Law of the People's Republic of China*, the *Civil Code of the People's Republic of China*, and other related provisions and norms that relate to the rights of people with mental disorders.

This chapter aims to: (1) evaluate the extent to which the provisions of relevant laws and regulations are implemented in relation to the CRPD; and (2) provide insights and recommendations on how to improve related laws and regulations to make them more harmonious with the CRPD and improve mental health care for persons with mental disorders and disabilities related to them in China.

4.2 An Overview of the Mental Health Services in China

Mental health is garnering more attention around the world. The Diagnostic and Statistical Manual of Mental Disorders (DSM-5) (American Psychiatric Association 2013), as developed by the American Psychiatric Association, defines mental disorders as having five elements: (a) a behavioural or psychological pattern or syndrome in an individual; (b) demonstrates underlying psychobiological dysfunction; (c) substantial suffering or disability (i.e., impairment in one or more important areas of functioning) are the consequences; (d) must go beyond simply an anticipated reaction to typical stresses and losses or a culturally approved reaction to a specific event (e.g. trance states in religious rituals); (e) primarily as a result of social deviation or disagreements with society.

Based on a national mental disorder epidemiological survey (Huang et al. 2019) in China, the lifetime prevalence of schizophrenia and psychotic disorders is 0.7%, the lifetime prevalence of any affective disorder is 7.4%, and the lifetime prevalence of dementia is 5.6%. Mental disorders may have negative, long-lasting impacts on people's health, education, and general well-being. They also place a significant burden on families and society. Given the high frequency and impairing nature of mental disorders, mental disabilities are not uncommon in China. Data from National Bureau of Statistics of China showed that more than 37.8 million people (2.68% of the population) lived with disabilities (National Bureau of Statistics of China 2021). Psychosis was associated with 4.16% of all disability among persons aged 15 years and over in China (Liu et al. 2019). Because mental disability has a higher impact than mental disorders, it is critical to safeguard the needs of individuals with mental disorders or disability due to impairments caused by mental illness in terms of daily living, medical treatment, rehabilitation, education, employment, and social integration.

China has paid more attention to mental health issues and invested more mental health resources over the past decade, but it still lags behind high-income countries. Inadequate mental health resources and uneven development of mental health care services are the predominant manifestations of the issue. In China, the number of psychiatrists and registered nurses reached 3.55 per 100,000 and 9.89 per 100,000, respectively, in 2020 (Ma et al. 2022). The resources of psychiatrists in China are around one-third of those in the

[1] In this chapter, the authors used different terms of mental disorder, impairments of function caused by mental disorders and disability resulting from the impairments where applicable.

United States and one-fifth of those in Japan although the number of registered nurses is comparable to those in the United States and are one-eighth of those in Japan (World Health Organization 2019). In addition, although there is still some uncertainty about the numbers of professionals who provide mental health services, such as psychotherapists, psychological counsellors, and social workers, even in developed areas. The lack of these professionals has also worsened the unmet needs of mental health services. Another major challenge in China is the uneven distribution of mental health resources. Most doctors and nurses are mainly in the Eastern areas and the bulk of high-quality medical resources are found in provincial and prefectural specialized hospitals.

The existing mental health treatment paradigm remains hospital-centric, and there are challenges to develop community-based mental health services. This status quo is connected to the classic psychiatric paradigm, which is based on the biological model of mental illness. To shift the priority of mental health care from specialist hospitals to community mental health, China has taken various steps, such as establishing local and municipal pilot projects and formulating the national action plans. The National Mental Health Work Plan (2015–2020) (National Health and Family Planning Commission et al. 2015) outlined the importance of developing community rehabilitation service systems for people with mental disorders and constructing model projects for mental health community rehabilitation facilities. The specification calls for "making a major push to develop socialized, comprehensive, and open models of rehabilitation for individuals with mental disorders or disability due to impairments caused by mental illness, as well as carrying out demonstration projects for community rehabilitation institutions to promote the reintegration of people with mental disorders into society (p. 48)." (National Health and Family Planning Commission et al. 2015)

Bearing in mind that mental health resources are still insufficient, that services do not meet demand, and that community-based rehabilitation systems for mental disorders have not yet been established, we attempt to describe the legal and regulatory safeguards for guardianship, involuntary treatment, rehabilitation, and employment—relevant rights and interests of people with mental disorders—and discuss how well these laws and regulations align with the CRPD in China.

4.3 Guardianship

Due to functional limitations, persons with mental disorders may need guardianship to protect their legal rights as their disorder progresses. The choices of the guardian have a significant impact on the social life of the person under guardianship, as well as the person's rights and interests. According to the principle of Article 12 of the Convention and the General Comment on Article 12, "persons with disabilities enjoy legal capacity on an equal basis with others in all aspects of life". The article highlights that the will and choices of persons with disabilities should be respected, and that the support and care for persons with disabilities should be guaranteed, and that there should be "no discrimination on the basis of disability". Article 12 also states that measures shall be taken to facilitate access by persons with disabilities to the assistance they may need in exercising their legal capacity.

The adult guardianship in China is based on a system of substitute decision-making. Article 21 of the *General Principles of the Civil Code* provides that an adult who is unable to account for his or her own conduct is a person having no capacity for civil conduct; Article 22 states that "an adult who is unable to fully account for his or her own conduct shall be a person with limited capacity for civil conduct". An adult who is unable to account for or fully account for his or her own conduct shall be represented in the performance of civil juristic acts by his or her agent (Article 21 and Article 22). People with mental impairments are among the range of adults subject to guardianship under civil law. An adult with full capacity for civil conduct may determine his or her guardian in writing in advance (Article 33). It has been argued that this provision rectifies the deficiencies of the *General Principles of the Civil Law* in the selection of a legislative model for adult guardianship and marks a change from legal guardianship to an intentional guardianship (Chen 2015). The idea of deliberate guardianship allows the person with the disease (or before it) to appoint his or her own guardian. In contrast to legal guardianship, the intentional guardianship model gives the ward the right to choose his or her own guardianship.

The principle of the best interest of the ward is emphasized in the General Rules. Article 22 of the General Provisions provides that "a person with limited capacity for civil conduct may independently perform civil juristic acts which are purely to benefit the adult or the performance of which is compatible with his or her intelligence and mental health". As per Article 35 of the General Provisions, "the guardian of an adult, while fulfilling the guardianship responsibility, shall respect the ward's true will to the largest extent, and safeguard and assist the ward in performing the civil juristic acts that are compatible with the ward's intelligence and mental health".

These two provisions give adults the opportunity to perform acts that are compatible with their level of impairment. This principle of the best interest is also reflected in the *Mental Health Act 2013*. For example, the guardian of a person with a mental disorder shall safeguard the legitimate rights and interests of the patient (Article 9). These provisions of civil law have a positive impact on the protection of guardianship, respecting the free will of the person under guardianship from a legal standpoint and allowing the guardian to make decisions in the person's best interests in the event of a loss of capacity to act.

The *Mental Health Act 2013* contains numerous regulations concerning the duties of guardians of people with mental disorders, particularly when a patient has committed acts that endanger the safety of others (The first item of the second clause of Article 30). Under this condition, a medical facility shall impose inpatient treatment if their guardians agree (Article 31). The guardian may request discharge at any time and the medical facility shall comply with such requests (Article 44). These provisions neither address the evaluation of a patient's capacity to provide informed consent nor grant him or her the right to delegate autonomy. The rights of patients with mental disorders can only be executed by a guardian after the patient has exhibited dangerous behaviour; however, the patient may regain autonomy after recovery. The existing legal provisions do not sufficiently consider the patient's right to independent and equal participation in decision-making. These issues may impair the rights of patients. In contrast, the Convention emphasizes the autonomy and independence of persons with disabilities related to mental illness, rather than limiting and excluding their participation via guardianship. In summary, the guardianship provisions of China's *General Civil Law and Mental Health Law* are insufficient to support a comprehensive adult guardianship system. The lack of specific operational provisions and limited legal provisions make it difficult to translate legislation into concrete judicial practice. Under the framework of intended guardianship, efforts are needed to better protect the rights and interests of people with mental disorders.

4.4 Involuntary Treatment

Access to treatment is a fundamental right of people with mental disorders. In many developed countries, legal safeguards for voluntary treatment have long been valued. Specifically, Article 25 in the CRPD highlighted that States Parties shall ".... require health professionals to provide care of the same quality to persons with disabilities as to others, including on the basis of free and informed consent by, inter alia, raising awareness of the human rights, dignity, autonomy and needs of persons with disabilities through training and the promulgation of ethical standards for public and private health care".

The "principle of voluntariness" has long been recognized in the civil law system in China. According to Article 4 of the General Principles of Civil Law, "in civil activities, the principles of voluntariness, fairness, making compensation for equal value, honesty and credibility shall be observed". However, specific provisions regarding treatment have not been addressed. The landmark law that explicitly states that inpatient treatment for patients is voluntary in the *Mental Health Act 2013* (Article 30). The right of individuals with mental disorders to make their own choices based on informed consent for consultation, treatment, and hospital discharge was first established by the act. The *Mental Health Act 2013* affirms that people with mental disorders have the right to control their own bodies and respects their human rights, in line with the CRPD. It is worth noting that the *Mental Health Act* took 27 years to develop and was finally put into effect in 2013. The *Mental Health Act 2013* comprises of 7 chapters and 85 articles. It clearly states that "personality, dignity, and personal and property safety of the patients with mental disorders are inviolable" (Article 4). In order to strike a balance between the public security and the rights of patients, Article 30 stipulates that patients shall be hospitalized if they meet the criteria for "dangerousness" (including two clauses: the first clause states that "having committed any act of harming himself or herself or having the potential to harm himself/herself" and the second clause states that "having committed any act of endangering the safety of others or having the potential to endanger the safety of others"), subject to the principle of voluntariness.

Mental health legislation has been in effect for nearly 10 years; yet the act and its implementation do not ensure human rights respect and enforcement. Legal justification for both voluntary and involuntary treatment, as well as the responsibilities of those involved in mental health, are crucial components of mental health legislation. A study based on a tertiary specialized psychiatric service system in Shanghai showed an increasing trend in involuntary treatment rates in the 4 years following the implementation of the mental health law, similar to what has been seen in Europe and Australia following changes to legislation (Gill et al. 2020; Jacobsen 2012). The pattern may be attributed to a lack of corresponding operational processes and of adequate community mental health services to function in accordance with the act.

Internationally, the necessity for involuntary treatment is still debated. Although the enforcement of the mental health legislation is in line with the principles of the CRPD, there are still aspects that need to be improved. A major problem is the lack of defined operational rules. The absence of defined operating regulations is a key issue. There is a vagueness in risk management definitions, as well as a lack of standard operating criteria. The immediate and severe danger to oneself and others is not emphasized. The capacity of people with mental disorders to make treatment decisions is also not addressed, and there is a lack of assessment methods in related laws. In addition, discharge criteria and review mechanisms are unclear, and patients may face difficulties with discharge, leading to a compromise of their rights.

4.5 Rehabilitation

Through habilitation and rehabilitation, people with mental disorders may achieve personal independence and full inclusion into society. According to Article 26 of the Convention, rehabilitation shall be "based on the multidisciplinary assessment of individual needs and strengths; support participation and inclusion in the community and all aspects of society; and shall promote the development of initial and continuing training for professionals and staff working in habilitation and rehabilitation services". The article reflects respect for the individual needs and abilities of persons with disabilities and re-emphasizes the principle of voluntariness. At the same time, the article indicates the government's obligation to develop training programmes for professionals to promote the rehabilitation of the disabled population.

The development of psychiatric rehabilitation in China started late due to the lack of adequate community resources. In recent years, with the development of rehabilitation-related laws and policies, the development of the psychiatric rehabilitation field has taken off. Chapter 4 of the *Mental Health Act 2013* articulates the rehabilitation of people with mental disorders, outlining the responsibilities of community rehabilitation institutions (Article 54), medical institutions (Article 55), villagers' or residents' committees

(Article 56), employers (Article 56), Disabled Persons' Federation organizations (Article 57), and guardians (Article 59) of people with disabilities due to mental disorders. As part of a pilot project on the management of designated service providers for the rehabilitation of people with disabilities, China's Ministry of Civil Affairs, the National Health and the Disabled Persons' Federation launched the Norms for Community Rehabilitation Services for Mental Disorders in 2020 (China's Ministry of Civil Affairs, National Health and the Disabled Persons' Federation 2020). Following that, a selection of provinces and cities serving as pilot projects issued corresponding norms. Sichuan Province, for instance, has created service guidelines and management standards that cover the treatment of mental illness, supported employment training, day-care, transitional housing, sheltered work, rehabilitation clubs, and long-term recovery (Tang et al. 2020).

With the change from a biomedical to a biopsychosocial model, community-based rehabilitation has become more important because it focuses on how social factors affect the care of people with mental disorders. A review of the course and outcome of schizophrenia in Asian countries revealed that the clinical outcome was better in Indian centres than in other centres, despite the fact that in Indian centres the proportion of patients who were never prescribed antipsychotics was higher than in other centres (Holla and Thirthalli 2015). The authors hypothesized that the involvement of family members in the care of individuals with schizophrenia may explain the regional variances. A WHO ten-country study on schizophrenia showing that the outcome of the disease was better in the low-income countries than in those in highly industrialized countries could also be considerable relevance in showing social-related impacts on the clinical outcomes of individuals with schizophrenia (Jablensky et al. 1992). Community-based rehabilitation that involves social supports, including but not limited to family members, should be considered for inclusion in comprehensive therapy plans. Community rehabilitation, in general, offers the geographic and social circumstances for recovery and contributes to the rehabilitation of the social functioning of persons with mental disorders. Evidence base showed that providing social skills training may facilitate mental rehabilitation in community settings since the psychological interventions improve social performance and general psychopathology in people with severe mental disorders (Turner et al. 2018). In addition to the challenge of community reintegration, another obstacle in community rehabilitation is how to protect the unique needs of diverse groups of individuals. People with disabilities related to mental illness have varying rehabilitation needs based on their socio-demographic features (Lu et al. 2018). The rehabilitation demands of children, women, and elderly individuals with mental impairments vary. Consider the rehabilitation of mentally disabled children as an example. The Second National Sample Survey of Persons with Disabilities in 2006 revealed that children with disabilities related to mental illness had low utilization of health services (44.35%), while there was high demand (98.26%) (Ding et al. 2021). Due to the fact that children and adults may have distinct disability features and health treatment needs, tailored rehabilitation services should be provided for children with disabilities (Hoffmann et al. 2015).

4.6 Employment

Employment is a crucial step in the rehabilitation process for people living with mental disorders to enhance their quality of life and increase their participation in society. According to Article 26 of the Convention, States Parties recognize the right of persons with disabilities to work on an equal basis with others; this includes the right to the opportunity to gain a living by work freely chosen or accepted in a labour market and work environment that is open, inclusive, and accessible to persons with disabilities. China has long been concerned with ensuring employment for persons with impairments. In 2007, the Employment of Persons with Impairments Regulations were enacted in China, prohibiting discrimination against people with disabilities in the workplace. The *Mental Health Act 2013* states that patients' right to employment should be guaranteed. According to the Act, patients' right to employment must be safeguarded. Article 58 of the Chapter 4 (Rehabilitation of Mental Disorders) in the Act states that "Employers should arrange for patients with mental disorders to engage in work within their capabilities in line with their actual circumstances, guarantee that patients receive equitable treatment, organize for patients to participate in appropriate vocational skills training, increase their employability, provide a suitable working environment for them, and encourage their achievements in their work".

People with mental disorders do not have satisfactory employment rates, though. Between 2007 and 2012, the employment rate for persons with disabilities related to mental illness fell from 56% to 34.7% (Shi and Wang 2013). The employment rate was lower than people with physical disabilities, such as speech and physical impairments (Shi and Wang 2013). Despite this, the employment of persons with mental disorders continues to be hampered by a lack of clear and effective legislation. The Government's civil affairs departments and Disabled Persons' Federation at all levels have also taken this subject seriously, issuing applicable rules and policies to improve work protection. In 2016, the "Outline of the 13th Five-Year Plan for Accelerating the Process of Prosperity of Persons with Disabilities", which was complemented by government laws and departmental normative guidelines, featured supported work for people with disabilities.

In 2019, China issued the "Specification of care services for intellectual, mental and severe physical disabilities at working age" (GB/T37516–2019) (State Administration for Market Regulation 2019). Persons with disabilities related to mental illness of working age are included in the scope of care services under the national standard, ensuring their care and support. Furthermore, the rule promotes self-care, social adaption, motor functions, vocational rehabilitation, and employment skills training for people with disabilities related to mental illness. These measures aimed to aid people with disabilities in finding work and ensure their equal participation in social life. The rule is China's first national standard for regulating disability care services, and it has favourable implications for rehabilitation and guides the vocational development of persons with mental disorders. As follows, municipalities are offering employment-specific approaches and action programmes. For instance, Guangdong Province's Three-Year Action Plan for Promoting the Employment of Persons with Disabilities (2022–2024) (General Office of the People's Government of Guangdong Province 2022) focuses on proposed employment support actions for individuals with intellectual, mental, and severe physical disabilities, as well as the development of supported employment products and service brands with local characteristics.

Among diverse employment alternatives, integrated employment is crucial for reducing social isolation. Evidence indicates that vocationally oriented rehabilitation, such as vocational peer support, may help people recover from mental disorders in many countries despite variable economic and labour performance markers (Maru et al. 2021; Warner 2009). Unsurprisingly, the provision of integrated employment can be a reflection of social inclusion. China's first regulatory policy on the integration of persons with disabilities related to mental illness into employment is the Guangdong Measures on Employment of Persons with Disabilities (People's Government of Guangdong Province 2019), introduced by the People's Government of Guangdong Province in 2019. Article 19 of the Measures states that "federations of persons with disabilities at all levels shall establish a framework for appointing supported employment counsellors for persons with disabilities, cultivate and support qualified organizations to provide supported employment services, and promote the gradual transition of persons with intellectual disabilities and persons with mental disabilities to employment in a regular employment environment with the assistance of supported employment counsellors." Unfortunately, concrete regulations or policy guidelines about how to implement the integrated employment of people with mental disorders are still missing.

4.7 Future Directions

We attempt to propose four response strategies based on the above discussion on legal safeguards for guardianship, involuntary treatment, rehabilitation, and employment. These strategies may bring laws and regulations more in line with the requirements of the Convention and to improve the situation of individuals with mental disorders or disability due to impairments caused by mental illness.

4.8 Guarantee the Participation of People with Mental Disorders in Decision-Making

The principle of making "no decision about me, without me" must be realized for and people with disabilities must participate in decisions concerning their rights and services which are developed to serve them. The rights of individuals with mental disorders or disability due to impairments caused by mental illness can be better protected if their voices are heard. As advocated in the CRPD, it is important to respect the inherent dignity, individual autonomy, and independence of persons with disabilities. We recommend that laws and regulations, action plans, and strategies relating to the rights of people with disabilities related to mental illness be established with full respect for individual autonomy and that the participation of people with disabilities and their representative organizations in public decision-making be guaranteed. It is necessary to make every effort to avoid and reduce stigma in order to create an inclusive environment for public participation. To achieve this goal, intervention projects that aim to reduce discrimination and stigma associated with mental disorders should continue to be carried out, and relevant research that is based on evidence should be carried out in China. Increasing social contact with patients and promoting public education are two of the most important strategies for reducing stigma associated with mental disorders. All sections of society should undertake active support measures to create inclusive communities. The ideal inclusive community may attract people with mental disorders to participate in the life of the community and to be integrated actively and freely in society.

4.9 Improve the Legal System and Formulate Operable Regulations

There is a continuing need for amendments to be made to the *Mental Health Act 2013* and other associated legal provisions, one of which is the formulation of regulations that are clearer and more operational. We suggest that the regulations on the risk assessment for hospitalization, guardianship, and supervision should be improved. First, to comply with the principle of least restriction, the law should emphasize the criteria of "immediate" and "serious" risk to reduce involuntary hospitalization even though it is impractical to eliminate it entirely. Second, it is critical to develop operational risk assessment tools and processes, establish clear guardianship standards, and offer patient stakeholders such as their guardians and medical staff legal training. Third, develop a monitoring system and an impartial legal process to audit the process of admission, hospitalization, and discharge. The legal system should play a role in protecting the rights of patients. We hope to achieve a balance between the rights of patients and the protection of the public security by finding a synergy between the rights and interests of patients with mental disorders and the community as a whole.

4.10 Promote Community Mental Health and Build Inclusive Rehabilitation Communities

Community mental health services may be the mainstream of the mental health service model in the future (Rosen et al. 2020). The development of community mental health is critical for reducing involuntary hospitalization and facilitating patient recovery. Hence, we suggest that the government should vigorously develop community mental health and provide community-based mental health services providing voluntary treatment. The place of community rehabilitation centres should be clearly defined from a legal perspective, emphasizing that community mental health can no longer be left in an auxiliary role. The enactment of the law can guarantee a shift from the hospital-led model to the community mental health services model, so that community mental health services and hospital services can develop in a new balance. Boosting the development of community mental health can help clarify the responsibilities of mental health institutions at all levels, thus further protecting the rights of people with mental disorders. Additionally, the government should invest additional mental health resources to ensure the establishment of community mental health institutions and provide training for the workforce of community mental health services, especially community rehabilitation professionals such as social workers and psychologists.

The government should work on developing integrated employment services to facilitate the social integration of individuals with mental disorders or disability due to impairments caused by mental illness. To begin, the government ought to work on individualized employment strategies. Priority should be given to assessing the employability of various groups of people as well as the integration needs of people who have disabilities related to mental illness. Accordingly, the government might consider developing a variety of occupations that are helpful for social inclusion for persons with disabilities. Second, the government should develop and emphasise jobs development policies and practices. Supported employment models, peer support, and other programmes should be supported and planned for. Affirmative programmes or incentives should be used to promote the employment of individuals with mental disorders or disability due to impairments caused by mental illness. The government should provide appropriate training and give clear guidelines for employers to make workplaces comfortable and convenient to individuals with mental disorders or disability due to impairments caused by mental illness. Next, the government ought to supply individuals with disabilities with job hunting and employment agencies, in addition to providing training in a variety of labour and vocational skills. Finally, a professional team should be established to provide employment services for persons with disabilities related to mental illness.

4.11 Conclusion

As CRPD has been implemented for 14 years, this chapter aims to sort out current practice in China's legal framework. China faces immense mental health challenges and opportunities as a result of its rapid economic growth and social structural changes. The economic burden caused by mental disorders is heavy because of China's large population and the high prevalence of mental disorders, as well as because of inadequate health care resources and their uneven development. Another major challenge is the predominance of hospital-based mental health care, and slow development of community mental health services. With the increased emphasis on mental health, China has attempted to shift from a biomedical service model to an integrated "bio-psycho-social" service model through the implementation of several strategies. The implementation of China's first mental health law, the promulgation of the Civil Code, and the publication of national mental health plans have played key and positive roles in protecting the rights of people with mental disorders.

We focused on the assessment of the extent to which legal safeguards for guardianship, involuntary treatment, rehabilitation, and employment issues for people with mental disorders are in harmony with CRPD. The existing legal framework provides some protections for guardianship, voluntary treatment, rehabilitation, and employment for people with mental disorders in China. To further protect the rights of people with mental disorders, we have proposed four response strategies, which are to (a) guarantee the participation of people with mental disorders in decision-making, (b) improve the legal system and formulate operable regulations, (c) promote community mental health and build inclusive rehabilitation communities, and (d) develop integrated employment services to promote social inclusion. The improvement of the rights of people with mental disorders requires a series of measures and involves joint efforts of all stages and areas of society. We hope that in the near future, legal protection for people with mental disorders in China will be closer to the principles of the CRPD.

References

American Psychiatric Association (2013) Diagnostic and statistical manual of mental disorders: DSM-5. American Psychiatric Publishing, Washington, DC

Chen B (2015) The development of right to civil litigation of persons with mental disabilities in practice: from mental health law to the UN convention on the rights of persons with disabilities. Disabil Rights Stud China 2:216–229, 297–298.

China's Ministry of Civil Affairs, National Health and the Disabled Persons' Federation (2020) Norms for community rehabilitation services for mental disorders [WWW Document]. https://www.mca.gov.cn/article/xw/tzgg/202101/20210100031781.shtml. Accessed 12 March 2022.

Ding R, Cheng Y, Zheng X (2021) Utilization and demand of health care service for children with mental disabilities in China. Chinese J Rehabil Theory Pract 27:243–248. https://doi.org/10.3969/j.issn.1006-9771.2020.00.002

General Office of the People's Government of Guangdong Province (2022) Guangdong Province's three-year action plan for promoting the employment of persons with disabilities (2022–2024) [WWW document]. http://www.gd.gov.cn/zwgk/wjk/qbwj/yfb/content/post_4039336.html. Accessed 12 March 2022.

Gill NS, Amos A, Muhsen H, Hatton J, Ekanayake C, Kisely S (2020) Measuring the impact of revised mental health legislation on human rights in Queensland, Australia. Int J Law Psychiatry 73:101634. https://doi.org/10.1016/j.ijlp.2020.101634

Hoffmann KD, Walnoha A, Sloan J, Buddadhumaruk P, Huang H-H, Borrebach J, Cluss PA, Burke JG (2015) Developing a community-based tailored exercise program for people with severe and persistent mental illness. Prog Commun Health Partnersh 9:213–227. https://doi.org/10.1353/cpr.2015.0045

Holla B, Thirthalli J (2015) Course and outcome of schizophrenia in Asian countries: review of research in the past three decades. Asian J Psychiatr 14:3–12. https://doi.org/10.1016/j.ajp.2015.01.001

Huang Y, Wang Y, Wang H, Liu Z, Yu X, Yan J, Yu Y, Kou C, Xu X, Lu J, Wang Z, He S, Xu Y, He Y, Li T, Guo W, Tian H, Xu G, Xu X, Ma Y, Wang L, Wang L, Yan Y, Wang B, Xiao S, Zhou L, Li L, Tan L, Zhang T, Ma C, Li Q, Ding H, Geng H, Jia F, Shi J, Wang S, Zhang N, Du X, Du X, Wu Y (2019) Prevalence of mental disorders in China: a cross-sectional epidemiological study. Lancet Psychiatry 6:211–224

Jablensky A, Sartorius N, Ernberg G, Anker M, Korten A, Cooper JE, Day R, Bertelsen A (1992) Schizophrenia: manifestations, incidence and course in different cultures. A World Health Organization ten-country study. Psychol Med Monogr Suppl 20:1–97. https://doi.org/10.1017/S0264180100000904

Jacobsen TB (2012) Involuntary treatment in Europe: different countries, different practices. Curr Opin Psychiatry 25:307–310. https://doi.org/10.1097/YCO.0b013e32835462e3

Liu Z, Huang Y, Chen H, Ma C, Zhang T (2019) A cross-sectional survey of mental disability attributed to psychosis among persons aged 15 years and over in China. Chinese Ment Health J 33:321–327. https://doi.org/10.3969/j.issn.1000-6729.2019.05.001

Lu X, Li X, Qiu Z, Ge J, Wang G, Huang K, Li A (2018) Needs and service of rehabilitation for people with psychiatric disability. Chinese J Rehabil Med 24:1252–1256. https://doi.org/10.3969/j.issn.1006-9771.2018.11.003

Ma N, Chen R, Zhang W, Wang, Bai Y, Su R, Li Z, Wang W, Wu X, Lu L (2022) The mental health resources in Chinese mainland by 2020. Chinese J Psychiatry 55:459–468. https://doi.org/10.3760/cma.j.cn113661-20220617-00158

Maru M, Rogers ES, Nicolellis D, Legere L, Placencio-Castro M, Magee C, Harbaugh AG (2021) Vocational peer support for adults with psychiatric disabilities: results of a randomized trial. Psychiatr Rehabil J 44:327–336. https://doi.org/10.1037/prj0000484

National Bureau of Statistics of China (2021) China statistical Yearbook-2021. China State Statistical Press, Beijing

National Health and Family Planning Commission, Central Commission for Comprehensive Management of Public Security, National Development and Reform Commission, Ministry of Education, Ministry of Public Security, Ministry of Civil Affairs, Ministry of Justice, Ministry of Finance, Ministry of Human Resources and Social Security, China Disabled Persons' Federation (2015) National Mental Health Work Plan of China (2015–2020)

People's Government of Guangdong Province (2019) Guangdong measures on employment of persons with disabilities [WWW document]. http://www.gd.gov.cn/zwgk/wjk/qbwj/yfl/content/post_2577705.html. Accessed 12 March 2022.

Rosen A, Gill NS, Salvador-Carulla L (2020) The future of community psychiatry and community mental health services. Curr Opin Psychiatry 33:375–390. https://doi.org/10.1097/YCO.0000000000000620

Shi D, Wang Q (2013) Trends on employment situation of the disabled in China. Disabil Res 4:76–79

State Administration for Market Regulation (2019) Specification of care services for intellectual, mental and severe physical disabilities at working age [WWW document]. https://www.samr.gov.cn/bzjss/sjdt/gzdt/201908/t20190828_306309.html. Accessed 12 March 2022.

Tang Z, Huang X, Wen H, Yang X, Huang G, Xiang H, Yang X, Tao Y, Zhou W, Wang D, Wang R, Liu Y, Li J, Tang M, Wang H, Yuan Z, Zhang Y, Yang X, Wang Q, Yao W, Chen G, Zhao G, Wang D, Deng F, Yang M, Xu K, Mu F, Liang H, Luo M, Luo J, Jiang D, Tang L (2020) Standard of community rehabilitation services for mental disorders (DB 51/T 2697-2020). Sichuan Mental Health 33:289–296

Turner DT, McGlanaghy E, Cuijpers P, van der Gaag M, Karyotaki E, MacBeth A (2018) A meta-analysis of social skills training and related interventions for psychosis. Schizophr Bull 44:475–491. https://doi.org/10.1093/schbul/sbx146

Warner R (2009) Recovery from schizophrenia and the recovery model. Curr Opin Psychiatry 22:374–380. https://doi.org/10.1097/YCO.0b013e32832c920b

World Health Organization (2019) Human resources for mental health [WWW document]. https://www.who.int/data/gho/data/themes/topics/indicator-groups/indicator-group-details/GHO/human-resources. Accessed 12 Feb 2022.

Egypt: Implementation of the CRPD in Mental Health Care

5

Tarek Okasha and Nermin Shaker

Contents

5.1 Introduction

The United Nations (UN) Convention on the Rights of Persons with Disabilities (CRPD) (United Nations General Assembly 2007) was adopted by the United Nations General Assembly in 2006 and came into force in 2008. The general idea of the CRPD is inclusion of people with disabilities into the society and communities instead of establishing special rules and institutions (Lord et al. 2010). The CRPD calls for the full realization of all human rights and fundamental freedoms for all persons with disabilities without discrimination of any kind based on disability. The CRPD does not explicitly define 'disability' but characterizes persons with disabilities as those who have 'long-term physical, mental, intellectual or sensory impairments which in interaction with various barriers may hinder their full and effective participation in society on an equal basis with others'. The CRPD is therefore completely applicable to the situation of people with long term mental impairments as well as with other kinds of disabilities. The CRPD set up the UN Committee on the Rights of Persons with Disabilities and requires state parties to report regularly on their application of the Convention (United Nations General Assembly 2007).

T. Okasha · N. Shaker (✉)
Okasha Institute of Psychiatry, Ain Shams University, Cairo, Egypt
e-mail: tarek.okasha@med.asu.edu.eg; nerminshaker@med.asu.edu.eg

N. Gill, N. Sartorius (eds.), *Mental Health and Human Rights*, Sustainable Development Goals Series, https://doi.org/10.1007/978-3-031-52179-9_5

UN-CRPD was ratified by the European Union in 2010 and, in total, by 185 states parties till 2022. Interpretative declaration was made by Egypt on the fourth of April 2007, and the CRPD was formally confirmed, and ratified on the 14th of April 2008. Egypt declared that its interpretation of article 12 of the CRPD is that persons with disabilities enjoy the capacity to acquire rights and assume legal responsibility but not the capacity to perform duties, under Egyptian law (Meadows et al. 2014).

5.2 Available Statistics of Disabilities in Egypt

There is little reliable data concerning the prevalence of disability in the Egyptian population. A 2002 study commissioned by the Japan International Cooperation Agency (2002) found that mental disabilities comprised almost 75% of all disability in Egypt with mobility impairment making up 15% and visual and hearing impairment constituting the remaining 11% (WHO 2011). The 2006 Egyptian census estimated that 1.8% of the Egyptian population is living with disabilities (WHO 2011). A 2011 study of the World Health Organization (WHO), UNICEF, and local civil society organizations estimated the percentage of persons with disabilities to be approximately 11%, or approximately 8.5 million persons (WHO 2011). The UN estimates a much higher figure, estimating that 12 million people are living with some type of disability (Meadows et al. 2014). Since the impact of disability extends to the families of the individuals, there are about 36 million persons who are affected by disability in Egypt, which makes up 35% of the total population, according to the United Nations Development Programme (Disability:IN 2022).

5.3 Legislation of Rights of People with Disability in Egypt

Egypt's current Constitution was approved in January 2014 and contains several articles that relate both directly and indirectly to disability.

Article 81 of Egypt's 2014 Constitution states: *"The State shall guarantee the health, economic, social, cultural, entertainment, sporting and educational rights of persons with disabilities strive to provide them with job opportunities, allocate a percentage of job opportunities to them, and adapt public facilities and their surrounding environment to their special needs. The State shall also ensure their exercise of all political rights and integration with other citizens in compliance with the principles of equality, justice and equal opportunities."* The employment quota of *Rehabilitation Law 39 (1975)*, amended under *Law 49 (1982)* was raised for disabled workers from 2% to 5% (Kassab et al. 2018).

The phases of evolution of the disability movement and rights can be viewed through four phases; institutionalization during the 50s until the end of the 70s. Then, shifting to a community focus and grass roots movement during the 80s until the 2000s, followed by integrating law into society recently, that led to issuing a new comprehensive law adopted by the Egyptian parliament in 2018. In 2018, law no. 10 was issued on the Rights of Persons with Disabilities, after being approved by the parliament. The new law offers many commitments by the government to persons with disabilities. It includes non-discrimination on the basis of disability or gender of the person with disabilities, and to ensure real equality in the enjoyment of all human rights and fundamental freedoms in all fields, respect their choices and how they express them by their own independent will, the right of persons with disabilities and their families to obtain all information that concerns them from all sectors (Kassab et al. 2018).

The adoption of a rights-based approach was the main shift in formulating changes to laws and policies. Inspired by international developments, societal perspectives surrounding disability began to evolve. Civil society began to turn to legislative and political frameworks as a necessary media to further mobilize and solidify rights for persons with disabilities (Miller 2011). By 2007, the international community, including Egypt, adopted the CRPD, which is the most recent treaty in international law and the only legally binding instrument about disability (Kassab et al. 2018).

The Egyptian parliament passed a new law [10/2018] replacing the old insufficient law 39/1975. The definition of disability is cornerstone in this law as it reveals how the society currently understands the problem:

> *"A person with a disability is a person who has a partial or full stable limitation, whether physical, mental, sensory, or that prevents him when dealing with barriers and surrounding environment from participating fully and effectively with society and on an equal footing with the others." [Law10/2018—Article 2].*

The Law addressed the notions of equality, discrimination, equal opportunities, the government responsibility towards persons with disabilities and social protection. It includes clear definitions of the previous terms with emphasis on rehabilitation and awareness about prevention of disability (Kassab et al. 2018).

It should be noted that it entails tax exemption and financial incentives to employing persons with disabilities, along with retaining the quota (5%), highlighting the importance of environment considerations for the needs of persons with disabilities, daily 1-h work time reduction, and exemption from health tests prior to hiring. The law addresses the punishment related to acts of discrimination, isolation, and violence in workplace, and gives tools for assertion and justice (Kassab et al. 2018).

Implementation of the law in Egypt is an ongoing evolving process, manifesting in issuing a medical card for persons with disabilities as part of accessing healthcare including mentally ill patients, integration of children with special needs in school and university education including children with mental disability, autism, ADHD, and learning disorders, in addition to proceeding in their rehabilitation and employment.

5.4 The Rights of Persons with Disabilities in the Context of Mental Health

Particular rights have historically been denied or restricted in the context of mental health, namely the right to equal recognition before the law, the right to personal liberty and security, and freedom from non-consensual medical treatment and experimentation. The right to legal capacity is central to human rights. It entails holding rights and duties (legal standing) and exercising those rights and duties (legal agency). Therefore, it is a precondition to the exercise of all human rights and fundamental freedoms. However, many groups of persons with disabilities have historically been denied their legal capacity. Persons with psychosocial disabilities, persons with intellectual disabilities and autism, for example, often have their legal capacity restricted on the basis of having a medical condition or impairment, having made a decision perceived as poor, or having deficient decision-making skills.

The CRPD challenges all these practices and introduces a paradigm shift in relation to the legal capacity of persons with disabilities. Its article 12 affirms the right of all persons with disabilities to equal recognition before the law, upholding their right to exercise legal capacity on an equal basis with others in all areas of life. States parties must refrain from denying persons with disabilities their legal capacity and must, rather, provide persons with disabilities access to the support necessary to enable them to make decisions that have legal effect, including decisions about treatment or admission for treatment (UN CRPD 2006).

5.5 Mental Health Legislation in Egypt

The existence of mental health legislation reflects the potential and willingness of a country to provide better mental health services and to move towards realizing better human rights standards (Loza and Omar 2017).

In Egypt, the earliest reference to the care in specialized institutions of people with a mental illness date back to Fatimid Egypt and the establishment of the Bimaristan in the thirteenth century, which still stands today in central Cairo. Throughout the Islamic era in Egyptian history, care of people with a mental illness appears to have been community based, while institutional care for those suffering from mental health problems was within general hospitals. The building of asylums away from residential areas, to separate those with mental illness from their communities, began only in the late nineteenth century. The beginning of the British protectorate in Egypt led to the modern practice of asylum care in 1880. The Abasseya hospital was built as an exemplary asylum. It was at this point that regulations organizing the involuntary admission of a person with a mental illness were needed. With only one asylum in Egypt, however, the regulations were internally set by the superintendent (Loza and Nawawi 2012).

The first Egyptian mental health legislation was introduced in 1944, this legislation addressed the involuntary detention of psychotic patients, second opinions, consent to treatment and appeals. According to law No. 41, 1944 mental patients have the right to leave the hospital if they want to. The law formed the basis of hospital practice of psychiatry for about 30 years. Nonetheless, by the 1980s psychiatric hospitals were detaining numerous patients who did not suffer from psychotic disorders (largely because of loopholes in the legislation), but rather had addictions or behavioural disorders; in fact, the involuntary detention of patients on moral grounds became common practice (Zaki 2009). By 2006, Egypt had 8000 inpatient beds for people presenting with mental illness, all on locked wards, and many of these patients had stayed for decades.

In 2009 Dr. Nasser Loza founded The Egyptian Society for the Rights of People with Mental Illness. His main focus was to advocate for the rights of people with mental illness, as well as, to fight stigma against patients and their families. In collaboration between the Egyptian Ministry of Health and the World Health Organization, and the Royal College of Psychiatrists along with other human rights entities, work on a new draft legislation that would protect the rights of people with mental illness and set guidelines for clinical practitioners was completed. Egyptian Parliament ratified *The Mental Health Act 2009* (Law 71, published in the Official Gazette, issue 20, 14 May 2009).

The Mental Health Act, 2009 brought basic conceptual changes to the care of people with a mental illness in Egyptian institutions. This, like its predecessor, focused on the rights of those with a mental illness, independent second opinions from psychiatrists and patients' right to consent to treatment. The real change in the environment of mental hospitals followed the policy of opening the gates to visitors, the press and international professional organizations, such as the Royal College of Psychiatrists, the Arab Board of Psychiatry, the Institute of Psychiatry in London and the World Federation for Mental Health, which all offered to support the work. In parallel to this, another important step was to campaign and raise awareness regarding the rights of people with a mental illness to live in the community. A media campaign was launched using television, billboards and educational material in schools. Initially, this started with the Ministry of Health's effort and funding, then the work gradually took off on its own, with non-governmental organizations (NGOs), human rights organizations and consumer representatives taking the lead. Training workshops were conducted throughout Egypt. By May 2009, the law was applied to all mental institutions in Egypt, and a *Code of Practice (2010—ministerial decree number 128)* was completed. Training workshops were conducted throughout Egypt. The application of the new Act appeared to be well accepted by most hospital-based professionals but not fully supported by psychiatrists, who had practiced without the implementation of the 1944 Mental Health Act for decades. Indeed, a body of resistance built up among clinicians, who felt that the new Act, by empowering patients, represented a threat to clinicians' judgement (Loza and Nawawi 2012).

Consequent to Egypt's *Mental Health Act 2009*, Abbaseya mental hospital discharged 15% of its patients, while Misr El Gedidah mental hospital discharged 41%, Al-Khankah 9%, Helwan 22%, Port Said 93%. Furthermore, one hundred percent of patients in Assuit mental hospital were discharged. According to the draft law, cities around Egypt would boast a National Center for Psychological Health, where judges and government officials would supervise the clinics and ensure that patients receive all their legal rights. Specialized mental hospitals still exist to treat mental patients, along with the new national centers and clinics.

Although the new law helped to evolve the concept of care in Egyptian hospitals and the treatment institutions became less stigmatized, there was a huge need for Egyptian society to bear the responsibility for promoting the concept and fostering the rights of people with mental illness. The Egyptian Society for the Rights of People with Mental Illness means to change this general attitude towards mental patients. It aims to help integrate mental patients in the community and combat the stigma associated with mental illness, and to advocate for the rights of those affected by mental illness in Egypt. Its vision is for fair treatment with dignity, with respect and to foster a better quality of life for all those affected by mental illness, their carers, families and friends.

The Egyptian experience underlines the importance of public education and community participation in the drafting of new legislation. Ideally, laws are ratified to fulfil society's need for regulation. Bringing in new ideas of human rights and empowerment of service users becomes a challenge when the predominant culture does not fully acknowledge the rights of people with a mental illness. Nevertheless, the process of drafting the Act—with repeated conferences and workshops, lengthy parliamentary debates in the upper and lower houses, and substantial media coverage—has influenced the wider community's perception of people with mental illness, their place in society and their role. Patients are their own best advocates. Bringing a long-stay patient to meet with Members of Parliament in the Egyptian parliament was probably the loudest call that led to Egypt's *Mental Health Act 2009*.

The Code of Practice of the Mental Health Act was redrafted in 2011 (ministerial decree number 210) by a working group, which chose to relax the requirements for patients' informed consent to treatment, from a written signed form to a written entry in the patient's notes stating that the patient has verbally consented. The new Code allows the compulsory use of psychotropic medication to facilitate bringing people to hospital from their private homes without prior permission from the district attorney. Involuntary electroconvulsive therapy (ECT) without second opinion for up to three initial sessions became legitimate. Attempts to discuss allowing patients suffering from mental and psychological ailments to receive treatment at special departments in public hospitals rather than the overloaded and socially-stigmatized mental hospitals was raised (Loza and Nawawi 2012).

In parallel with mental health legislation, implementation of the mental health reforms and mental health policy in Egypt was done aiming at integrating mental health into the health sector in the period from 2002–2009. An integrated approach to mental health policy development in Egypt, the policy objectives of the programme were fourfold: firstly, to conduct detailed situation appraisal of mental health within Egypt; secondly, to use that information to develop appropriate and integrated mental health policy and plans; thirdly, to develop mechanisms for sustainable implementation of policy across the country, using locally available resources and integrated into local systems; and fourthly, to monitor and evaluate progress to fine tune implementation. The multi-faceted and comprehensive programme combined situation appraisal to inform planning and establishment of a health sector system for coordination. Also, it included supervision and training of staff at each level (national, governornorate district and primary care) through workshops; production of toolkits and development of guidelines and standards. The programme encouraged intersectoral liaison at national, governorate, district and local levels; public education; and integration of mental health into health management systems. Specific efforts to improve forensic services, rehabilitation services and child psychiatry services were also done (Loza and Nawawi 2012). In the context of preserving the rights of the mentally ill during the COVID-19 pandemic, Egypt provided a unique specialized hospital for COVID-19 positive psychiatric patients. In June 2020, the head of the Ministry of Health and Population allocated Al Fatimia Cairo Hospital as the first to admit psychiatric patients infected with COVID-19. Thrifty-four cases were admitted during the first two waves. They included patients diagnosed with schizophrenia, bipolar disorder, dementia, and intellectual disability. (Okasha et al. 2022).

5.6 Mental Health Legislation in the Arab world

The main source of information on the status of mental health legislation in the Arab world is the World Health Organization's Mental Health Atlas. First developed in 2001, it provides comprehensive estimates of global mental health resources and policies. The data are collected through a survey sent to key mental health focal points in every member state of the World Health Organization (WHO). The World Health Organization's Mental Health Atlas (2020) mentioned that 70% of responding countries in the Eastern Mediterranean Region (EMR) reported the existence of stand-alone mental health laws ($N = 14$) compared to 11 countries (61% of responding countries) in 2017. In addition, 31% of them reported that their law had been updated since 2017. Regarding the degree of compliance of mental health laws with international human rights instruments, 80% of responding countries in the EMR ($N = 15$) considered that their law promotes the following standards: (1) transition towards community-based mental health services (including mental health integrated into general hospitals and primary care; (2) promotion of the rights of people with mental health conditions and psychosocial disabilities to exercise their legal capacity; (3) promotion of alternatives to coercive practice; (4) provision for procedures to enable people with mental health conditions and psychosocial disabilities to protect their rights and file appeals and complaints to an independent legal body; (5) provision for regular inspections of human rights conditions in mental health facilities by an independent body. The proportion of EMR countries reporting full compliance increased from a little under 32% in 2014 to 91% in 2017, then dropped to 80% in 2020. The proportion of responding EMR countries reporting that a dedicated authority or independent authority did not exist decreased from 47% in 2017 to 20% in 2020. Meanwhile, the reported existence of an independent authority or body providing irregular inspections increased from 12% in 2017 to 20% in 2020. Similarly, EMR countries reported that a dedicated authority or independent authority or body providing regular inspections increased from 24% in 2017 to 35% in 2020. In Egypt, the National Council for Mental Health is the independent authority or body providing regular inspections of human rights conditions in mental health facilities.

On summarizing the status of mental health legislation, implementation and compliance with human rights instruments in the EMR countries reported by WHO Atlas 2020, it was found that 76% ($N = 16$) reported the existence of a stand-alone and/or integrated law for mental health, 58% ($n = 12$) reported that their laws were fully compliant with human rights instruments, and 39% of Member States stated that their laws were in the process of implementation. However, only 29% reported having a mental health law that was in the process of implementation and was fully compliant with human rights instruments.

The majority of the countries in the region are classified as middle or low income countries (World Bank Group 2012). Despite this, even politically stable high income countries in the region, such as the United Arab Emirates (UAE), have laws that lack safeguards when it comes to involuntary admission and compulsory treatment, or do not apply their laws consistently (Alhassani and Osman 2015). Furthermore, among the few countries that have a modern mental health law that is in line with international human rights standards, implementation is weak. In the Arab world, mental health legislation stands a long way from realizing the objectives of the CRPD.

In Egypt, an assessment of the Abbasseya Mental Health Hospital, one of the largest psychiatric hospitals in Cairo, using the WHO Quality Rights Assessment Tool—which uses the CRPD as a framework—showed that the majority of human rights violations concerned: the right to an adequate standard of living (Article 28 of the CRPD); the right to enjoy the highest attainable standard of physical and mental health (Article 25); freedom from torture or cruel, inhumane and degrading treatment or punishment, as well as from physical violence and abuse (Articles 15 and 16); and the right to exercise legal capacity and personal liberty (Articles 12 and 14) (Fawzy

2015). Even if the *Mental Health Act of 2009*—which brought forward many positive changes for ensuring the rights of patients (Loza and El Nawawi 2012)—were to be firmly implemented as imagined by the General Comment, CRPD Articles 12 and 14 would remain unfulfilled.

An assessment using the same tool showed similar results in Tunisia (WHO and Ministry of Health 2008; Rekhis 2015) and Somalia (WHO 2010; Currie 2012). Somalia's prolonged conflict has contributed to the neglect of the mental health system and a high prevalence of mental health disorders, even compared with other low income countries.

The General Comment on Article 12 states that persons with disabilities will always have capacity and dismisses all kinds of substituted decision-making, including involuntary admission and treatment under any circumstances. In the context of Arab culture, the family often participates in decision-making on matters related to health and social welfare, forming a doctor–patient–family relationship as opposed to a doctor–patient relationship (El-Islam 2005). Article 12 says that people with disabilities should be provided with '*the support they may require in exercising their legal capacity*', and the family can be interpreted as being one form of such support. Indeed, various mental health acts across the Arab world involve family members in the application for involuntary hospitalization (Loza and Omar 2017). During the drafting of the CRPD, 20 Arab countries included a reservation to Article (Pearl 2013).

5.7 The Role of Mental Health Legislation in Consolidating the Rights of People with Mental Illness in the Arab World

Mental health legislations provide a legal framework for overcoming stigma and discriminatory practices through the provision of guidelines for integrating mental health services within the community, definition of governmental and professional responsibilities and liabilities, and establishing human rights-based criteria for the protection of patients and prevention of abuse (Okasha 2003). The WHO (2003) mandates that mental health legislations should guarantee the right for privacy, informed consent, confidentiality, freedom from abusive treatment and the right for non-discrimination. The absence of any control or monitoring mechanism allows for different types of malpractices in mental health care. Compared to other WHO regions (the Americas, Europe, South East Asia and the West Pacific region), the African and the EMR countries are still lagging behind when it comes to the existence of a mental health policy, the updating of that policy, whether the policy fully complies with human rights criteria, and whether there is an authority to monitor this compliance. Thus, more vigorous work is needed in these four areas to enhance the professional status of mental health services and to give mental health care more credibility and trust, thus reducing the stigma against mental illness (WHO 2017).

Okasha (2003) and El-Islam (2008) reported that it is quite common to find private practitioners with online degrees from unaccredited institutions delivering mental health care. In Palestine, mental health care is provided by psychologists with bachelor's and master's degrees, and social workers who lack proper clinical exposure and are unable to handle patients with complicated psychiatric conditions (Jabr et al. 2013). This inevitably affects the quality of mental health services and increases the likelihood of professional maltreatment, which, in turn, serves to further exacerbate the stigma against such services. In Lebanon, patients' rights and dignity are often violated through their isolation from their community for long periods of time and through the practice of unpaid labor within the institution, coined as occupational therapy by hospital personnel (Kerbage et al. 2016). In the United Arab Emirates, three mental health laws were developed (mental health in general, health of the elderly and child protection law), entailing the protection of the human rights of the patient and regulating compulsory admission to mental health facilities; however, no unified procedure has yet been identified to ensure consistent implementation of these laws (Haque 2020).

5.8 Mental Health Legalization in the Context of Islamic Law (Shari'ah)

According to Shariʿah, the lunatics (Majinum) have impaired judgment and will and so they cannot be held accountable for their actions. There is tripartite classification of insanity in the Islamic law: (a) absolute or continuous, (b) intermittent, and (c) partial. In the case of intermittent insanity, it must be proven that the mental disorder was active at the time of the criminal act for the defendant to be found not guilty by reason of insanity. Otherwise, if the disorder was in remission and not active, the perpetrator is fully responsible for his acts. A pivotal issue addressed in the Islamic law, in the interface between law and psychiatry, is the concept of involuntary admission of mental health patients. According to the principle of Al-Hajjer, the state can undertake the financial management of a person's fortune, if he does not manage it "properly." By extending the application of this legal procedure, Shariʿah accepts the necessity of involuntary hospitalization. This necessity lies on the patient's "need for therapy" (including patients with substance use disorders) and not on the criterion of dangerousness (Tzeferakos and Douzenis 2017). El-Islam (2008) talked about a 'legislation-free professional-family-patient liaison approach' in some countries such as Qatar and Kuwait, where it is extremely rare for a hospital or a family to be taken to court by patients for illegal detention or violation of human rights.

With regards to patient confidentiality in Shariah, a clinician may not be required to testify against the patient and a doctor forced by law to disclose confidential matters. Shariah also divides mental competence into two: the competence of entitlement and the competence of performance. The age of mental competence, entering a contract, committing oneself to a mental hospital, and making a will are generally different from secular law. The issue of interdiction upon a person and guardianship rules for the mentally ill vary based on the views of different Shariah schools (Haque 2020).

For child custody, secular law includes legal guardianship, whereas in Shariah, there is a difference between custody (caring/residential responsibility) and legal guardianship (full responsibility for child's welfare, including decisions for money, contracts, and career). Legal guardianship always belongs to the father. The custody of a male child is the right of the mother until the child can take care of his/her own self, which has been approximated at 7 years of age. In the case of a female child, the mother's rights of custody extend until the child reaches puberty, with rights being subject to conditions such as remaining faithful and being attentive to her children. Suicide including euthanasia is a major sin and is unlawful in Sharia. One must remember that Sharia contributes to Egypt and UAE laws but is not the only source. If there are specific provisions for a certain issue, the courts will follow that provision, but in the absence of such a provision, Shariah laws may prevail (Haque 2020).

References

Alhassani G, Osman OT (2015) Mental health law profile: The United Arab Emirates. BJPsych Int 12(3):70–72. https://doi.org/10.1192/s2056474000000489

Currie J (2012) Assessment of the Mental Health Ward, Hargeisa Group Hospital in Somalia, using the WHO Quality Rights Tool Kit. Project report, International Diploma in Mental Health Law and Human Rights. http://www.who.int/mental_health/policy/qualityrights/Somalia_qrs_report

Disability: IN (2022). www.disabilityIN.org

El-Islam MF (2005) Some cultural aspects of the Arab patient–doctor relationship. Int Psychiatry 7:18–20

El-Islam MF (2008) Arab culture and mental health care. Transcult Psychiatry 45(4):671–682. https://doi.org/10.1177/1363461508100788

Fawzy ME (2015) Quality of life and human rights conditions in a public psychiatric hospital in Cairo. Int J Human Rights Healthcare 8:199–217. https://doi.org/10.1108/IJHRH-02-2015-0006

Haque A (2020) Mental health laws and reflections on culture: the case of united arab emirates. J Muslim Mental Health 14(1). https://doi.org/10.3998/jmmh.10381607.0014.103

Jabr S, Morse M, El Sarraj W, Awidi B (2013) Mental health in Palestine: country report. Arab J Psychiatry 24(2):174–178. https://doi.org/10.12816/0001376

Japan International Cooperation Agency (2002) Planning and evaluation department 'country profile on disability: Arab Republic of Egypt'. http://digitalcommonsilr.cornell.edu/gladnetcollect/233/

Kassab A, Orfy AE, Al-Helewa AK, Alsawahli H, Barsoum G (2018) Employing people with disability in Egypt. The Public Policy HUB The School of Global Affairs and Public Policy, The American University in Cairo

Kerbage H, El Chammay R, Richa S (2016) Mental health legislation in Lebanon: nonconformity to international standards and clinical dilemmas in psychiatric practice. Int J Law Psychiatry 44:48–53. https://doi.org/10.1016/j.ijlp.2015.08.031

Lord JE, Suozzi D, Taylor AL (2010) Lessons from the experience of UN convention on the rights of persons with disabilities: addressing the democratic deficit in Global Health governance. JL Med Ethics 38:564

Loza N, El Nawawi M (2012) Mental health legislation in Egypt. BJPsych Int 9:64–66

Loza N, Nawawi M (2012) Mental health legislation in Egypt. Int Psychiatry 9:64–66. https://doi.org/10.1192/S1749367600003246

Loza N, Omar MH (2017) The rights of persons with mental disabilities: is the UN convention the answer? An Arab perspective. BJPsych Int 14(3):53–55

Meadows L, Bamieh LA, Lord JE (2014) Egypt. In: African disability rights yearbook. Pretoria University Law Press, Pretoria, pp 169–184

Miller EK (2011) Tailors of law: transitioning disability rights in Egypt. A master thesis, The American University in Cairo

Okasha A (2003) Mental health services in the Arab world. Arab Stud Q 25(4):39–52

Okasha T, Rabie M, Shaker NM, Mohsen N, El-Habiby M, El-Gabry DA, Gaber E, Ali N, Ali M, Sayed M (2022) Mental health services in Egypt during the COVID-19 pandemic. Middle East Curr Psychiatry 29:102. https://doi.org/10.1186/s43045-022-00270-5

Pearl AL (2013) Article 12 of the United Nations convention on the rights of persons with disabilities and the legal capacity of disabled people: the way forward? Leeds J Law Criminol 1:1–30

Rekhis M (2015) Rights of people with mental disorders: realities and perceptions. MD thesis, Université de Tunis el Manar. http://www.who.int/mental_health/policy/quality_rights/qr Tunisia

Tzeferakos GA, Douzenis AI (2017) Islam, mental health and law: a general overview. Ann General Psychiatry 16:1–6. https://doi.org/10.1186/s12991-017-0150-6

United Nation Convention on the Rights of Persons with Disabilities and Optional Protocol. https://www.un.org/disabilities/documents/convention/convoptprot-e.pdf

United Nations General Assembly (2007) Convention on the rights of persons with disabilities. http://www.refworld.org/docid/45f973632.html

World Bank Group (2012) World development indicators. World Bank Publications

World Health Organization (2003) Mental health legislation and human rights. World Health Organization (Mental Health Policy and Service Guidance Package), Geneva

World Health Organization (2010) A situation analysis of mental health in Somalia. http://applications.emro.who.int/dsaf/EMROPUB_2010_EN_736.pdf?ua=1. Accessed 5 May 2016

World Health Organization (2011) World report on disability (2011): Technical appendix A' 295. https://www.who.int/publications/i/item/9789241564182

World Health Statistics (2017) Monitoring health for the SDGs, sustainable development goals. Geneva: World Health Organization; 2017. Licence: CC BY-NC-SA 3.0 IGO

World Health Organization (2020) Mental health atlas 2020. https://www.who.int/publications/i/item/9789240036703

World Health Organization & Ministry of Health 2008 WHO-AIMS report on the mental health system in Tunisia. https://cdn.who.int/media/docs/default-source/mental-health/who-aims-country-reports/tunisia_who_aims_report.pdf?sfvrsn=3ddd1efb_3&download=true

Zaki MM (2009) Egyptian legislation on the compulsory treatment of persons with psychiatric disorders: the old and the new. Int Psychiatry 6:57–58

6 Fiji: Mental Health Care and Law in an Island Nation

Balram Pandit, Michael Evans, and Neeraj Gill

Contents

6.1 Introduction

Fiji is the most populated of the South Pacific Island countries with 884,887 persons in the 2017 census (Fiji Bureau of Statistics 2018). The Exclusive Economic Zone includes an archipelago of approximately 322 islands spanning 1.26 million square kilometres. Most of the Fijian population is concentrated on two islands, Viti Levu and Vanua Levu. The capital city of Fiji is Suva on the island of Viti Levu (Foster & Macdonald 2024). Fiji was annexed by the British in 1874 and remained a British colony until it gained independence as a nation within the Commonwealth of Nations in 1970 (Newbury 2011). The subsequent political development of Fiji was a tumultuous journey culminating in multiple departures from, and reinstatements to the Commonwealth. Most recently, Fiji was reinstated to the Commonwealth in 2014 following its national election and com-

B. Pandit (✉)
Ministry of Health and Medical Services, Suva, Fiji
e-mail: balram.pandit@health.gov.fj

M. Evans
Mental Health and Specialist Services, Gold Coast Health, Gold Coast, Australia

School of Medicine and Dentistry, Griffith University, Gold Coast, Australia
e-mail: michael.evans4@health.qld.gov.au

N. Gill
Mental Health and Specialist Services, Gold Coast Health, Gold Coast, Australia

School of Medicine and Dentistry, Griffith University, Gold Coast, Australia

Mental Health Policy Unit, Health Research Institute, University of Canberra, Canberra, Australia
e-mail: neeraj.gill@griffith.edu.au

N. Gill, N. Sartorius (eds.), *Mental Health and Human Rights*, Sustainable Development Goals Series, https://doi.org/10.1007/978-3-031-52179-9_6

mitment to a democratically elected government (Australian Government Department of Foreign Affairs and Trade 2022).

6.2 Fijian Healthcare System

The Fijian healthcare system operates three geographical divisions including the combined Central and Eastern Divisions, Western Division and Northern Division under the Ministry of Health (Singh et al. 2013). There are three divisional hospitals: Lautoka Hospital, Labasa Hospital and Colonial War Memorial Hospital. There are two specialist hospitals including the dedicated psychiatric facility St. Giles Hospital and the Tamavua/Twomey Hospital. The Tamavua/Twomey hospital has three units including the Leprosy and Dermatology hospital, the Tuberculosis Unit and the National Rehabilitation Medicine Hospital. Furthermore, there are sub-divisional hospitals, health centres and nursing stations. There are village clinics serving more rural and remote areas (Singh et al. 2013).

Multiple rounds of decentralisation have been undertaken by the Fijian ministry of health (Mohammed et al. 2016). The most recent round starting in 2009 with an attempt at geographical decentralisation with the aim to provide improved health services in the Suva sub-division then eventually the other divisions (Mohammed et al. 2016). The aim of decentralisation is to create a more responsive, efficient and robust community-based model of treatment with the ability to tailor to the needs of the local area (Sreeramareddy and Sathyanarayana 2019). Unfortunately, the transfer of ambulatory care from hospitals to health centres has led to several issues including pharmaceutical shortages, inequitable distribution of financial resources and high workforce turnover (Mohammed et al. 2016). A critique of Fiji's decentralisation process is the lack of autonomy bestowed upon the peripheral health facilities in terms of finance and local initiatives—this is an ongoing area of development.

The Fijian healthcare system is guided by the National Strategic Planning Process (Singh et al. 2013). Furthermore, there is an evolving National Mental Health Strategic Plan guiding the trajectory of mental health services. Currently, mental health care remains a largely centralised process via the 100 bed facility St. Giles Hospital in the national capital region. However, several community services have recently been established. There are now three divisional Stress Management Wards at Colonial War Memorial (Suva, Central), Latouka (Western) and Labasa (Northern) hospitals and dedicated divisional community mental health outreach teams. Furthermore, there has been significant work to upskill workers in sub-divisional, health centres and nursing stations to address the mental health needs of local communities (Singh et al. 2013). St. Giles Hospital is a tertiary centre taking referrals from each of these services and now provides adult, child and youth and forensic psychiatric care. There are two consumer-driven support services the Psychiatric Survivors Association and Youth Champs 4 Mental Health (Ministry of Health and Medical Services 2018).

6.3 Mental Health Legislative Framework

During its period of colonial rule, mental health care in Fiji was governed by the *Mental Treatment Act, 1940*. This Act was informed by the *British Lunacy Act, 1890* which governed mental health treatment in Britain until it was repealed by the *Mental Health Act (1959)*. Like the *Lunacy Act, 1890*, the *Mental Treatment Act, 1940* reflected the institutional nature of psychiatric treatment during this time in Fiji (Singh et al. 2013). The *Mental Treatment Act, 1940* essentially focused solely on in-patient treatment within St. Giles Hospital (Saxton et al. 2018).

In 2010, the acting government of Fiji signed the United Nations Convention on the Rights of Persons with Disabilities (CRPD) which was then formally ratified in 2017 (United Nations Human Rights Treaty Bodies (n.d.). The CRPD was the consequence of decades of work by the United Nations to set out the rights and principles for people living with a disability. For example, articles 12, 14, 15, 18, 25 and 26 of the UNCRPD outline the right to: equal legal capacity, liberty and security, freedom from torture, freedom of movement, enjoyment of the highest standard of health and rehabilitation towards maximum independence (United Nations 2006). Upon signing the CRPD, Fiji was obliged to contemporise their mental health legislation to comply with the principles of the convention (Saxton et al. 2018). In 2010, the *Mental Health Decree, 2010*, later referred to as the *Mental Health Act, 2010*, was announced by the government of Fiji to replace the *Mental Treatment Act, 1940* (O. Chang 2016).

The *Mental Health Act, 2010* is more compliant with the CRPD in several domains. Firstly, Part 2 (section 13) requires the National Mental Health Advisor to assist with the following functions: policy development, coordination and promotion of decentralisation of mental health services, development of the mental health workforce, formulation of treatment guidelines and creation of specialist mental health services. This role fosters accountability and ensures that efforts to further improve the quality and access to culturally appropriate mental health treatment are prioritised.

Part 5 outlines the treatment principles and reinforces several priorities: highest quality of care in the least restrictive environment, timely access to care, care to assist people to live, work and participate in the community, to address cultural and religious needs and the provision of culturally appropriate care including consideration of age, gender, religion, culture and language. Furthermore, Part 5 dictates that all efforts must be made to involve patients in the assessment and treatment of their condition including the risks, benefits and alternatives of interventions in an understandable and supported manner. Embodying these principles in the Act aligns care with the aforementioned CRPD articles 12, 14, 15, 18, 25 and 26. Importantly, this part of the Act transitions the focus from involuntary in-patient care to the provision of care in the least restrictive setting including community treatment with direct consumer stakeholder involvement.

Part 9 establishes the Mental Health Review Board and the formal processes to review mental health treatment facilities and in-patient and community treatment orders. The Act enforces a periodic review system of the treatment and care of consumers under these orders and requires annual written reporting of the standard of care provided in mental health facilities empowered by the Act. It formalises the process by which consumers may request an additional review of their treatment order and requires healthcare providers to ensure requests for review are submitted to the board. This part of the Act helps to ensure accountability and respect for consumer liberty in line with the CRPD articles. Unfortunately, the Act does not formalise the requirement for transparent and public reporting of the use of treatment orders. Furthermore, the mandatory annual reporting on facilities is addressed to the Permanent Secretary without specifying the need for this reporting to be available publicly.

6.4 Burden of Disease and Treatment Gap

Several psychosocial risk factors are particularly prominent for the Fijian population. In Fiji, 24.1% of the population lived below the national poverty line in 2019 (The World Bank, 2022). Additionally, in 2017, 44.1% of the population were living in rural locations (Fiji Bureau of Statistics 2018). Rurality is a well-established risk factor for increased completion of suicide in Fiji (Morris and Maniam 2000).

The path to modernity and materialism in Fiji has caused conflict and compartmentalisation of traditional philosophy and culture that, by contrast, emphasise a simple and austere lifestyle. The emphasis on individualism has resulted in a reduction of traditional support systems, which has increased social isolation (Pandit et al. 2018). Also, rapid urbanisation and large-scale migration from rural areas leaves many without community supports (Jacob 2009).

Substance misuse is a significant population issue identified by the Fijian government including cannabis, alcohol and the psychoactive depressant plant kava (Singh et al. 2013). Furthermore, there are significant waitlists to seek mental health support and treatment (WHO Regional Office for the Western Pacific 2011).

Fiji does not formally report epidemiological data relating to the prevalence of mental disorders. However, St. Giles Hospital, is reported to have treated a total of 1902 in-patients and outpatients during 2010 (Singh et al. 2013). Based on the 2004 World Mental Health Survey prevalence of severe mental disorders, it is estimated that at least 18,000 adults in Fiji would have a severe mental disorder. This means that, based on the 2010 treatment rate, only approximately 10% of people with a severe mental health disorder received treatment through St. Giles Hospital (Singh et al. 2013). This clearly indicates that there is likely a large burden of mental health disorders in Fiji with a significant treatment gap. Most patients treated through St. Giles Hospital in 2010 had a diagnosis of schizophrenia or a mood disorder (Singh et al. 2013).

In 2008, WHO launched the mental health gap action programme (mhGAP) in response to the wide gap between the resources available and the resources urgently needed to address the large burden of mental, neurological and substance use disorders globally (World Health Organisation 2008). The aim of the mhGAP is to upscale mental health services especially in low-income countries. The mhGAP includes efforts to provide evidence-based resources and training to non-specialist medical practitioners to build capacity to achieve better mental health services in local communities (Hoadley et al. 2020). A recent achievement in capacity building is the establishment of Fiji National University's postgraduate diploma in mental health (O. A. Chang et al. 2015). Furthermore, in 2022 a comprehensive, 3 year Masters in Psychiatry (MMED-PSY) programme was established which is scheduled to start from 2024 at Fiji National University (FNU). Moreover, a recently added postgraduate diploma in mental health nursing programme at FNU has started strengthening psychiatric nursing capacity.

6.5 Moving Forward

Decentralisation of services from stand-alone mental hospitals to community-based recovery-oriented accessible services is paramount for protection and promotion of human rights of people with mental health issues as highlighted in the Comprehensive WHO Mental Health Action Plan 2013–2030 (World Health Organization 2021). With its limited and volatile resources, Fiji has been attempting to decentralise its mental health services. However, an effective decentralisation has not yet been realised. With increasing mental health awareness, the demand for care has increased, though, the capacity of the main mental health facility (St. Giles Hospital) has reduced from 136 beds in 1884 to the current 100 beds.

Fiji ranks among the top ten countries as a percentage of total population for migration (United Nations ESCAP 2020). This has led to brain drain from Fiji and has affected the health sector too. Currently, St. Giles is operating only with nearly 50% of its nursing staff and medical officers.

The Community Recovery Outreach Programme (CROP) designed to be operating in the community is temporarily back to St. Giles premises due to infrastructure issues at the current location and a newer location is being actively searched. The frequency of outreach clinics in Suva-Nasauri corridor (at Samabula, Valelevu and Nasauri health centres) has reduced from weekly to monthly. Nonetheless, St. Giles-based Community Mental Health Team (CMHT) has started conducting clinics in Korovou (Tailevu province), St. Vincent home, Hope centre and does home visits, case reviews in the community, and engages in workplace and faith-based mental health awareness activities. A few centres are supported by doctors currently practising as General Practitioners who have completed a postgraduate diploma in mental health. Additionally, CMHT has been successfully supporting an eight-bed virtual hospital (a relatively newer facility where eight patients are provided with home-based services as CMHT visits them on a daily basis and provides services expected at hospital). CMHT is also involved in liaising with the ministry of Women, Children and Poverty Alleviation to find accommodation for homeless patients. Social Security Allowances and a bus pass for travel is also arranged by CMHT for poor patients, after home assessment. The mhGAP trained medical officers and nursing staff posted in different divisions are also encouraged and empowered to actively assist in the care of persons with mental health problems, so that required health services can be delivered early and closest to their place of residence.

St. Giles Forensic unit is not only providing in-patient and out-patient services at hospital but also conducts clinics in Suva, Korovou and Lautoka correction centres and remand homes.

There is motivation and movement towards adopting a new model of care. Opportunities for required additional training and upskilling of healthcare professionals have recently strengthened with local availability of newer university postgraduate programmes and more frequent, need-based symposiums and workshops are being organised in collaboration with overseas partner individuals and organisations.

After a long wait, vacant senior positions (Medical Superintendent St. Giles Hospital and National Mental Health advisor) have been filled and serious efforts are being made to provide quality services. As the team aspires to develop St. Giles Hospital into a Regional Institute of Mental Health Care and Research (RIMCaRe), renovation of current infrastructure is happening and newer structures with specific facilities for special populations are being planned. Safer and patient friendly environments with padded rooms, special beds and renovated wards with better aesthetics and ambience are being created. Work is progressing on delivery of effective Tele-Health Services, Amendment of Mental Health Act-2010 and guidelines for media and mental health and Tele-mental health. Efforts are also being made to revive the National Mental Health Advisory Council, Mental Health Review Board and Board of visitors which were adversely affected during the COVID-19 pandemic.

Current mental health services have a good mixture of staff and availability of interpreters to understand and meet the cultural needs of clients. Culturally appropriate tools in native languages for assessment of mental health issues are being developed. Family members are not only informed but also involved as they form an integral part of the intervention process and are an important ally in long-term patient care. Also, Fijian "Talanoa" sessions (where hierarchy breaks and everyone sits on the same traditional mat) and religious places are locally emerging platforms for mental health awareness activities (Pasefika Proud n.d.).

There is dearth of rehabilitation services in Fiji. Currently, it is mainly St. Giles-based Occupational Therapy centre which is supporting this service in collaboration with government and non-government organisations. Fiji has been mulling over to build a "halfway home" and rehabilitation unit for a long time. A new idea in the form of "Mind Farm"—a community-based rehabilitation facility linked to tertiary and primary mental health care services is being planned. Mind Farm is proposed to home rehabilitation services for patients with substance abuse problems, rehab services for patients with chronic illness, halfway home, occupational therapy workshop, block for staff and volunteers and market network for its produce/products. This facility placed in a rural setting aims at multidisciplinary assessment of individual needs and strength of its clients will be supported not only by government but also by the community members, accredited skilled volunteers and NGOs. Supervision by health staff will be minimum and clients/residents will have increased liberty of movement and autonomy.

The Fijian health system respects privacy, confidentiality and rights of clients. Clients and primary care givers are parts of management strategy formulation. Clients provide written informed consent for treatment, exercise their right of access to records, right to make advance directives and right to appeal against detention.

Largely, Fijian employers are anti-discriminatory and claim to offer equal opportunity based on competency of individuals with or without mental health issues. Insurance sectors are also aware of rights of individuals with mental health issues; however, their policies can be disadvantageous to people with established mental health condition.

6.6 Conclusion

With the limited resources, Fiji is striving to meet its commitment to the CRPD. The mental health act was revised in 2010 to align with the

CRPD and further amendments are being planned to promote rights of people with mental health problems. However, the amendments in the mental health act need to be accompanied by budget and resources for adequate implementation. The Ministry of Health and Medical Services 2020–2025 Strategic Plan recognises mental health as a priority and the very first strategic priority aims to improve the physical and mental wellbeing of all citizens, with particular emphasis on women, children and young people (Ministry of Health and Medical Services 2020). Moving forward, it relies mainly on channelising existing resources in communities and effective collaboration with local and overseas partners, with a resolve to create a better and just society for persons with mental health problems.

References

Australian Government Department of Foreign Affairs and Trade (2022) Fiji country brief. https://www.dfat.gov.au/geo/fiji/fiji-country-brief. Accessed 24 Mar 2023

Chang O (2016) Fiji's Mental Health Decree 2010. BJPsych Int 13(2):41. https://doi.org/10.1192/S2056474000001112

Chang OA, Allen MM, Pandit B (2015) Capacity building for Pacific Island countries: the challenges and benefits of developing a postgraduate clinical training programme. Australas Psychiatry 23(6 Suppl):32–34. https://doi.org/10.1177/1039856215608294

Fiji Bureau of Statistics (2018) 2017 Population and housing Census. https://www.statsfiji.gov.fj/statistics/2007-census-of-population-and-housing.html

Foster, S & Macdonald, BK (2024) Fiji. Encyclopedia Britannica. https://www.britannica.com/place/Fiji-republic-Pacific-Ocean

Hoadley B, Gaikwad K, Allen M, Kowalenko N, Chang O (2020) Addressing the specialist workforce CAMH skill-gap: providing and evaluating iCAMH training in Fiji and Papua New Guinea. Australas Psychiatry 28(1):27–30

Jacob KS (2009) Public health in low- and middle-income countries and the clash of cultures. J Epidemiol Community Health 63(7):509. https://doi.org/10.1136/jech.2009.086934

Mental Health (2018) Ministry of Health and Medical Services. https://www.health.gov.fj/mental-health/

Ministry of Health and Medical Services (2020) Strategic Plan 2020–2025. https://www.health.gov.fj/wpcontent/uploads/2020/05/Strategic-Plan-2020-2025-1.pdf

Mohammed J, North N, Ashton T (2016) Decentralisation of Health Services in Fiji: a decision space analysis. Int J Health Policy Manag 5(3):173. https://doi.org/10.15171/IJHPM.2015.199

Morris P, Maniam T (2000) Suicide in Fiji: a review of the literature. Asia Pac J Public Health 12(1):46–49. https://doi.org/10.1177/101053950001200110

Newbury C (2011) History, hermeneutics and Fijian ethnic 'paramountcy': reflections on the deed of cession of 1874. J Pac Hist 46(1):27–57

Pandit B, Fatima FB, Dadd L, Balaratnasingam S, Gill NS (2018) Suicide prevention in Fiji: social and clinical issues. Fiji J Public Health 7(1):22–25

Pasefika Proud (n.d.) National Fijian Wellbeing Plan 2022–2025. https://www.pasefikaproud.co.nz/assets/Uploads/Lalawa-Fijian-WellBeing-Plan-2022-WEB.pdf

Saxton K, Allan JA, Gill NS (2018) Mental health as a human right: challenges and opportunities in Fiji. Fiji J Public Health 7(1):38–40

Singh S, Chang O, Funk M, Shields L, Andrews A, Hughes F, Sugiura K, Drew N (2013) WHO proMIND: profiles on mental health in development: Fiji. World Health Organization, Geneva

Sreeramareddy CT, Sathyanarayana T (2019) Decentralised versus centralised governance of health services. Cochrane Database Syst Rev 2019(9):CD010830. https://doi.org/10.1002/14651858.CD010830.PUB2

The World Bank (2022). World Bank Statement: Update on Fiji 2019–2020 Household Income and Expenditure Survey. https://thedocs.worldbank.org/en/doc/592481a9b487107114a733bce2d6bc44-0070012022/original/220425-WB-Statement-FijiPovertyRevision-final.pdf

United Nations (2006) Convention on the rights of persons with disabilities and optional protocol. https://www.un.org/disabilities/documents/convention/convoptprot-e.pdf

United Nations, Economic and Social Commission for Asia and the Pacific (ESCAP) (2020) Asia-Pacific Migration Report. https://www.unescap.org/sites/default/files/APMR2020_FullReport.pdf

United Nations Human Rights Treaty Bodies (n.d.) Ratification Status for Fiji. https://tbinternet.ohchr.org/_layouts/15/TreatyBodyExternal/Treaty.aspx?CountryID=60&Lang=en. Accessed 25 Mar 2023

WHO Regional Office for the Western Pacific (2011) The Fiji Islands health system review. WHO Regional Office for the Western Pacific. http://iris.wpro.who.int/handle/10665.1/5534

World Health Organisation (2008) Mental Health and Substance Abuse: Mental Health Gap Action Programme. https://www.emro.who.int/mnh/mental-health-gap-action-programme/index

World Health Organization (2021) Comprehensive mental health action plan 2013–2030. World Health Organization. https://apps.who.int/iris/handle/10665/345301

France: Psychiatric Care, Human Rights, and the CRPD

7

Cecile Hanon and Benoit Eyraud

Contents

7.1 Introduction

In August 2021, the Committee on the Rights of Person with Disabilities examined the reports submitted by French state administration and civil society. The committee's rapporteur, Jonas Ruskus, was outspoken in his criticism of the inadequacies of French public policies in implementing the Convention on the Rights of Persons with Disabilities (CRPD): "The measures taken by France do not reflect the human rights-based model of disability that is defended by the CRPD." (United Nations 2021)

The rapporteur mentions in particular the difficulties posed by the roadmap on psychiatry and mental health referring to a medical model of disability, and the non-harmonization of the 2005 law with the Convention, and then explicitly cites the failure to comply with Article 12 of the Convention (United Nations 2021). Fifteen years after its adoption by the United Nations General Assembly, 10 years after its ratification by France, the appropriation of the CRPD is judged severely by this

Supplementary Information The online version contains supplementary material available at https://doi.org/10.1007/978-3-031-52179-9_7.

C. Hanon (✉)
Regional Resource Center of old age Psychiatry, APHP, University of Paris, Paris, France
e-mail: Cecile.hanon@aphp.fr

B. Eyraud
University of Lyon, Max Weber Center, CNRS, Lyon, France

N. Gill, N. Sartorius (eds.), *Mental Health and Human Rights*, Sustainable Development Goals Series, https://doi.org/10.1007/978-3-031-52179-9_7

UN monitoring body. This severity seems to be based not so much on the question of the application of an international standard but on that of the "human rights-based model of disability" (Arnardóttir and Quinn 2009; Sabatello and Schulz 2014). This criticism questions not only the modalities of dissemination of an international legal convention, but also the non-reception of a model of disability that is presented as being based on the human rights norm. These issues relating to the dissemination of new norms in the field of disability have been the subject of analyses concerning the production and domestication of supra-national norms or of rights-based approaches (Bregain 2018; Vanhala 2015).

Even though France recognizes itself as a model country in terms of human rights, it is paradoxical to see that the weak reception of the convention is not analyzed (Zuber 2014). It is notable that there are only a few publications on the reception of the Convention in the field of psychiatry and mental health even if the international controversy has been discussed (Eyraud et al. 2018).

In this chapter, we look back at some of the elements that illustrate the poor reception of the CRPD in the field of psychiatry and mental health in France, and more generally at the place taken by human rights in the history of psychiatry in France.

7.2 The Reference to Human Rights in Mental Health Laws in France: Some Historical Milestones

In this first part, we will review the links between psychiatry and attention to human rights in the French context (Pascal and Hanon 2014).

7.2.1 The Reference to Human Rights Before the CRPD

It is well known that the "birth of mental medicine" in France took place in the context of the French Revolution, in the aftermath of the Declaration of the Rights of Man and the Citizen (Castel 1976). The abolition of the "lettres de cachet" was the first gesture leading to the release of detainees without explicit justification; then the removal of chains and the use of straitjackets made of cotton, at the Salpètrière in 1793, constituted the symbolic founding act of psychiatry.

> "The insane, far from being culprits who should be punished, are patients whose painful state deserves all the respect due to suffering humanity and whose lost reason should be restored by the simplest means" (Pinel 1809).

The affirmation of the pathological nature of insanity had two consequences: it entered the domain of medicine, and in fact, it became susceptible to treatment. Pinel then proposed to implement what he called "moral treatment," i.e., treatment that would concern consciousness, in the sense of the mind, of human experience. This term "moral" is not to be understood here as morality nor good manners. Later, it will be called "psychological."

7.2.1.1 The Law of 1838

The reference to human rights was still present when the law of 1838 was discussed. Detention was both a medical and an administrative measure (i.e., it was the director of a hospital or the prefect who, based on a medical decision, took the admission measure, and not a judicial body). In his comments on the bill, the doctor JP Falret refers to "the rights of humanity":

> "It will no doubt be objected that the lights of the special doctor can be obscured by personal interest, and that the law must protect the unfortunate insane against the greed of families and that of the directors of establishments devoted to this type of patient. This objection may unfortunately sometimes be well founded, and in every respect I earnestly hope that it will be possible to prevent such criminal abuses, and that they will be rigorously punished whenever they are discovered. But by what means can the existence of these offences against individual freedom and the rights of humanity be revealed? That is the difficult problem to solve." (Garabe 2004)

This law will allow the recognition of a new specialty, alienism, which will include a double competence on insanity (being a medically pathological condition and being treatable) but also on the way to reconcile the protection of the insane and that of society.

After the First World War, in 1921, the first open psychiatric department opened at the Sainte Anne Hospital in Paris, where patients were admitted at their request and not under the regime of the 1838 law, for the treatment of neuroses by the so-called psychodynamic therapies. Between 1870 and 1939, more than 15 projects to reform the law of 1838 will be put forward, without ever leading to a modification of the text.

7.2.1.2 The Law No. 90-527 of 27 June 1990 on the Rights and Protection of Persons Hospitalized for Mental Disorders

The reference to human rights was again mobilized at the time of the reform of 27 June 1990. This law introduced semantic changes: the term "internment" was replaced by "full-time hospitalization." It should be noted that in France, at the end of the 1960s, a model for the organization of psychiatric care was put in place, the "sectorisation" model.

Resulting from the 1960 circular, this model emphasized the need for continuity of care, both geographically and in terms of time. Thus, for a given population (70,000 inhabitants) and a given geographical area, a set of care facilities are allocated (hospital beds, outpatient clinic, day hospital, emergency room, etc.), within which the same care team works. For the first time, the importance of having care facilities outside the hospital emerged, and ambulatory structures and teams founded the basis of the patient pathway of care. Community care was born and raised to the essential and this model is still in place today.

This law is thus inscribed by the Minister of Health in the context of the celebration of the bicentenary of the French Revolution and the proclamation of the rights of man and of the citizen. It constitutes an opportunity for society to question itself on the rights of patients and particularly that of the mentally ill. The Minister also specifies that this law aims to bring French legislation into line with the recommendations of the Council of Europe of February 22, 1983, relating to the legal protection of persons suffering from mental disorders and placed as involuntary patients.

In fact, a certain number of decisions of the European Court of Human Rights, including the famous Winterwerp judgment in 1979, concerning the Netherlands, had led the Council to take up this issue and invite the countries to better adapt their legislation to the European Charter of Human Rights (Eyraud and Velpry 2015).

The medical justification of forced care stated is explicitly predominant. What counts is the need for care and not the dangerousness of an individual. However, the legal choice between the medical need for care and the social need to protect public order has not been clarified. Progressively, it appears that the 1990 reform is not sufficient to the ECHR, which condemns France on several occasions, in particular in the Baudoin judgment of November 18, 2010 (Baudouin v. France, no. 35935/03).

7.2.1.3 The Law of 2002 on Patients' Rights

With this law, the notion of consent is placed at the heart of care and is once again strongly affirmed: no care is possible without the free and informed consent of the person. No care, except… mental care. Indeed, mental pathology is an exception to this rule and remains governed by the 1990 law when consent cannot be obtained or is altered. Of course, mental care remains possible with consent and freewill! This law also clarifies the notion of trusted person and facilitates access to the medical file.

7.2.2 Law Reforms in the Field of Psychiatry in France Since the International Adoption of the CRPD

Since 1990, all official reports have pointed out the need to link the decision to hospitalize without consent to a psychiatric assessment systematically carried out prior to the decision, and two types of positions have clashed: those who see hospitalization without consent as a purely sanitary measure, and those who see it above all as a security measure that deprives people of their liberty, who will advocate judicial competence—an option supported by users' associations (Rhenter 2010).

In November 2010, following a "priority question of constitutionality" raised by a disabled people's organization, the "Groupe Information Asile" (GIA), the French Constitutional Council declared that the provisions of the Public Health Code relating to hospitalization without consent were unconstitutional in terms of fundamental human rights.

Moreover, the infringements of freedom of movement and respect for private life, protected by Articles 2 and 4 of the Declaration of the Rights of Man and of the Citizen of 1789 had to be adapted to the objectives of protecting health and preventing infringements of public order. Indeed, over the last 20 years, France has witnessed an unprecedented development of organizations of psychiatric care users, with various objectives (self-support, representation, contestation, affirmation of differences) and several degrees of institutionalization (Troisoeufs and Eyraud 2015).

The GIA specialized in the systematic use of legal proceedings and had developed a litigation strategy to change the law, and thus the French Constitutional Council took into consideration a societal sensitivity to fundamental human rights: the influence of supra-national human rights law, notably via the European Court; the mobilization of civil society and the democratization of access to fundamental rights (Eyraud et al. 2023).

7.2.2.1 The Law of 2011 on the Rights and Protection of Persons Under Psychiatric Care and the Conditions of Their Care (Amended on 27 September 2013)

Following the declaration of unconstitutionality for psychiatric care without consent, the GIA defended their complete judicialization. We cite here the Winterwerp judgment of 1979, in which the Court set out the principles that authorize the internment of a person on grounds of mental disorder, including the need for regular review of the appropriateness of such internment, and placed the obligation to comply with them on national laws. This ruling will lead to reforms in various European countries.

In reaction to the decision of the Constitutional Council in November 2010, the French legislator reformed the 1990 Act. Several provisions relating to non-consensual care were passed without any real consultation, in particular the introduction of a judicial judge to control non-consensual care measures. The introduction of a judicial tribunal within the care without consent procedure was done in a hurry, in the middle of the summer of 2011, while most of the care workers were on holiday, and without any reference to the CRPD.

This law introduced two major changes:

1. The introduction of a systematic control, a posteriori, by the judge of freedoms and detention for any hospitalization without consent extended beyond 12 days. The introduction of the judge concerns the development of the law as a "militant weapon" (Israël 2009). Thus, the legislator literally "enters" hospitals for the first time, and the liberty and detention judge holds a hearing within the hospital in rooms specifically created for this purpose. Lawyers have access to closed wards or even intensive care rooms to meet their "clients." While the primary objective of this law was to pave the way for better representation of patients' rights, it has received a mixed reception. A significant proportion of patients were distressed about the need to be heard by a judge when they have not committed any offense (Rossini and Verdoux 2015).

Nowadays, there seems to have been little improvement in the way patients are informed about and have access to their rights and to the judge.

The reception of this new law by carers was also reserved. While some are sensitive to a certain form of sharing of responsibility for the use of restraint with judges; many do not consider themselves to be working in a place of detention, like a prison, and they do not consider patients to be prisoners. The majority of psychiatrists agreed that a reform was necessary, that a form of control was positive and could keep arbitrariness at bay, diffuse responsibilities and enrich decision-making, but not like this. Added to this is an enormous administrative burden, generated by the multiplication of medical certificates in chronically understaffed departments, which encroaches on the time spent by the doctor with their patients.

2. The change in semantics and the replacement of the notion of "hospitalization" by that of "psychiatric care" without consent, which can then be implemented not only inside the hospital but also outside, i.e., on an outpatient basis. This new possibility of forced care in the community provoked strong controversy. How can one imagine that a person can be forced to take medication at home, to go and see their doctor at the medical-psychological center, to go to a day hospital or even to undergo psychotherapy?

   And yet, this type of care was originally the wish of family associations, suffering with their loved ones and having difficulty getting them into care.

Today, more than 10 years after the reform, things have improved and stakeholders have integrated the value and necessity of judicialization of care without consent. Societal sensitivity to human rights has been acquired; but still without any reference to the CRPD.

7.2.2.2 The Law of 2022 on Seclusion and Restraint

This new reform of forced care reinforces the rights of patients by instituting judicial control in cases of seclusion or physical restraint. These measures are decided as a last resort, based on a reasoned decision by a psychiatrist, to prevent immediate or imminent harm to the patient or others, in a manner that is appropriate, necessary, and proportionate to the risk. Strict monitoring and traceability are required, with medical certificates drawn up every 12 h for seclusion and every 6 h for restraint. This type of measure is referred to the judge after 48 or 72 h to check its legality. A family third party must be informed of the implementation and, if necessary, the continuation of the measure.

These new, complex, and even more administratively burdensome provisions have a particularly dissuasive dimension. The aim is to encourage a sharp reduction in the number and duration of seclusion and restraint measures and to seek less restrictive alternatives for patients.

7.3 The Reception of the CRPD in France Since 2006

The low influence of the CRPD in mental health laws in France is part of a general slow reception of this Convention in different areas of disability. Why is this? Probably because the CRPD has been of more interest and concern to disabled people's organizations, professionals such as lawyers, social workers, trustees but not to psychiatrists and other mental health carers.

7.3.1 The Reception in Other Fields of Disabilities

Adopted by the general assembly of the United Nations in 2006, the CRPD was ratified by France in 2010. It can be said that it has not been widely disseminated and that it has had limited publicity in French society culturally and professionally. For example, the legislator remained unaware of its role and potential impact, even though important reforms were being implemented in France, in various fields of interest and well beyond non-consensual care, such as guardianship law (Law of 2007) or the adaptation of society to aging (Health Autonomy Law of 2015). As early as 2005, legislative reforms regarding the care of people with disabilities were occuring but this appears to have had limited impact on the field of mental health care.

7.3.1.1 The Law of 2005 for Equal Rights and Opportunities, Participation, and Citizenship of People with Disabilities

Like the CRPD, this law sets out the principle according to which "any disabled person is entitled to the solidarity of the whole of the national community, which guarantees, by virtue of this obligation, access to the fundamental rights recognized for all citizens as well as the full exercise of their citizenship." In order to achieve this, disability policy puts in place two complementary mechanisms:

- the necessary compensation for disability through a financial allowance
- the obligation of accessibility in order to enable mobility in all situation of the collective life (establishments open to the public, professional premises, housing, transport and public spaces, means of communication, exercise of citizenship and access to law)

This law also leads to a broader approach to disability. In 2005, this approach was not very widespread nor developed in medical culture, especially in psychiatry. If this law was a success for the development of many social services, it did not lead to an articulation between the different legislations.

7.3.1.2 Guardianship Law and Legal Capacity

The 2007 law on the legal protection of adults did not take into account the existence of the CRPD. However, since the publication of General Comment No. 1 in 2014, various actors have become interested in the controversy generated by the promotion of "universal legal capacity."

Divergent voices have been raised, showing the paradox of this interpretation. The universality of legal capacity brings people with disabilities into the common law in a certain way, but how can we reconcile the recognition of their vulnerability and their sometimes different needs for help and support?

In 2016, the "Défenseur des droits" (defendeur of the rights), which is an independent administrative authority, recommended an evolution of the French system of "substitute" decision-making towards a system of "assisted" decision-making. After Catalina Devandas' visit in 2017, the 2019 Law was enacted leading to a number of key changes such as no longer restricting the right to vote for people with disabilities and facilitating access to marriage for people under guardianship (Raoul-Cormeil 2020).

7.3.2 Some Initiatives Inspired by the Interpretation of the CRPD

Despite the limited legislative consideration of the convention in mental health laws, various experiments can be mentioned: the use of the WHO QualityRights Tool Kit; the development of psychiatric advance directives; and an experimental scientific and citizen-based approach of the convention, the Capdroits initiative.

7.3.2.1 The WHO QualityRights Tool Kit

The QualityRights tool kit is a program for assessing quality and respect for rights in mental health facilities. It enables the development of a targeted initiative adapted to the desired scale: a department, a facility, a hospital group, etc. It offers tools for on-site observation and diagnosis and for developing a targeted training plan for users, carers/families, and/or professionals.

In France, it is supported and developed by the WHO Collaborating Centre of Lille-Métropole—www.epsm-lille-metropole.fr—which conducts multi-professional observation visits throughout France in facilities that are willing to take it. Training modules are organized for users of care services and their carers, and professionals, in order to train observation teams.

The QualityRights tool kit highlights care practices that may not be respectful of human rights and of the CRPD and proposes the implementation of measures to correct them.

The overall aim of the QR tool kit is to promote the best care and avoid coercive measures. Nevertheless, it pragmatically recognizes the reality of their existence and remains both realistic and consistent with the terms of the CRPD. Legal remedies for restrictions of liberty exist and are readily available since the 2011 law, in that they have become automatic and mandatory.

7.3.2.2 Psychiatric Advance Directives

Psychiatric advance directives are only just beginning to emerge in care practices; they are still only distributed to a limited extent in France and have no legal value. They allow for the anticipation of a state of crisis, in a calm manner and in conjunction with one's care team, at a time of stability in a person's life. This is the paradigm of shared medical decision-making, and the hope of a reduction in restraint measures, insofar as this form of anticipation authorizes acceptance and fluidity of care, on the part of both patients and carers. Their implementation in various European countries has largely shown their effectiveness.

To date in France, they are the result of local initiatives and practices and are being implemented gradually throughout the country. For example, in 2021, a team of doctors and users in the Ile de France region, in collaboration with the Psycom association, drafted the "Kit mon GPS" (Prevention and Care Guide), accessible at www.psycom.org

Let's hope that they can be developed and ensure a better representation of individual wishes together with legitimate, relevant, and personalized care, in coherence with life histories and autonomy in the respect of human rights.

7.3.2.3 A Scientific and Citizen-Based Approach: The Capdroits Research Initiative

Collectives of scholars (sociologists, lawyers, philosophers), practitioners (psychiatrists, social workers, etc.) and users worked on the CRPD from 2015. They produced and publicized, in public media in 2018, a manifesto entitled "All capable all vulnerable," a work resulting from a long common reflection on Article 12 of the CRPD (Annexe 1).

They continue to do research-action-participation to allow a better anchoring of the CRPD and human rights in contemporary French society. All their work and articles are accessible on https://confcap-capdroits.org.

Thus, even though the French mental health laws have not taken into account the CRPD directly, various initiatives lead to its scattered appropriation in the context of mental health in France (Risse et al. 1999).

7.4 Conclusion

The CRPD is not yet sufficiently well known in France, despite the sustained efforts of disabled people's organizations, whereas it seems to be discussed among a few legal, philosophical, ethical, and sociological academic circles. This lack of knowledge seems to be specifically important among mental health practitioners. It looks even more paradoxical since the history of French psychiatry has sometimes been built in resonance with progress in human rights awareness. We have evoked in this chapter some stages of this history and have tried to shed light on the reluctance of psychiatric professionals to grasp this new convention.

This lack of knowledge can be explained undoubtedly by the fact that the psychiatric community was not associated with the development of this convention, and that psychiatric knowledge seems to have been ignored by the promoters and drafters of the convention (Appelbaum 2016). But more generally, they seem to ignore the complexity and diversity of psychiatric practices.

For example, the European Psychiatric Association (EPA) position paper published in 2018 expresses concern about the misleading and erroneous image of psychiatry described in the Special Rapporteur's report. Thus, the EPA Executive Committee and the Ethics Committee find "unacceptable the negative image of psychiatric care presented by the report when the Special Rapporteur inexplicably blames current psychiatric practices for unmet mental health needs… Psychiatry is caricatured as tainted by human rights abuses, using narrow biomedical methods, and driven by the pharmaceutical industry. The prescription of psychotropic drugs with proven efficacy is presented as a failure of the mental health system, but this evidence-free view ignores the beneficial effects of the drugs, often combined with psychotherapy, for users. By ignoring the evidence of the effectiveness of psychotropic drugs, this report undermines the efforts of all mental health workers and risks causing families or individuals to discontinue effective, even life-saving treatment." (Galderisi et al. 2018)

In France, 80% of psychiatric care is provided in the community, on an outpatient basis (Coldefy and Gandre 2020). Many carers promote a dynamic of empowerment, respect for autonomy, and recovery. Restraint measures are applied within the hospital as a last resort and in harmony with international recommendations around its use.

The radical questioning of these coercive measures is an undeniable challenge for care in the community. It should not contribute to weakening the health system and reducing access to care for the most vulnerable. A better understanding of the human rights of people with mental health conditions and psychosocial disabilities requires more dialogue between international human rights lawyers, disability organizations, and the mental health care community.

References

Appelbaum PS (2016) Protecting the rights of persons with disabilities: an international convention and its problems. Psychiatr Serv 67(4):366–368

Arnardóttir OM, Quinn G (eds) (2009) The UN convention on the rights of persons with disabilities: European and Scandinavian perspectives. Brill, Netherlands

Bregain G (2018) Pour une histoire du handicap au XXe siècle: approches transnationales (Europe et Amériques). Presses universitaires de Rennes, France

Castel R (1976) L'ordre psychiatrique: l'âge d'or de l'aliénisme. Editions de minuit, Paris

Coldefy M, Gandre C (eds) (2020) Atlas de la santé mentale en France. IRDES, Paris

Eyraud B, Velpry L (2015) La liberté d'aller et venir comme révélateur du tournant juridique des régulations du soin en santé mentale: une mise en perspective internationale. Revue de droit sanitaire et social 6:951–962

Eyraud B, Minoc J, Hanon C (eds) (2018) Choisir et agir pour autrui, Controverse autour de la convention de l'ONU pour les droits des personnes handicapées, Ed John Libbey Eurotext, Paris

Eyraud B, Lainé A, El Ayoubi R, Parriaud-Marin A (2023) L'adaptation sociétale à la reconnaissance de droits humains fondamentaux: l'exemple du contrôle judiciaire systémique des soins sans consentement. Revue française d'éthique appliquée 13:117–130

Galderisi S, Gorwood P, Gaebel W, Kurimay T, Dom G, Beezhold J, Wasserman D, Bailey S, Hanon C, Heinz A, Sartorius N, van der Gaag RJ, Vavrusova L, Wise J (2018) United Nations convention on the rights of persons with disabilities needs to be interpreted on the basis of scientific evidence regarding psychiatry. Eur Psychiatry 51:87–89. https://doi.org/10.1016/j.eurpsy.2018.05.008

Garabe J (2004) Historique des soins psychiatriques. In: Pascal JC, Hanon C (eds) Consentement et contrainte dans les soins en psychiatrie. Ed John Libbey Eurotext Paris, p 3

Israël L (2009) L'arme du droit. Presses de Sciences Po. France. https://doi.org/10.3917/scpo.israe.2009.01

LOI no 90-527 du 27 juin 1990 relative aux droits et à la protection des personnes hospitalisées en raison de troubles mentaux et à leurs conditions d'hospitalisation NOR: SPSX8900129L, JORF n°150 du 30 juin 1990. https://www.legifrance.gouv.fr/jorf/id/JORFTEXT000000349384. Accessed 8 March 2023

Pascal JCH, Hanon C (eds) (2014) Consentement et contrainte dans les soins en psychiatrie. Ed John Libbey Eurotext, Paris

Pinel PH (1809) Sur les moyens de répression en usage contre les aliénés. In: Traité médico-philosophique sur l'aliénation mentale, 2nd edn. Ed J. Ant. Brosson, Paris, p 496

Raoul-Cormeil G (2020) La notion de personne vulnérable en droit civil. Cahiers de la recherche sur les droits fondamentaux 18:47–54

Rhenter P (2010) La réforme des hospitalisations psychiatriques sans consentement: un éclairage historique. J Français de Psychiatrie 38:12–15

Risse T, Risse-Kappen T, Ropp SC, Sikkink K (eds) (1999) The power of human rights: international norms and domestic change, vol 66. Cambridge University Press, New York

Rossini K, Verdoux H (2015) Étude du vécu et de la compréhension par les patients hospitalisés sans consentement de l'audience devant le juge des libertés et de la détention. L'Encéphale 41(4):332–338

Sabatello M, Schulz M (2014) A short history of the international disability rights movement. In: Human rights and disability advocacy. University of Pennsylvania Press, Philadelphia, pp 13–24

Troisoeufs A, Eyraud B (2015) Psychiatrisés en lutte, usagers, Gemeurs, …: une cartographie des différentes formes de participation. Rhizome 58:3–4

United Nations (2021) France has not yet integrated the human rights-based approach to disability, regrets the Committee on the Rights of Persons with Disabilities. https://www.ungeneva.org/fr/news-media/meeting-summary/2021/08/la-france-na-pas-encore-integre-lapproche-du-handicap-fondee-sur?fbclid=IwAR227S9DY4cheTVklYq1iIADHU1nRh4YNroejkTZlBb5tSnLbrveex7Ja2M. Accessed 28 Feb 2023

Vanhala L (2015) The diffusion of disability rights in Europe. Hum Rights Q 37:831–853

Zuber V (2014) Le culte des droits de l'homme. Gallimard, Paris

Georgia: Steps for the Implementation of the Convention on the Rights of Persons with Disabilities

8

Eka Chkonia and Simon Surguladze

Contents

8.1 Introduction

Stigma and discrimination against people with mental disorders are the most significant problems in mental health. Many forms of stigmatization are still common in former communist countries (Ougrin et al. 2006).

Domestic discrimination toward people with psychiatric diagnoses is widespread; it often leads to the social isolation of a person and the family and rejection, even from close friends and relatives. Institutional discrimination includes examples such as frequent and inappropriate involuntary hospitalization, disregard of ethical issues (e.g., the right to informed consent), prolonged hospitalization, poor infrastructure, and quality of care in mental health facilities, are also regular practices (The Public Defender's Office, Special Reports 2019–2021).

Historically, using psychiatry as a means of repression has been reported in various countries, and most recently, well described in the Union of Soviet Socialist Republics (USSR) and allied countries. While an explanation might be found in the fact that their prevailing ideology was focused on establishing the ideal society, it was in fact used as a tool of repression. According to available data, thousands of dissenters were hospitalized for political reasons during the Soviet time. Psychiatric incarceration and involuntary treatment were used against the "unreliable" individuals who opposed the social or political situation in the country. The Soviet government frequently used the practice of involuntary confinement of dissidents. Psychiatry was used as an ideological instrument to hinder the activity,

E. Chkonia (✉)
Department of Psychiatry, Tbilisi State Medical University, Tbilisi, Georgia
e-mail: e.chkonia@tsmu.edu

S. Surguladze
South London & Maudsley NHS Trust, London, UK
e-mail: simon.surguladze@slam.nhs.uk

N. Gill, N. Sartorius (eds.), *Mental Health and Human Rights*, Sustainable Development Goals Series, https://doi.org/10.1007/978-3-031-52179-9_8

actions, and thoughts that "threaten" the stability and morals of society. The "concept of sluggish schizophrenia" developed by the Moscow School of Psychiatry (with Academician Andrei Snezhnevsky) provided a handy framework to explain this behavior (Van Voren 2012).

The new Mental Health Law in Georgia was introduced in 2007 with several later revisions. The Mental Health Law replaced the Law on Psychiatric Care adopted in 1997 and instituted several new practices, such as making a court decision for any involuntary hospitalization obligatory. Several by-laws introduced practical procedures, for example, procedures related to the use of physical restraint. In 2009, Georgian experts analyzed the law's implementation, and several further modifications were adopted; in 2013–2014, the process was continued, and some other changes were made in the Spring of 2014 by the Parliament of Georgia, particularly related to procedures on forensic psychiatric treatment (Parliament of Georgia 2014. adoption time: 26 July 2014).

According to the 2007 law, Georgia as a democratic state, recognizes that mental health is a fundamental aspect of human health and is an indispensable condition for the well-being of society. Therefore, the protection of the rights of people with mental disorders is an obligation of the State. The Mental Health Law requires humane treatment, which should exclude degrading measures and assures accessible, appropriate treatment with complete, objective, timely and understandable information about the diagnosis and proposed intervention (Law of Georgia on Psychiatric Care (n.d.), On the state of protection of human rights and freedoms in Georgia (2022).

The Public Defender's special reports on the mental health of Georgia declared that conditions and therapeutic environments existing in the psychiatric institutions cannot ensure patients' dignified life or protection of their rights. The problems include the ignoring of patients' involvement in the treatment plan, absence of privacy, lack of psychosocial treatments, the inadequate patient-to-staff ratio in wards with high risk of violent and aggressive behavior, inattention to reproductive health, non-compliance with sanitary standards in some facilities and the use of "traditional" practices for physical and chemical restriction of patients, which are not based on the updated clinical and treatment guidelines (The Situation in Human Rights and Freedoms in Georgia 2019).

From year to year, the monitoring bodies report that the patients of psychiatric institutions are not protected from violence and inhuman and degrading treatment (The Situation in Human Rights and Freedoms in Georgia 2020). Compulsory medical interventions used in psychiatric hospitals carry an elevated risk of arbitrariness. Rapid tranquillization and physical restraint are frequent and not always documented, increasing the chances of subjectivity and mistakes (The Situation in Human Rights and Freedoms in Georgia 2021).

International society has a long history of promoting the human rights of people with disabilities. However, the most influential instrument, the Convention on the Rights of Persons with Disabilities (CRPD), was adopted in 2006. This critical international document was ratified by Georgia in 2014. The Public defender office is the responsible body for the popularization, defending and monitoring of the CRPD (Monitoring mechanisms for implementation of the Convention on the Rights of Persons with Disabilities (CRPD) Bulletin 2017). In 2015, based on the decision of the Constitutional Court, the country conducted a substantial legislative reform (e.g., the legal capacity model, involuntary treatment). The implementation of the reforms requires an individual approach to the psychosocial needs of the person. The current legislation conforms to convention standards with minor exceptions (Human Rights Education and Monitoring Center 2016).

8.1.1 Criteria and Procedures of Involuntary Treatment

Article 14 of CRPD obliges States Parties to ensure that a person with disabilities has equal rights with others to enjoy the right to liberty and security and that the existence of a disability shall in no case justify a deprivation of liberty. States Parties shall ensure that if persons with disabilities are deprived of their liberty through any process, they are, on an equal basis with others, entitled to guarantees in accordance with international human rights law and shall be treated in compliance with the objectives and principles of this Convention, including provision of reasonable accommodation (Convention on the Rights of Persons with Disabilities, n.d.Article 14—Liberty and security of the person).

The current Mental Health Law institutes new practices regarding involuntary and compulsory treatments. The court decision is obligatory for involuntary hospitalization. Furthermore, various by-laws have been introduced for practical procedures, such as procedures related to physical restraint use (Law of Georgia No 3341 of 20 March 2015, n.d.).

The Law guarantees that people with mental disorders should enjoy other rights and freedoms provided for by the legislation of Georgia. People with mental disorders can reject medical treatment; this right is limited in the cases provided for in Articles 16, 18, and 221 of the Law, when the person may exhibit a real danger to himself or others.

According to the Law (Article 16), the methods of physical restriction of patients include the following rules: A psychiatrist shall be authorized to use restriction methods against a hospitalized patient if there is a real danger that the patient will harm himself or others, and it cannot be otherwise avoided; a decision on using physical restriction against a patient shall be made by the physician on duty, justified in the medical record and terminated immediately upon the elimination of the danger; the rules and procedures for using methods of physical restriction shall be established by an instruction approved by an appropriate order of the Ministry of Health (Order No. 92/N 2007).

The Law differentiates involuntary and compulsory hospitalization. Involuntary inpatient psychiatric care shall be provided when a person is unable to make a conscious decision due to a mental disorder and he cannot be provided with psychiatric care without hospitalization; where a delay in psychiatric care poses a danger to the life and/or health of the patient or other persons, and by his/her actions, the patient may cause significant material damage to himself or to others (Mental Health Law of Georgia, n.d.).

Compulsory psychiatric treatment concerns patients who committed a crime. A court hearing is authorized to use compulsory psychiatric treatment on the two following grounds. Firstly, when a person is unable to make a conscious decision due to a mental disorder, and the provision of psychiatric support is impossible unless they are hospitalized, and secondly, there is a risk that due to a mental disorder, a person will damage, threaten, and/or harm himself and/or other persons.

A person shall be placed only in a hospital where special security is provided and a system of measures ensuring risk mitigation, resocialization, and improvement of psychiatric health is implemented (Chkonia 2022).

The Public Defender welcomed the changes in the law regarding voluntary and compulsory treatment. The monitoring of psychiatric hospitals in 2021 revealed that implementing the rules and regulations improved mental health inpatient practices, but still, in some cases, the above articles are ignored (The Public Defender's Office, Special Reports 2019–2021).

8.1.2 Legal Capacity

The successful ratification of the United Nations Convention implies substantial reforms in law on guardianship and the replacement of guardianship with the supported decision-making model. According to the Civil Code, "Guardianship grants the authority to make decisions about the personal and property rights and interests of the adult, who, due to his health condition, cannot independently exercise his rights and fulfil his duties." The criteria for guardianship are based on the diagnoses, and persons with "mental retardation" and "mental disorders" could be entirely deprived of their rights (Civil Code of Georgia 2022).

After ratification of the CRPD, the parliament of Georgia, the Constitutional Court of Georgia, declared the guardianship model unconstitutional, and in 2015, the supported decision-making model was introduced. Supported decision-making allows individuals with disabilities to make choices about their own lives with support from a team of people they choose.

A survey conducted in 2019, which intended to study the consequences and satisfaction with the new model among patients with mental disorders and their caregivers showed that, although there are significant gaps in legislation and implementation, the replacement of the guardianship model with the supported decision-making model was a positive step for the protection of the rights of persons with mental disabilities (Qelekhsaeva 2019). The major challenges are involving people with mental disabilities in the decision-making process, changing the "traditional" practices due to inappropriate training of mental health professionals, and supporting informed choices. The participants noted that the existing practices in most of the cases remained the same, and it is necessary to increase awareness regarding the new regulations. Insufficient information about the changed legislation could not guarantee thorough rights protection. Therefore, people with mental disabilities cannot fully enjoy the rights granted by the new law.

8.1.3 Future Perspectives of Human Rights Promotion

The challenges with the implementation of the major principles of the convention could be a lack of rules defined by the law and regulations, and an absence of inspections to control the performance of the rules. The countries from the WHO European Region, including Georgia, agree that promoting mental health and preventing and treating mental disorders are fundamental to safeguarding and enhancing the quality of life, well-being, and productivity of individuals, families, workers, and communities.

The Ministry of Health has prepared a specific 2022–2030 strategy for promoting mental health reforms in the country. Ensuring the well-being of the Georgian population and addressing mental health disorders through a mental health strategy is critical to Georgia's sustainability. This strategy is in line with the principles defined by the CRPD and the content of the European Union Framework for the United Nations Convention on the Rights of Persons with Disabilities.

The Mental Health Strategic Plan 2022–2030 includes seven major priorities (Resolution No. 23 of the Government of Georgia of January 18, 2022, on the approval of the Mental Health Strategy of Georgia for 2022–2030). Alongside establishing strong governance for the mental health system and deinstitutionalization, which can be essential for enhancing human rights promotion, the second priority is to "ensure patients' rights with assertive actions."

These actions aim to:

1. Adopt a new law on mental health in line with international standards.
2. Train and create a certification system for all staff of all levels working in mental health concerning patients' rights.
3. Increase the sanctions for human rights infringements in the criminal code.
4. Have a team with independent specialists and lawyer(s) in the Ministry in charge of mental health to manage complaints.
5. Modify the law to allow patients' lawyers to meet their customers at any time in mental health services and structures.
6. Extend the competence of the Georgian Public Defender to all mental health structures and services (Mental Health Strategy of Georgia for 2022–2030).

With the implementation of the current strategy, mental health care will be improved with substantial emphasis on promoting human rights and the respect and dignity of people with mental disorders.

8.2 Conclusion

Developing and implementing a human rights-based approach to caring for people with mental disorders in countries with a long history of totalitarian ideology and institutionalisation requires consistent effort and substantial reforms in legislation and service delivery practices.

References

Chkonia E (2022) Past, present, and future of involuntary admission in Georgia. Eur Psychiatry 65(S1):S38. https://doi.org/10.1192/j.eurpsy.2022.133

Civil Code of Georgia (2022) Consolidated publications: 15 Dec 2022. https://matsne.gov.ge/ka/document/view/31702?publication=122

Convention on the Rights of Persons with Disabilities (n.d.) Article 14—liberty and security of the person. https://social.desa.un.org/issues/disability/crpd/article-14-liberty-and-security-of-person

Human Rights Education and Monitoring Center (2016). https://emc.org.ge/2016/06/07/emc-82/

Law of Georgia No 3341 of 20 March 2015 (n.d.). https://matsne.gov.ge/en/document/download/24178/12/en/pdf

Law of Georgia on Psychiatric Care (n.d.). https://matsne.gov.ge/en/document/download/24178/12/en/pdf

Mental Health Law of Georgia (n.d.). https://matsne.gov.ge/ka/document/view/24178?impose=parallelEnRu&fullscreen=1&publication=17

Monitoring mechanisms for implementation of the Convention on the Rights of Persons with Disabilities (CRPD) Bulletin (2017). https://www.ombudsman.ge/res/docs/2019041015072211483.pdf

On the state of protection of human rights and freedoms in Georgia (2022). https://ombudsman.ge/res/docs/2023033120380187763.pdf

Ougrin D, Gluzman S, Dratcu L (2006) Psychiatry in post-communist Ukraine: dismantling the past, paving the way for the future. Psychiatr Bull 30(12):456–459. https://doi.org/10.1192/pb.30.12.456

Qelekhsaeva N (2019) Master thesis: consequences of the Legal Capacity Reforms. http://eprints.iliauni.edu.ge/id/eprint/8659

Regarding the approval of the instruction on the rules and procedures for the use of physical restraint methods for patients with mental disorders, Order No. 92/N (20 March 2007). https://matsne.gov.ge/ka/document/view/69838?publication=0

Resolution No. 23 of the Government of Georgia of January 18, 2022, on the approval of the Mental Health Strategy of Georgia for 2022–2030 (n.d.). https://matsne.gov.ge/ka/document/view/5357283?publication=0

The Public Defender's Office (2020) The situation in human rights and freedoms in Georgia. https://ombudsman.ge/res/docs/2022040413242699860.pdf

The Public Defender's Office, Special Reports (2019–2021). https://ombudsman.ge/

The Situation in Human Rights and Freedoms in Georgia (2019). https://ombudsman.ge/res/docs/2020040215365449134.pdf

The Situation in Human Rights and Freedoms in Georgia (2021). https://ombudsman.ge/eng/saparlamento-angarishebi

Van Voren R (2012) The abuse of psychiatry for political purposes. In: Oxford University Press eBooks. Oxford University Press, Oxford, pp 237–254. https://doi.org/10.1093/med/9780199213962.003.0015

Germany: Human Rights in Psychiatry

9

Andreas Heinz, Erik Lukas Bode, Melissa Gül Halil, and Sabine Müller

Contents

9.1 Introduction

In the beginning of the twentieth century, Kraepelin and other German psychiatrists constructed a classification system that is still influential today (Kraepelin 1913). Lesser known is that Kraepelin also reacted to social unrest following World War 1 and used antisemitic stereotypes to stigmatize and discriminate some of the democratic revolutionaries that helped to abolish the monarchy following the defeat of the German army (Heinz 2017). Kraepelin's successor Rüdin played a key role in the compulsory sterilization campaign during the Nazi era, which also involved the murder of over a hundred thousand persons with mental illness (Aly 2013). One of the victims of compulsory sterilization, Dorothea Buck, a renowned artist, started self-organization of persons subjected to psychiatry interventions and, together with Thomas Bock, commenced the so-called trialogue, in which persons with mental illness experience, relatives and professionals share experiences on an equal level (Buck-Zerchin 1990; Buck-Zerchin 2002; New York Times 2022). While psychiatry reform came relatively late in Germany compared to Italy and the United Kingdom, in Germany it was promoted by self-help groups and backed by the Federal Parliament (Bundestag), resulting in a comprehensive inquiry (Psychiatrie-Enquete) that lasted from 1971 to 1975 (Aktion Psychisch Kranke 2001). The recommendations of this comprehensive inquiry have only partly been met. Large institutions in the countryside were only partly dissolved, even though the number of patients treated in such institutions drastically declined from usually several thousand to a few

A. Heinz (✉) · E. L. Bode · M. G. Halil · S. Müller
Department of Psychiatry and Neurosciences, Charité—Universitätsmedizin Berlin, CCM, Berlin, Germany
e-mail: andreas.heinz@charite.de; erik-lukas.bode@charite.de; melissa.halil@charite.de; mueller.sabine@charite.de

N. Gill, N. Sartorius (eds.), *Mental Health and Human Rights*, Sustainable Development Goals Series, https://doi.org/10.1007/978-3-031-52179-9_9

hundred. In the general hospitals, psychiatric wards were established that aimed at serving persons from the community, i.e., the local sector.

Following reunification in 1990, a drastic cut in psychiatry beds was established, reducing inpatient facilities by about 50% and drastically shortening the duration of stay. This was accompanied by legal changes in laws governing the acute treatment of a person who poses a danger to herself or others due to mental illness. For example, in Berlin 1985, the respective law (Psychisch-Kranken-Gesetz (PsychKG), Federal Constitutional Court 2017) explicitly stated for the first time, that the presence of mental illness per se was no reason for compulsory treatment, and that only posing a direct danger to oneself or others justified compulsory admission to a psychiatric hospital. At this time, one of the authors (A.H.) worked in a self-organized psychiatric complaint center and met a person who had been admitted for 18 years against his will to a mental institution. This person had helped to word the new legal text that required a judge to check whether a person indeed poses a threat to herself or others due to mental illness.

This law and the other legally binding documents discussed in the following sections are not applied when a person committed a crime and, instead of being imprisoned, is transferred to the so-called forensic psychiatry because this person is not considered guilty due to mental illness. The laws governing forensic psychiatry are legally separated from laws governing the treatment of acute mentally ill persons and those with chronic disabilities.

Regarding acute mental disorders, each federal state in Germany has its own legislation. Compulsory admission to a psychiatric hospital and compulsory treatment is largely but not completely identical across federal states, which has repeatedly been criticized, by the authors of this chapter, among others. Persons with chronic disabilities, such as dementia or persistent psychotic disorders can be placed under legal guardianship if they are no longer able to manage important matters of their lives themselves. In this case, treatment against the current will of the person is only possible if they pose a severe danger to their own health and do not have insight into that risk due to mental illness, for example, in the case of a person with dementia no longer eats or drinks adequately.

Altogether, the German legal system does not distinguish between psychiatrically classified mental disorders and mental disorders caused by a physical disorder or medication side effects, for example, delirium due to herpes encephalitis or alcohol withdrawal, or psychosis due to antiparkinsonian dopaminergic medication or stress-associated dopamine dysfunction as in many cases of schizophrenia. Nevertheless, in purely somatic wards and institutions, the complex legal system that applies to mental disorders is not applied and compulsory treatment is justified by a paragraph referring to "acute danger" ("Gefahr im Verzug"), which allows short-term interventions that are not agreed upon by a judge (Section 34 StGB, Federal Ministry of Justice 2019). This, on the other hand, is not possible in any institution associated with psychiatry.

9.2 Historical Development of Laws in Germany Following the UN Convention for the Rights of Persons with Disabilities (United Nations 2006)

The convention was agreed upon in 2006 by the General Assembly of the United Nations and was ratified by 185 states including the European Union until May 2022 (United Nations 2006). The German Federal Constitutional Court (Bundesverfassungsgericht) has repeatedly based its decisions regarding human rights in psychiatry on the UN-CRPD. For example, in March 2011, it ruled on the case of a man in forensic psychiatry with implications for general psychiatry. This man had tried to murder his wife and daughter with a hammer and was judged to be incapable of guilt due to psychotic paranoia. He refused to accept medical treatment with antipsychotics/neuroleptics when in forensic psychiatry. The Federal Constitutional Court ruled that this person understands the implications of the treatment, the potential side effects, and the consequences of rejecting treatment, namely that he will continue to be confined in forensic psychiatry due to a lack of change in his mental condition. The Federal Constitutional Court thus ruled that this person has insight into his condition and can refuse medical treatment accordingly (2 BvR 882/09, Federal Constitutional Court 2017). The Federal Constitutional Court nevertheless stated that this ruling does not mean that the "freedom to be ill" has to be considered completely independent of the actual "free will" of the person and her possibility to act accordingly. However, any compulsory treatment in such situations should only aim at reestablishing the ability of the person to form their own free decision. The Federal Constitutional Court did not see this decision in conflict with the UN-CRPD and claimed that the UN-CRPD restricts the legality of compulsory interventions in order to protect persons from conflicts of interests, abuse, or disrespect of their personal rights.

In the following, the German Federal Constitutional Court generalized its decision from compulsory treatments in forensic psychiatry to acute compulsory treatments of mental illness. The relevant paragraphs of the PsychKG of the federal states Baden-Wuerttemberg (2 BvR 633/11, Federal Constitutional Court 2017), and Saxonia (2 BvR 228/12, Federal Constitutional Court 2017) were found to be unconstitutional. The Federal Constitutional Court ruled that compulsory treatment can only be allowed if a person is incapable of consenting and poses a direct threat to herself, if the treatment is a last resort and other less restrictive treatments have failed to show any effect, and if the treatment is of sufficient efficacy and not associated with significant hardship for the person with mental illness. In the following years, all of the laws of federal states in Germany governing compulsory admission and treatment have been reformed. In most federal states, they now include an option for compulsory admission in an "open" setting, after it has been shown that acute wards with open doors reduce (and do not increase) absconding and violence (Huber et al. 2016; Cibis et al. 2017).

In the following years, the federal law regulating legal guardianship has been declared partly illegal by the German Federal Supreme Court (Bundesgerichtshof). This decision was based on the decisions of the German Federal Constitutional Court. From 2011 to 2013, there was no legal opportunity for compulsory treatments. In this time, a significant increase of fixations and of aggressive incidents was observed (Flammer and Steinert 2015). In 2013, the law governing legal guardianship was changed and it was ruled that a legal guardian can only agree with medical interventions against the natural (not the free) will of the person with mental illness if: I) The person lacks insights or cannot act according to this insight in his or her situation; II) it has sufficiently been tried to find other ways to deal with the medical problem; III) the compulsory treatment is necessary to avert a substantial risk to the health of the afflicted person; IV) there is no other way to avert this potentially damaging situation, and V) the benefit of the intervention is substantially larger than the risk for the person treated in this way (Section 1906a (1), Bürgerliches Gesetzbuch (BGB) 2002). Also, in the following it was ruled that every person under legal guardianship should independently have a legal counselor (Verfahrenspfleger) who informs the person about her or his rights. Furthermore, medical experts providing the expertise for the decision of the respective judge should never have treated the person or provided expertise and should not work in the same institution in which the person is treated.

In 2016, the Federal Constitutional Court dealt with a legal complaint regarding the federal law to avert substantial harm to a person under legal guardianship (1 BvL 8/15, 26.07.2016, Federal Constitutional Court). In this case, it was not legally possible to give the patient medical treatment against her will although treatment was urgently necessary. The reason for this was that according to legal articulations of the existing law, compulsory treatment could only follow compulsory admission, and compulsory admission was only possible if the person would otherwise leave the clinic.

However, in this case, the patient was unable to leave the ward because of her poor general condition. She suffered from a severe autoimmune disease, psychosis, dementia, and breast cancer. She refused to have medical treatment for her autoimmune disease and for breast cancer, and rejected any kind of nutrition, because she wanted to die. However, compulsory treatment was not legally allowed because she was not able to leave the ward. Accordingly, there was no necessity for legal admission, and therefore compulsory treatment could not be allowed. While this may sound like complicated legalistic argumentation, the German Federal Constitutional Court explained some fundamental principles in its ruling. It claimed that inpatients who cannot leave the ward due to physical problems can be legally treated against their current "natural will" as they have a human right to live and to be bodily unharmed, which is guaranteed in the German constitutional law (Article 2, Section 2, Grundgesetz (GG) für die Bundesrepublik Deutschland 2021). The court stated explicitly that the state cannot leave a helpless person without adequate support but instead needs to establish a system of support and protection that can include as an ultima ratio also compulsory treatment. The German Federal Constitutional Court thus discussed how to weigh autonomy and the right to be bodily unharmed on the one hand and severe physical harm in case of not treating a medical disease on the other. Again, the German Federal Constitutional Court stated that this decision is in accordance with the UN-CRPD Article 12. It rejected the interpretation of the Committee on the Rights of Persons with Disabilities (CRPD) (see also Freeman et al. 2015) and stated that its interpretation of the UN-CRPD, while relevant in this context, is not legally binding and does not include the competence to interpret the UN-CRPD exclusively. Particularly, the German Federal Constitutional Court criticized that the Committee does not discuss how to proceed in case of a complete absence of the free will of the afflicted person who is helpless and should not be left alone in such a situation.

9.3 Summary

Compulsory treatment in Germany is strictly regulated by law and always requires a judge to make the final decision. Medical expertise is always to be provided by an independent psychiatrist, who does not work in the same institution. This is true both for (1) laws of different federal German states that govern the acute protection of persons with mental illness who pose harm to themselves or others due to a lack of insight caused by the mental illness as well as (2) for persons with chronic mental illness and lack of insight who are exposed to substantial physical harm and hence placed under legal guardianship. A lawyer is not regularly provided in the German system; however, a legally experienced person is provided in all cases of legal guardianship as an independent legal consultant to the patient (Verfahrenspfleger). Later rulings also specified that orders of physical restraint for more than 30 min have to be controlled by a judge (except during nighttime).

Despite these rather tight legal procedures, four points of criticism should be addressed: Firstly, legal guardians are not regularly trained in participatory decision-making, which should be obligatory. Secondly, the legal consultants (Verfahrenspfleger) often appear to be rather passive and do not actively inform patients about all their rights. This should be changed by systematic education and training of these persons, with educational material being provided by organizations of patients, relatives, and professionals in the trialogue tradition. Thirdly, open wards as legal standard are only required by most but not all federal states of Germany. In Germany, they have not been implemented by more than roughly 10% of all hospitals. Finally, in several parts of Germany, many psychiatry hospitals are still located far away from communities, which in the countryside is hard to change but nevertheless should be promoted even in such situations, including daycare clinics and ACP-Teams that provide medical care in the homes of afflicted persons instead of transferring them into inpatient treatment.

References

Aktion psychisch Kranke (2001) 25 Jahre Psychiatrie-Enquete. Tagungsberichte, vol 27. Psychiatrie-Verlag, Bonn

Aly G (2013) Die Belasteten: "Euthanasie" 1939–1945. Eine Gesellschaftsgeschichte (1. neue Ausg.). Fischer, Frankfurt/M.

Buck-Zerchin D (1990) Auf der Spur des Morgensterns. List Verlag, Frankfurt/M.

Buck-Zerchin D (2002) Lasst euch nicht entmutigen. Anne Fischer Verlag, Norderstedt

Bürgerliches Gesetzbuch (BGB) (2002) BGB mit Allgemeinem Gleichbehandlungsgesetz, Produkthaftungsgesetz, Unterlassungsklagengesetz, Wohnungseigentumsgesetz, Beurkundungsgesetz und Erbbaurechtsgesetz, 90th edn. Beck-Texte im dtv, München

Cibis M-L, Wackerhagen C, Müller S, Lang U, Schmidt Y, Heinz A (2017) Comparison of aggressive behavior, compulsory medication and absconding behavior between open and closed door policy in an acute psychiatric ward. Psychiatr Prax 44(3):141–147. https://doi.org/10.1055/s-0042-105181

Federal Constitutional Court (2017) Pressemitteilung Nr. 107/2017 vom Dezember 2017. Mündliche Verhandlung in Sachen "Fixierung im Ramen der öffentlich-rechtlichen Unterbringung" am Dienstag, 30. Januar 2018, 10.00 Uhr, und am Mittwich, 31. Januar 2017, 10:00 Uhr. http://www.bundesverfassungsgericht/SharedDocs/Pressemitteilungen/E/2017/bvg17-107.html. Accessed 31 Jan 2018

Federal Ministry of Justice (2019) German criminal code (Strafgesetzbuch—StGB). https://www.gesetze-im-internet.de/englisch_stgb/. Accessed 10 Sept 2022

Flammer E, Steinert T (2015) Impact of the temporaneous lack of legal basis for involuntary treatment on the frequency of aggressive incidents, seclusion and restraint among patients with chronic schizophrenic disorders. Psychiatr Prax 42(5):260–266. https://doi.org/10.1055/s-0034-1370069

Freeman M, Kolappa K, Almeida J, de Kleinman A, Makhashvili N, Phakathi S et al (2015) Reversing hard won victories in the name of human rights: a critique of the general comment on article 12 of the UN convention on the rights of persons with disabilities. Lancet Psychiatry 2(9):844–850. https://doi.org/10.1016/S2215-0366(15)00218-7

Grundgesetz (GG) für die Bundesrepublik Deutschland (2021) Mit Einigungsvertrag (ohne Anl.), ParlamentsbeteiligungsG, Artikel 10-G, BundeswahlG, ParteienG, BundesverfassungsgerichtsG, Parlamentar. Geschäftsordnungen, EuropawahlG, Menschenrechtskonvention, EUV, AEUV, EU-Grundrechte-Charta, 69th edn. C. H. Beck, München

Heinz A (2017) A new understanding of mental disorders. MIT Press, Boston

Huber C, Schneeberger A, Kowalinski E, Fröhlich D, Felten S, von Walter M et al (2016) Suicide risk and absconding in psychiatric hospitals with and without open door policies: a 15 year, observational study. Lancet Psychiatry 3(9):842–849. https://doi.org/10.1016/S2215-0366(16)30168-7

Kraepelin E (1913) Psychiatrie. Band 3. J.A. Barth, Leipzig

New York Times (5 Sept 2022) Dorothea Buck, 102, dies; Nazi victim and voice for mentally ill. New York Times. https://www.nytimes.com/2019/10/18/health/dorothea-buck-dead.html

United Nations (2006) Convention on the rights of persons with disabilities. https://treaties.un.org/Pages/ViewDetails.aspx?src=TREATY&mtdsg_no=IV-15&chapter=4&clang=_en. Accessed 5 Sept 2022

Mexico/Latin America: Mental Health and Human Rights

10

Nicolás Martínez-López
and Marlen Abigain Gómez-Mendiola

Contents

10.1 Introduction

There are approximately 85 million people with disabilities in Latin America, representing 14.7% of the population and one in five households. For this reason, in recent years, the countries that make up Latin America have worked hard to promote and protect the human rights of people with disabilities, in order to ensure their dignity as persons and their participation in society on equal terms (Banco Mundial 2021).

The Convention on the Rights of Persons with Disabilities (CRPD) is a human rights treaty adopted by the United Nations General Assembly on December 13, 2006 with the purpose to proclaim justice, peace, and dignity of persons with disabilities, with equality of rights (Comisión Presidencial coordinadora de la Política del Ejecutivo en materia de Derechos Humanos 2011). Most Latin American countries, such as Mexico, Panama, or Argentina, signed the Convention months after it was promulgated; however, some countries, such as Venezuela, were not party to it until 2013 (Naciones Unidas 2011) (See Table 10.1).

The Convention prompted changes in different areas, mainly the incorporation of non-discriminatory language, as well as autonomy for people with disabilities, leaving aside the welfare model that limited both civil and political rights (Dhanda 2009). Previously, terms or expressions were used, both in civil and criminal matters, which focused more attention on physical or mental deficiencies, such as "mentally incapable or disabled" (Panama), different capacities (Mexico), or physically, sensorial, and psychically handicapped (Colombia) (Stang Alva 2011).

N. Martínez-López (✉) · M. A. Gómez-Mendiola
Clinical Epidemiology Laboratory, Ramón de la Fuente Muñiz National Institute of Psychiatry (INPRFM), Mexico City, Mexico

N. Gill, N. Sartorius (eds.), *Mental Health and Human Rights*, Sustainable Development Goals Series, https://doi.org/10.1007/978-3-031-52179-9_10

Table 10.1 Latin American countries which signed the Convention on the Rights of Persons with Disabilities by year

Year	Country
2007	El Salvador, Jamaica, México, Nicaragua, Argentina, Brazil, Belize, Bolivia, Chile, Colombia, Costa Rica, Cuba, Barbados, Bolivia, Ecuador, Guatemala, Guyana, Honduras, Nicaragua, Panamá, Paraguay, Perú, Dominican Republic, Trinidad and Tobago, Uruguay, Surinam
2009	Haití
2010	Granada, Saint Vincent, and the Grenadines
2011	Saint Lucia
2013	Venezuela

At the legislative level, the Convention has made it possible to establish significant changes in legal concepts that have allowed Latin American legal systems to advance, mainly in concepts such as capacity, involuntary commitment, interdiction and not guilty by reason of insanity defense (Espejo Yaksic 2021). Although each of the Latin American countries has adopted its own mechanisms to enforce the provisions of the Convention in each of these concepts, this chapter will focus on changes in countries such as Argentina, Colombia, Chile, Ecuador, Salvador, Panama, Peru, and Mexico.

10.2 Capacity

Article 12 of the Convention establishes that persons with disabilities have the right to recognition of their legal capacity on an equal basis with others. Therefore, the States have the obligation to recognize without discrimination the right to legal capacity of persons with disabilities, and to implement mechanisms that allow necessary support required by a person to exercise his or her capacity (Espejo Yaksic 2021).

In Argentina, the Convention was the pillar for the decree and approval in 2010 of Law 26.657 on mental health, which established in its Article 3, the right of the patient in making decisions related to medical care and treatment. However, its main change was reflected in the Civil Code, since it incorporated in the Article 152 Ter, to established that in any judicial declaration dealing with matters related to incapacity, the protection of the rights of the person should always be prioritized, with the least possible interference in the exercise of their autonomy (Rajmil and Llorens 2015; Ministerio de Salud 2013; Comisión Nacional Asesora para la Integración de Personas Discapacitadas 2010). As a result, in 2011, the National Executive Branch drafted a reform bill to update and unify the civil codes for the issuance of reforms for the legal capacity concept (Comisión Interamericana de Derechos Humanos 2014).

Other countries such as Peru, Costa Rica, and Colombia have made reforms for the elimination of the disqualification of capacity of a person with disabilities. Colombia had previously enacted Law 1306 in 2009, which dictated the rules for the legal representation of incapable persons, establishing the definition of mental disability as a person who did not understand the scope of the acts due to their mental limitations. However, in 2019 it approved Law 1996, which establishes specific measures to guarantee the right to legal capacity, replacing the substitution of will with support at the time of decision-making, specifically allowing a person to designate who can assist him/her in making decisions on legal matters, thereby promoting the autonomy of persons with disabilities (Cortés 2019; Ministerio de Justicia y del Derecho 2019).

Peru enacted Law No. 299973, in 2012, called General Law of Persons with Disabilities, recognizing the rights of persons referred to as deaf and dumb or visually impaired. Then in 2018, it enacted Legislative Decree No. 1384, which likewise promotes and guarantees the right to recognition of the capacity of persons with intellectual disabilities, establishing that everyone has the right to express their freedom in an autonomous manner (Chunga Castro 2021).

Ecuador was one of the first countries to modify its legal framework based on the Convention, creating the Organic Law on Disabilities in 2012, which incorporated the definition of the term person with disabilities. In 2018, it issued Resolution 011-ST-2019, which establishes that any person with a physical, hearing, visual, intellectual, and psychosocial disability is legally capable of carrying out legal acts on their own (Friend Macías and Álava Díaz 2019). Mexico was also one of the countries that changed the assignment of a guardian to supported decision-making, establishing that they can be the family support networks, community support, personal assistants, etc. as long as they are based on the trust of the person and guarantee respect for the dignity and decision-making of the person with disabilities (Comisión de Derechos Humanos del Distrito Federal 2008; Consejo Nacional para Prevenir la Discriminación 2013; Suprema Corte de Justicia de la Nación 2022). In 2011, a Human Rights reform was published in Mexico, with the objective of ensuring the dignity of people (Comisión Nacional de Derechos Humanos 2014).

Similarly, advances in human rights continue and are updated regularly, as is the case of The Salvador, which in 2021 enacted the Special Law for the Inclusion of Persons with Disabilities, which is complemented by the Convention, which promotes the protection and recognition of the rights and the ability of the person to obtain a decent job based on respect for their human rights, thus promoting labor inclusion (Organización Internacional del Trabajo 2021).

For this reason, it is an issue that is gradually taking shape and continues to adapt to society; however, progress both at the legislative and social levels continues to be of great relevance, especially because the capacity can intersect with other concepts.

10.3 Involuntary Commitment

Involuntary internment has been another figure that has undergone changes inspired by the Convention. Although there are diverse types of disabilities, those with mental disorders are among the most discriminated against in different areas, in addition to the lack of recognition of their human rights. Involuntary internment is the last therapeutic resource when the user or patient cannot request admission to a health institution by himself/herself due to his/her mental disorder, and this is requested by a family member or guardian (Vega et al. 2010). This procedure has been the subject of several analyses since most of the time it has been in violation of human rights due to the nature with which it is carried out, especially because it is related to the issue of capacity. The most frequent causes of involuntary internment are in cases related to psychotic breaks, mania, depression, addictions, disorders mainly with a high level of stigma, which causes it to be considered that the person who suffers from them does not have the power to make decisions (Gutiérrez Luna 2009).

In this regard, Argentina, following the ratification of the Convention in 2010, promulgated the National Law on Mental Health (Law 26. 657) and later in 2015, the Civil and Commercial Code, establishing in both the need to protect not only the rights of people with a disability (related to a mental disorder), but also to respect their autonomy, emphasizing the need for informed consent, something that previously was not taken into account. This gave the power to each person to make their own decisions related especially in the matter of treatment, adding especially to the Civil Code, that the capacity of a person is not altered or modified even if he/she is hospitalized in a health institution (López et al. 2017; Ministerio de Salud 2013; Ainzenberg and Reyes 2009).

In this sense, this Law also showed progress in the cases of hospitalization, being considered as a therapeutic resource, which would only be carried out when it would bring benefits to the patient, respecting above all the right to autonomy and information. It also establishes the requirements that must be met, and which must be collected during the first 48 h, being in the first place a multidisciplinary evaluation that justifies the reason for the internment, signed by at least two health professionals, one of them being a psychologist or psychiatrist, search of data that identifies the patient and informed consent of the person or the legal representative. In the case of involuntary commitment, it is specified that these will only be given when there is a risk for the person himself or for third parties, and that besides having the general requirements of an internment, it must be specified, within the multidisciplinary evaluation, the risk considered as a reason to require the involuntary commitment and the absence of other alternative treatments. Furthermore, there is a maximum term of 10 h to notify the judge so that they can evaluate that the requirements established by law are fulfilled. Finally, it is important to emphasize that mental health internments must be carried out only in general hospitals (Ministerio de Salud de la Nación 2013).

Chile enacted Law No. 20. 584 in 2012, which regulates the rights and duties of patients in their health care, specifying that the dignity, autonomy, and equality of the person are the fundamental rights that must be respected by health care providers, especially the right to informed consent to grant or deny their willingness to accept any procedure. In order to determine that a patient is at risk, there must be a diagnosis certified by a psychiatrist establishing the type of risk, in addition to the fact that if the treatment is suspended, it would lead to a worsening of the patient's health condition (Gobierno de Chile 2016; Bustamanete Donoso and Cavieres Fernández 2018).

However, involuntary commitment should never exceed the time established by the physician, which should be determined as closely as necessary, being the least restrictive possible (Figueroa San Martín 2017b). As a result of this, alternatives have emerged such as advance directives, in which the patient can accept or reject medical, preventive, palliative treatments, or in general any decision that has to do with treatment. The advance directive is established at a time when the person is stable and which gives them the power to be respected in terms of their autonomy and their right to decide (Figueroa San Martín 2017a). Argentina, México, Uruguay, Colombia, and Brazil are countries that already have specific legislation regulating these advance directives (Da Silva Fontes and Da Silva 2019).

Ecuador is another country that has adopted measures to ensure equal rights. The Organic Law on Disabilities was the first legislation subsequent to its addition to the Convention, where it not only made changes in the definitions of disability, but also changed terms such as "demented" or "handicapped" (Nasimba Loachamin 2017). Although there are no specific offenses related to the involuntary placement of a person in health institutions, Ecuador has made changes to its regulations within the Organic Integral Criminal Code (Asamblea Nacional República del Ecuador 2014; Consejo nacional de Igualdad de Discapacidades 2014), to include situations related to illegal deprivation of Liberty, establishing the following:

> Article 10: Prohibition of deprivation of liberty in unauthorized centers—Any form of deprivation of liberty in facilities or places not legally authorized is prohibited, as well as any form of arrest, coercion, or deprivation of liberty derived from administrative disciplinary proceedings.
>
> Article 161: Kidnapping—The person who deprives of liberty, retains, conceals, snatches, or transfers to another place one or more persons, against their will, shall be punished with imprisonment for a term of 5 to 7 years.

More recently, in 2019, Peru enacted Law No. 30947 called the Mental Health Law, which mentions informed consent as a requirement for commitment and hospitalizations, leaving the possibility of not requiring it in emergency cases or in criminal proceedings (Chunga Castro 2021). However, the law reflects the vision of the Convention with respect to human rights, which was previously lacking. In 2008, there was the first precedent of a judgment of the Constitutional Court, against the judgment granted in the Honorio Delgado-Noguchi case. In this judgment, psychiatrists belonging to the Addictions Department of the Institute of Mental Health "Honorio Delgado-Noguchi" were sued, requesting the restitution of the personal liberty of patients hospitalized against their will, who were also denied the right to information, recreation and family visits (Instituto de Democracia y Derechos Humanos de la Pontificia Universidad Católica del Perú 2012; Tribunal Constitucional 2009).

In Mexico, the General Health Law establishes that involuntary commitment must be the last therapeutic resource, always in accordance with ethical principles, and that it must be requested by a family member, guardian, or interested person, as long as evaluations are carried out by a medical specialist who determines that it is indeed the last resort to safeguard the patient's health (Von Aguilar and Martínez López 2020; Cordero Oropeza et al. 2021). For 2014, the Mexican Official Standard NOM-025-SSA2-2014 was enacted, which established the procedural requirements depending on the type of admission required, whether voluntary or involuntary, and although it refers that doctors are the ones who request it, in the case of involuntary admission, the signature of the family member or representative is required. When the person is in better condition, they must be informed of their involuntary admission so that in any case, they can give their duly informed consent and thus move to a voluntary admission (Von Aguilar and Martínez López 2020; Secretaría de Salud [SSA] 2015).

In 2021, Mexico made an amendment to the General Health Law on mental health and addictions, in which it added that informed consent will be an essential part of a person's right to health, so that all health professionals have the obligation to communicate all the necessary information related to the objective of the treatment, benefits, alternatives, and risks, so that the patient can make a decision and give his or her consent in a free and, above all, informed manner. In addition, it also states that in cases where the person cannot give this consent, nor does he/she have an advance will, the health professional will proceed to preserve life (only in cases where life is at risk and administering the treatment is the only way) recording in the report and justifying it to the Ethics Committee and the judicial authority (Cámara de Diputados 2022). In addition, hospitalization in health services must be the last therapeutic resort, which must be carried out in a general or pediatric hospital and at no time may it be prolonged for non-health reasons, specifying that all persons with mental and substance use disorders shall have the capacity to consent or refuse permission for treatment.

10.4 Interdiction

Interdiction is the restriction of legal capacity, allowing a judge to give the person a guardian or representative to make decisions for him/her, that although aims to protect the person, the reality is that it restricts the person's right to autonomy (Lara 2015; Treviño Barrios 2020). As mentioned above, the basic principles of the Convention are respect for human dignity, autonomy, freedom to make decisions, and equality of opportunity (Organización de las Naciones Unidas 2007). However, the interdiction limits these rights of persons with disabilities. For this reason, regulatory changes have been important for the full enjoyment of the rights established by the Convention.

Thus, in 2016, Costa Rica through Law No. 9379 called Law for the Promotion of Autonomy of Persons with Disabilities, recognized legal capacity as one of the fundamental rights of persons with disabilities, introducing in this law the concept of personal assistance and thereby eliminating the interdiction, being one of the main precedents for the promotion of the rights of persons with disabilities, thereby protecting the full enjoyment of autonomy under equal conditions (Espejo Yaksic 2021). The Program for the Promotion of Personal Autonomy of Persons with Disabilities (PPAPPwD) was also created, which facilitates the promotion of inclusion in various contexts, especially in generating all those conditions that help a person with a disability to exercise his or her right to autonomy (Ministerio de Planificación Nacional y Política Económica 2020).

In 2018, Peru established Decree No. 1384 where it recognized the legal capacity of persons with disabilities over 18 years, repealing the interdiction and curatorship for reasons of disability, and establishing the application of reasonable accommodation necessary for the support of their legal capacity. In addition, the Decree reestablished the legal capacity of all those persons who were in a state of interdiction (Espejo Yaksic 2021; El Congreso de la República 2018).

Colombia was another country that eliminated this concept in 2019, through Law No. 1996, thus complying with the provisions of the Convention. This law guarantees not only access to all persons with disabilities who previously had rights restrictions, but also promotes inclusion for the elimination of barriers, such as interdiction, which did not allow the full enjoyment of autonomy and decision-making (Espejo Yaksic 2021).

The importance of this new law is that it not only promotes that the person has the capacity to decide, but it also establishes mechanisms to guarantee this (Navas Agudelo 2020), such as the following:

1. Support mechanisms: Support persons who provide the necessary measures to enable the person with a disability to exercise his or her legal capacity.
2. Advance directives: Document where the person establishes in advance his or her decision on personal matters, whether health or patrimonial.
3. Judicial adjudication of support: Request to a judge for the designation of a person to act as a decision-maker, as long as it is proven that the person does not have mechanisms to exercise his or her will or communicate it.

Mexico, in 2011, made a reform in Article 1 of the Constitution, which provides that human rights of persons with disabilities are recognized in the Constitution in line with the international treaties where Mexico is a party (Treviño Barrios 2020; González Alcántara and Von Aguilar 2020). Consequently, the pro persona principle began to gain strength in cases involving interdiction trials, since the application of this concept determined the so-called civil death of a person, due to the loss of legal personality (González Alcántara and Von Aguilar 2020) which was the opposite of the objective of the Convention. Therefore, this principle determined that the application of the rule that most benefited a person should always be chosen.

In this regard, the habeas corpus 1368/2015 established that:

> "… the recognition of legal capacity is linked to the enjoyment of many other human rights such as: the right of access to justice, the right to equality and non-discrimination, due process, the right to a hearing, the right to an independent life, the right to privacy, the right to freedom of expression, the right to participation and inclusion in society, and the right to a fair trial."

With this background, including the case of Ricardo Aldair[1] in 2014, the First Chamber of the Supreme Court of Justice determined that in effect the figure of interdiction was unconstitutional, that is, it was in violation of human rights, specifically the right to equality and non-discrimination, being more of a paternalistic model and not of respect for human rights (Treviño Barrios 2020; González Alcántara and Von Aguilar 2020).

Although, little by little, work has been done to modify legislation in order to recognize legal capacity, which in turn is closely related to the issue of interdiction, these issues must continue to be updated. As described, there are more and more countries that are basing their rules and laws to safeguard the rights of its inhabitants. Thanks to this work, on September 01, 2022, the Parliament of Persons with Disabilities approved a bill to eliminate the figure of interdiction from the Civil Code of Mexico City (Yo También. Discapacidad con todas sus letras 2022).

10.5 Not Guilty by Reason of Insanity Defense

The Convention not only brought changes in the civil or constitutional sphere, but also in the criminal sphere, specifically what is established in Article 13:

> Article 13: "… States Parties shall ensure that persons with disabilities have access to justice on an equal basis with others, through the provision of procedural and age-appropriate accommodations, to facilitate the effective seh including at the investigative and other preliminary stages."

This specific article takes us into one of the concepts that involves people with disabilities with the criminal justice system, which is the not guilty by reason of insanity defense. There is no global definition to understand what is the not

[1]Ricardo Aldair was the first case in Mexico where it was recognized that interdiction restricted decision-making and deprived the right to exercise legal capacity. See: https://cdhcm.org.mx/wp-content/uploads/2014/02/ricardo-adair.pdf

guilty by reason of insanity defense, as it depends on each Criminal Code, however, according to the Mexican Legal Dictionary, this term is defined as:

> "Not guilty by reason of insanity defense can be configured in three ways: (1) biological or psychiatric, which expresses only the sources of the incapacity—deaf-mutism, dementia or insanity, etc.—without mentioning the consequent inability to understand or determine oneself; (2) psychological, which expresses this incapacity without mentioning its sources; and without alluding to the consequent incapacity to understand or determine oneself; and (3) the psychiatric-psychological-legal or mixed, in which the more or less ample indication of the sources follows one of its effects in terms of the deprivation of the consciousness to commit a crime or of the possibility of acting in accordance with the law. But whatever the formula, the conditioning factors of not guilty by reason of insanity defense are two: the insufficient mental development and the lack of mental health." (Instituto de Investigaciones Jurídicas 1982)

Being a party to the Convention, Mexico made the necessary modifications and adjustments in 2011 by enacting the General Law on Inclusion of Persons with Disabilities, in which the State has the obligation to protect, promote, and ensure human rights. Similarly, in 2014, the National Code of Criminal Procedure was published, which incorporated the principle of equality before the law and the implementation of reasonable accommodation to the procedure (Gómez Mendiola 2020; DOCUMENTA 2019). Through this reform, the Special Procedure for persons with disabilities is eliminated to give way to the application of the ordinary procedure, thus giving rise to procedural equality, i.e., following the same process but adopting measures to ensure access to justice for persons with disabilities, whether as victims, witnesses, or accused (DOCUMENTA 2019).

Also, among the mechanisms that were implemented was the addition of a technical consultant who can identify the barriers that each person may face within a procedure, and thus propose the necessary adjustments to ensure that the person can access justice on equal terms (Lizama & Sheinbaum 2019). Furthermore, there was a request for adherence to the Protocol of Action for those who impart justice in cases involving the rights of persons with disabilities and a document issued by the Supreme Court of Justice of the Nation which refers to the use of a multidisciplinary team, being specialists in the fields of medicine, psychiatry, law, social work, psychology, sociology, among others for the verification of a disability, in order to establish the necessary adjustments to the procedure (Suprema Corte de Justicia de la Nación 2014).

By 2016, the National Law of Criminal Execution established the guidelines for the execution of penalties and security measures imposed as a result of a judicial decision, establishing that when it is a measure of deprivation of liberty, this must be in establishments intended for this purpose, that is, those established by the health authority. However, it is a practice that is little used to date (Hegglin 2017; Diario de la Federación 2016).

Argentina has also been one of the countries that has addressed the issue of not guilty by reason of insanity defense, especially with regard to security measures in the criminal justice system. Argentina signed the Convention in 2008, and gave it constitutional status in 2014, i.e., it granted recognition to persons with psychosocial and intellectual disabilities (Hegglin 2017). In 2015, the Criminal Procedure Code of the Nation was enacted, which established that in cases where a person with a psychosocial disability or who could be not guilty by reason of insanity defense is found, the necessary adjustments would have to be applied without including deprivation of liberty, as previously established in the previous Code, where imprisonment was imminent (Hegglin 2017).

While the not guilty by reason of insanity defense helps as an exclusion of guilt in cases involving persons with disabilities, it is also true that it is not always adequately applicable or not universally understood. An example of this is the case of Peru, which in 2014 enacted Law No. 301551, which amended Article 20 of the Criminal Code and added that all personnel of the Armed Forces and National Police, may be declared not guilty by reason of insanity defense when, in the performance of their duty, cause injury or death due to the use of weapons (Pontificia Universidad Católica del Perú 2014).

Some other countries, such as Costa Rica, adopted the psychological model and in 2012, established in its Criminal Code, the performance of psychological-psychiatric evaluations to analyze the not guilty by reason of insanity defense from a more multidisciplinary point of view (Hernández Arguedas 2015). Countries such as Venezuela are still working to guarantee access to justice for cases of the not guilty by reason of insanity defense (Chirino and Giménez 2019).

Another example is Panama, which adopts the social model and thus gives persons with disabilities the right to be able to decide on various aspects; however, work is still being done to modify the law so that in cases of not guilty by reason of insanity defense, the deprivation of liberty as a security measure, becomes a placement in a mental health institution appropriate to the person. In recent years, the Committee on the Rights of Persons with Disabilities of the United Nations has stressed the importance of no longer taking dangerousness as the starting point for the decision to deprive the allegedly not guilty by reason of insanity defense person of his/her liberty. (Rodríguez Vásquez 2016).

Thus, the application of the Convention on the Rights of Persons with Disabilities is more important today, not only in Latin America, but globally. Not guilty by reason of insanity defense has shown an important change since the ratification of the Convention, and there are more and more precedents that grant not only a change in the criminal proceedings, but also in the persons with a disability who become involved in these proceedings.

10.6 Discussion and Conclusion

Signing and ratifying the convention as a binding instrument has provided the impetus for different member states of the UN in Latin America to reform their legislation to ensure that the rights of people with mental disorders are not violated. However, in the face of various obstacles such as stigma and a lack of sufficient budget, among other factors, the implementation in each area and each country has been complicated.

With respect to legal capacity, it is notable that these are not being met as urgent issues within the legislation in Latin American countries, much less now with the economic and political crisis that has followed the pandemic by COVID-19, generating a climate in which various initiatives do not progress or remain in the legislative pipeline. In addition, most of the countries within the Latin American context retain a stigmatizing vision regarding the decision-making that someone with psychosocial or intellectual disabilities may have, rarefying the climate in which these new legal instruments can be applied.

In interdiction, although the right path is to repeal and eradicate it from the language of civil and family law (Espejo Yaksic 2021; Ministerio de Planificación Nacional y Política Económica 2020; Ministerio de Justicia y del Derecho 2019), clear adjustments are needed as advance directives and reasonable adjustments that can be exercised efficiently. Within the labor and financial institutions, through the property and notary institutions, the practices fail to be regulated leading to this civil death sentence in the face of a protectionist vision. Fortunately, this concept has made greater progress in Latin America in terms of its repeal, which leaves room to generate reasonable adjustments so that legal capacity can operate although there is still a long way to go in this aspect.

Involuntary commitment is a particularly complicated issue not only for its control or elimination, but also for the complexity of establishing it clearly, that is to say; in Latin America, a person with a medical emergency, whether psychiatric or not, requires a legal framework capable of providing access to the right to health, either voluntarily or temporarily involuntary, which, given the interpretation of the UN Committee on Article 12 is challenging (Organización de las Naciones Unidas 2007). Involuntary commitment must have clearly established safeguards and with the possibility of advance directives, since in the case of not being able to attain informed consent of a person with a medical or psychiatric medical emergency, they would be left devoid of access to health care. Unfortunately, in many countries the vision is dichotomous regarding the elimination of involuntary treatment. Therefore, in this case, the reforms in the different Latin American countries have fallen short (Cámara de Diputados 2022) or even hinder access to proper care (Ainzenberg and Reyes 2009). There has to be a legal framework that allows care in case of a psychiatric medical emergency, which may be a brief involuntary commitment with strong safeguards, as the last resort.

Moreover, the stigma that prevails in the rest of medical specialties, makes it impossible to provide adequate care in general hospitals as is the objective. In view of this situation, actions and budget are required to train first contact physicians, to have psychiatric beds in general hospitals and to build the appropriate legal scaffolding to eradicate the abuse of this concept (Siebenförcher et al. 2020).

Finally, the not guilty by reason of insanity defense is the concept that has the least progress in Latin America, generating a series of difficulties for its implementation by the authorities and mental health experts, leading to the deprivation of liberty and other human rights abuses of people with psychosocial or intellectual disabilities (DOCUMENTA 2019; Cortés 2019). That is why, in the case of the not guilty by reason of insanity defense, rather than eliminating this concept, a clear and adequate definition must be generated. It requires an adequate deconstruction in order to clarify, based on evidence, that the presence of a psychosocial or intellectual disability is not directly proportional to the idea of not guilty by reason of insanity defense. A case in point is what we established in the analysis of the paraphilic disorders of ICD-11 (Martínez-López et al. 2019) and its landing in the context of Mexico, clearly establishing that it is not comparable to suffer a paraphilic disorder with the concept of not guilty by reason of insanity defense. Cognitive capacity may be transiently altered in some mental disorders and that it is the work of the expert and the need of the law to establish the trajectories to follow in the face of a need for access to justice and participation in the trial with reasonable adjustments such as urgent interventions of internment and upon resolution of the crisis to continue the trial (Martínez-López et al. 2020).

In conclusion, in Latin America and in the face of the current global economic and political crisis, the outlook for reforms for the adequate application of the convention is still an evolving process. A beginning has been made but there is a long way to go.

References

Ainzenberg M, Reyes R (2009) El reconocimiento del derecho a la Autodeterminación en el Ordenamiento. Jurídico Argentino: La consagración de las Directivas Médicas Anticipadas en la Ley 26.529. Buenos Aires. http://www.derecho.uba.ar/extension/dma_msa_rdr.pdf.

Asamblea Nacional República del Ecuador (2014) Código Orgánico Integral Penal. Ecuador. https://www.asambleanacional.gob.ec/es/system/files/document.pdf.

Banco Mundial (2021). https://documents1.worldbank.org/curated/en/099140012012142009/pdf/P1753830860ccc05c0a4400a141537f3421.pdf. Accessed 17 Sept 2022.

Bustamanete Donoso J, Cavieres Fernández A (2018) Internación psiquiátrica involuntaria. Antecedentes, reflexiones y desafíos. Revista Médica de Chile 146:511–517

Cámara de Diputados (2022) Proyecto de dictamen de la minuta con proyecto de decreto que reforma, adiciona y deroga diversas disposiciones de la Ley General de Salud, en materia de Salud Mental y Adicciones. http://sil.gobernacion.gob.mx/Archivos/Documentos/2022/03/asun_4342261_20220324_1648136647.pdf.

Chirino L, Giménez M (2019) Criminal conduct and its relation to imputability as an element of crime. Iustitia Socialis. Revista Arbitrada de Ciencias Jurídicas 4(6):28

Chunga Castro KM (2021) El internamiento y la hospitalización involuntaria de personas con discapacidad psicosocial en el ordenamiento jurídico peruano. [Tesis de licenciatura] Pontificia Universidad Católica del Perú.

Comisión de Derechos Humanos del Distrito Federal (2008) Informe especial sobre la situación de los derechos humanos de las personas con discapacidad en el Distrito Federal 2007–2008. México. https://cdhcm.org.mx/wp-content/uploads/2014/02/informe-personas-con-discapacidad.pdf

Comisión Interamericana de Derechos Humanos (2014). https://www.documenta.org.mx/wp-content/uploads/2020/04/Informe-sobre-la-situacio%CC%81n-de-los-derechos-de-las-PcD-en-AL-2014.pdf. Accessed 17 Sept 2022.

Comisión Nacional Asesora para la Integración de Personas Discapacitadas (2010) Convención sobre los derechos de las personas con discapacidad. Primer Informe. https://www.uba.ar/download/extension/discapacidad/convenciondiscapacidad.pdf. Accessed 18 Aug 2022.

Comisión Nacional de Derechos Humanos (2014). http://www.pudh.unam.mx/perseo/reforma-constitucional-de-derechos-humanos-hacia-un-nuevo-derecho-en-mexico/. Accessed 22 Aug 2022.

Comisión Presidencial coordinadora de la Política del Ejecutivo en materia de Derechos Humanos (2011). https://www.corteidh.or.cr/tablas/28147.pdf. Accessed 9 Sept 2022.

Consejo nacional de Igualdad de Discapacidades (2014) Normas Jurídicas en Discapacidad. CONADIS, Ecuador. https://www.consejodiscapacidades.gob.ec/wp-content/uploads/downloads/2014/08/Libro-Normas-Jur%C3%ADdicas-en-DIscapacidad-Ecuador.pdf.

Consejo Nacional para Prevenir la Discriminación (2013). https://www.conapred.org.mx/userfiles/files/LSD_IV_CapacidadJuridica_INACCSS.pdf. Accessed 25 Aug 2022.

Organización de las Naciones Unidas (2007) Convención sobre los Derechos de las Personas con Discapacidad y su protocolo facultativo. https://www.un.org/disabilities/documents/convention/convoptprot-s.pdf

Cordero Oropeza M, Robles R, Berenzon S, Medina-Mora ME (2021) Community-based mental health services in Mexico. Consortium Psychiatricum 2(3):53–62

Cortés AL (2019). https://www.funcionpublica.gov.co/eva/gestornormativo/norma.php?i=99712. Accessed 13 Sept 2022.

Da Silva Fontes R, Da Silva A (2019) Directivas anticipadas de voluntad: recorrido histórico en América Latina. Bioética 27:–91

Dhanda A (2009) Constructing a new human rights lexicon: convention on the rights of persons with disabilities. Int J Human Rights 5(8):43–60

Diario de la Federación (2016) Ley Nacional de Ejecución Penal. México. https://www.diputados.gob.mx/LeyesBiblio/ref/lnep.htm.

DOCUMENTA (2019) Guía de principios de actuación para garantizar el acceso a la justicia de las personas con discapacidad. Agencia de los Estados Unidos para el Desarrollo Internacional (USAID). Available at: https://www.documenta.org.mx/wp-content/uploads/2020/04/Gui%CC%81a-de-acceso-a-la-justicia-de-PcD.pdf.

El Congreso de la República (2018) Publican Decreto Legislativo 1384 que reconoce plena capacidad jurídica en las personas con discapacidad y elimina la interdicción. https://www.gob.pe/institucion/conadis/noticias/21984-publican-decreto-legislativo-1384-que-reconoce-plena-capacidad-juridica-en-las-personas-con-discapacidad-y-elimina-la-interdiccion. Accessed Sept 2022.

Espejo Yaksic N (2021). La capacidad jurídica para las personas con discapacidad en América Latina: avances legislativos y jurisprudenciales. Eurosocial. [Online] Available at: https://eurosocial.eu/bitacora/la-capacidad-juridica-para-las-personas-con-discapacidad-en-america-latina-avances-legislativos-y-jurisprudenciales/. Accessed 13 Sept 2022.

Figueroa San Martín F (2017a) Internamientos involuntarios y tratamientos forzados en psiquiatría: Autonomía y no discriminación como estándar de derechos humanos. Anuario de Derechos Humanos 13:111–121

Figueroa San Martín F (2017b) Voces de usuarios y sobrevivientes de la psiquiatría contenidas en la convención sobre los derechos de las personas con discapacidad: un nuevo paradigma abre camino en Chile. Revista Latinoamericana en Discapacidad, Sociedad y Derechos Humanos 1:123–142

Friend Macías R, Álava Díaz M (2019) La capacidad jurídica de los discapacitafos intelectuales y sus derechos como consumidores en Ecuador según la Cnvención de los Derechos de las Personas con Discapacidad. USFQ Law Rev 6(1):131–146

Gobierno de Chile (2016) Ley de Derechos y Deberes del paciente. N° 20.584. Superintendencia de Salud. Chile. Available at: https://www.ssmso.cl/tmpArchivos/participacion/Escuelas/Leyes/Ley%20de%20Derechos%20y%20Deberes%20de%20los%20pacientes%20Superintendencia%20de%20Salud.pdf

Gómez Mendiola M (2020) Revisión Sistemática: Trastornos mentales en personas declaradas inimputables. [Tesis de licenciatura]. Universidad Nacional Autónoma de México

González Alcántara JL, Von Aguilar L (2020) El Estado de Interdiccón en México. Esbozos metodológicos en su declaración. In: Salud Mental Forense. Tirant Lo Blanch, México, pp 65–83

Gutiérrez Luna M (2009) Internamiento involuntario de incapaces. Circunvalación del Hipocampo 1:1

Hegglin MF (2017) Las medidas de seguridad en el sistema penal argentino: su contradicción con principios fundamentales del Derecho Penal y de la Convención sobre los Derechos de las Personas con Discapacidad. In: Inimputabilidad y medidas de seguridad: reflexiones sobre América Latina en torno a los derechos de las personas con discapacidad. UBIJUS, México, pp 15–20

Hernández Arguedas F (2015) La imputabilidad e inimputabilidad desde el punto de vista médico legal. Medicina Legal de Costa Rica 32(2):83–97

Instituto de Democracia y Derechos Humanos de la Pontificia Universidad Católica del Perú (2012). https://idehpucp.pucp.edu.pe/images/publicaciones/manual_salud_mental02.pdf. Accessed 6 Sept 2022.

Instituto de Investigaciones Jurídicas (1982) Diccionario Jurídico Mexicano., Tomo V. Universidad Nacional Autónoma de México, México

Lara CR (2015) Legal interdiction, models of disability regulation and "interpretation in conformity": a victim case. Isonomía 42:171–196

López F, Mercurio E, Silva D (2017). https://salud.gob.ar/dels/entradas/consentimiento-informado-y-autonomia-en-salud-mental. Accessed 3 Sept 2022.

Martínez-López JN et al (2019) Legal and policy implications in Mexico of changes in ICD-11 paraphilic disorders. J Sex Med 16(10):1623–1637

Martínez-López JN et al (2020) Reconceptualización de la inimputabilidad. In: Martínez-López JN (ed) Salud Mental Forense. Tirant Lo Blanch, México, pp 445–456

Ministerio de Justicia y del Derecho (2019). LEY 1996 DE 2019. Available at: https://www.minjusticia.gov.co/programas-co/conexion-justicia/Documents/LineamientosGuiasDocumentos/LEY%201996%20DE%202019_I.pdf. Accessed 19 Aug 2022.

Ministerio de Planificación Nacional y Política Económica (2020). https://www.mideplan.go.cr/mideplan-evalua-el-programa-promocion-de-la-autonomia-personal-para-personas-con-discapacidad#:~:text=Este%20programa%20busca%20contribuir%20para,y%20ejecutar%20sus%20propias%20decisiones. Accessed 7 Sept 2022.

Ministerio de Salud (2013). Ley Nacional de Salud Mental N° 26.657. Decreto Reglamentario 603/2013. http://iah.salud.gob.ar/doc/Documento224.pdf. Accessed 15 Sept 2022.

Naciones Unidas (2011). https://acnudh.org/wp-content/uploads/2010/12/Foll-Discapacidad-ESP.pdf. Accessed 12 Sept 2022.

Nasimba Loachamin R (2017) El derecho a la libertad y la seguridad de las personas con discapacidad. Defensoría del Pueblo de Ecuador. Available at: https://repositorio.dpe.gob.ec/bitstream/39000/2171/1/DEOI-DPE-011-2017.pdf.

Navas Agudelo N (2020). https://lozanovila.com/el-fin-de-la-interdiccion-en-colombia-de-un-proceso-inconveniente-a-un-regimen-incierto/. Accessed 10 Sept 2022.

Secretaría de Salud (2015). NOM-025-SSA2-2014: Para la prestación de servicios de salud en unidades de atención integral hospitalaria médico-psiquiátrica. México.

Organización Internacional del Trabajo (2021). http://www.businessanddisability.org/es/news/nueva-ley-promueve-la-inclusion-laboral-de-las-personas-con-discapacidad/. Accessed 25 Aug 2022.

Pontificia Universidad Católica del Perú (2014). https://idehpucp.pucp.edu.pe/opinion_1/inimputabilidad-e-impunidad-a-proposito-de-la-ley-n-30151/. Accessed 20 Sept 2022.

Rajmil AB, Llorens LR (2015) Apuntes acerca del régimen de capacidad de las personas humanas en el Código Civil y Comercial de la República Argentina (Ley 26.994). IUS 9(36):89–117

Rodríguez Vásquez J (2016) Internamiento e inimputabilidad en el derecho penal peruano: statu quo y crítica. Ministerio Público de la Nación 11:149–161

Siebenförcher M et al (2020) Psychiatric beds and prison populations in 17 Latin American countries between 1991 and 2017: rates, trends and an inverse relationship between the two indicators. Psychol Med 5(52):936–945

Stang Alva MF (2011). https://repositorio.cepal.org/bitstream/handle/11362/7135/1/S1100074_es.pdf. Accessed 12 Sept 2022.

Suprema Corte de Justicia de la Nación (2014) Protocolo de Actuación para quienes imparten Justicia en casos que involucren Derechos de personas con discapacidad. México. Available at: https://www.scjn.gob.mx/registro/sites/default/files/page/2020-02/protocolo_discapacidad.pdf.

Suprema Corte de Justicia de la Nación (2022). https://www.scjn.gob.mx/derechos-humanos/sites/default/files/Publicaciones/archivos/2022-08/CAPACIDAD%20JURI%CC%81DICA%20DIGITAL_3a%20vuelta%20y%20presentacio%CC%81n.pdf. Accessed 28 Aug 2022.

Treviño Barrios S (2020). https://www.sitios.scjn.gob.mx/cec/blog-cec/la-interdiccion-un-acto-prohibido-por-el-articulo-22-constitucional. Accessed 5 Sept 2022.

Tribunal Constitucional (2009). Sentencia num 05842-2006.[Online]. Available at: https://tc.gob.pe/jurisprudencia/2009/05842-2006-HC.pdf.

Lizama & Sheinbaum (2019) Protocolo de atención a personas con discapacidad intelectual y psicosocial. Tribunal Superior de Justicia de la Ciudad de México. Available at: https://www.documenta.org.mx/wp-content/uploads/2020/09/Protocolo-de-atenci%C3%B3n-a-personas-con-discapacidad.pdf.

Vega C, Bañón R, Fajardo A. (2010) Internamientos psiquiátricos. Aspectos medicolegales. Atencion primaria 42(3):176–182. https://doi.org/10.1016/j.aprim.2009.07.012

Von Aguilar L, Martínez López JN (2020) Internamiento Involuntario en México. In: Salud Mental Forense. Tirant Lo Blanch, México, pp 143–149

Yo También. Discapacidad con todas sus letras (2022). https://www.yotambien.mx/actualidad/parlamento-de-las-personas-con-discapacidad-2022-aprueba-propuesta-para-eliminar-interdiccion-del-codigo-civil-de-la-cdmx/#:~:text=El%20Parlamento%20de%20las%20Personas,C%C3%B3digo%20Civil%20de%20la%20CDMX&text=En%20vez. Accessed 20 Sept 2022.

Scotland: CRPD and Mental Health Legislation

11

Jill Stavert

Contents

11.1 Introduction

The UN Convention on the Rights of Persons with Disabilities 2006 (CRPD) challenges previous human rights approaches to interventions involving persons with mental disability (meaning psychosocial, cognitive, and intellectual disability) (Minkowitz 2017; Clough 2018; Stavert 2018). Importantly, the CRPD requires states proactively ensure that persons with disabilities are able to enjoy rights on an equal basis with others without disabilities (Stavert 2021). The message is that through support where this is required [e.g. support for the exercise of legal capacity ('supported decision making')][1] a level playing field is created so that persons with mental disabilities are able to enjoy rights on an equal basis, either fully or as restricted as others.

The CRPD approach particularly challenges the foundations of mental health legislation. Traditionally, such legislation has tended to focus on the authorisation and regulation of non-consensual psychiatric detention and treatment based on diagnosis and little else. It often fails to consider the wider needs of per-

J. Stavert (✉)
Centre for Mental Health and Capacity Law, Centre for Mental Health Practice, Policy and Law Research, School of Health and Social Care, Edinburgh Napier University, Edinburgh, Scotland, UK
e-mail: j.stavert@napier.ac.uk

[1] Article 12 CRPD.

N. Gill, N. Sartorius (eds.), *Mental Health and Human Rights*, Sustainable Development Goals Series, https://doi.org/10.1007/978-3-031-52179-9_11

sons with mental disabilities. The Committee on the Rights of Persons with Disabilities (the CRPD Committee) in interpreting the CRPD has stated that non-consensual psychiatric measures reinforce inequalities in rights enjoyment for persons with mental disability by allowing their rights to liberty and autonomy to be disproportionately limited in a way that does not apply to those without mental disability (Committee on the Rights of Persons with Disabilities 2014, 2015). The CRPD also requires that states look beyond respecting only the civil rights associated with regulating the use of non-consensual interventions to the whole range of a person's human rights which includes their economic, social, and cultural rights that support their wider needs (Stavert and McGregor 2018).

Any state seeking to achieve CRPD compliance in relation to mental health care and treatment must therefore take these considerations into account. An illustration of the enormity of the challenge faced by states can be seen in relation to Articles 12 and 14 CRPD requirements which seek to address the inequalities mentioned above. Article 12(2) CRPD identifies the right to exercise legal capacity on an equal basis with others in all aspects of life. Articles 12(3) and 12(4) require that such equality is achieved through states providing access to appropriate supported decision-making to overcome difficulties with making and communicating decisions. This must be accompanied by safeguards to ensure that the person's rights, will, and preferences are enjoyed equally with others. Article 14 requires that persons with mental disabilities are only deprived of their liberty on the same basis with others. The CRPD Committee has stated that mental health laws which single out persons with mental disability for detention and non-consensual psychiatric treatment are discriminatory and must therefore be abolished and replaced by supported decision-making measures (Committee on the Rights of Persons with Disabilities 2014, 2015). Considerable debate exists as to whether such a proposition should be adopted in its entirety (Martin et al. 2014, 2016; Freeman et al. 2015; Wilson 2022)[2] but the fact remains that CRPD state parties must be mindful of their obligation to give effect to the rights identified in the treaty.

This chapter will focus on the compatibility of existing mental health legislation in Scotland with the CRPD and what is required to bring about CRPD alignment. This is something which has been extensively considered by a recent legislative review which will also be discussed. There will also be a brief consideration of other English-speaking jurisdictions which wholly or partially follow the United Kingdom (UK) legal tradition, all of which have also undergone recent legislative reviews requiring thought to be given to CRPD compliance. However, in order to provide Scotland's mental health law in its constitutional framework such framework will first be described.

11.2 Scotland's Legislative and Human Rights Framework

11.2.1 Scotland and the European Convention on Human rights (ECHR)

In Scotland (a devolved regional within the UK), mental health policy and legislation competence is devolved to the Scottish Government and Scottish Parliament, respectively, and its content, interpretation, and implementation must be in accordance with European Convention on Human Rights (ECHR).[3] If an individual's ECHR rights

[2] Indeed, not all UN treaty bodies fully agree with radical approach of the CRPD Committee. See, for example, UN Human Rights Committee (2014) General Comment 35 Article 9 (Liberty and Security of the Person) CCPR/C/GC/35 and Subcommittee on Prevention of Torture and Other Cruel, Inhuman or Degrading Treatment or Punishment (2016) *Approach of the Subcommittee on Prevention of Torture and Other Cruel, Inhuman or Degrading Treatment or Punishment regarding the rights of persons institutionalized and treated medically without informed consent* CAT/OP/27/2.

[3] ss 2, 3, and 6 Human Rights Act 1998; ss 29(2) and 57(2) Scotland Act 1998.

are violated, then these rights may be enforced through Scottish courts and tribunals.

This is somewhat different to UK-wide legislation[4] where the law and its implementation must, so far as it is possible, be ECHR compliant. Any incompatibility in its legislative content simply results in a court making a 'declaration of incompatibility' and it is in the discretion of the UK Government and Parliament whether or not to remedy this.[5]

The ECHR therefore strongly influenced the principles and criteria governing decisions about non-consensual interventions under the Mental Health (Care and Treatment) (Scotland) Act 2003 (Mental Health Act). However, the UK ratified the CRPD in 2009 which required a reconceptualisation of traditional approaches to the rights of persons with mental disability (Minkowitz 2017; Clough 2018). This has the potential to significantly change the nature and form of mental health law in Scotland, as indeed it does in any jurisdiction that is a CRPD state party (Stavert 2018, 2021).

11.2.2 Scotland and the CRPD

CRPD state parties are required to give effect to the rights identified in the treaty nationally. For individuals to be able to legally enforce the human rights in a particular treaty across the UK, however, there must also be enabling legislation. Whilst the Human Rights Act 1998 achieves this for the ECHR this is not the case for the CRPD. That being said, devolved legislation and Scottish Ministers' actions should not place the UK in breach of its CRPD obligations.[6]

The CRPD also has indirect effect in Scotland. Across the UK, the case law of its courts either dictates or is highly influential in interpreting legislative provisions. The ECHR, in turn, must be interpreted by UK courts and tribunals in accordance with the case law of the European Court of Human Rights which should take account of the CRPD, as a higher source of international law, when interpreting ECHR rights (although there has been little evidence of this). However, this lack of enforceability of CRPD rights does not mean that the treaty has been invisible in Scotland. Indeed, it has been visible for several years. Importantly, CRPD compliance was an integral component of the 2019–2022 Scottish Mental Health Law Review (Scottish Mental Health Law Review (Scott Review) 2022) and the 2018–2019 Independent Review of Learning Disability and Autism in the Mental Health Act (Rome Review) (2019). Moreover, the Scottish Government confirmed in 2021 that it would give effect to the recommendation of its National Taskforce for Human Rights Leadership (National Taskforce for Human Rights Leadership 2021; Scottish Government 2023) that, along with other international human rights treaties, the CRPD would be given legal effect in Scotland. Although the nature and extent of this incorporation is yet to be determined, this is likely to ensure that CRPD rights will be, at least to some degree, enforceable through Scottish courts and tribunals in the future.

However, despite the apparent visibility of the CRPD in Scotland and its perceived potential, existing mental health legislation falls somewhat short of its requirements.[7]

11.2.3 Scotland's Existing Mental Health Legislation

The Mental Health Act authorises and regulates the use of civil non-consensual measures relating to persons with 'mental disorder' defined as persons with mental illness, personality disorder and learning disability.[8] It also regulates the treatment

[4]In other words, legislation made by the UK Parliament which applies to England, Wales, Scotland, and Northern Ireland.

[5]s 4 Human Rights Act 1998.

[6]ss 35(1) and 58(1) Scotland Act 1998.

[7]This chapter focuses on mental health legislation in Scotland, but it should be noted that treatment for 'mental disorder' may also occur, subject to certain conditions and safeguards, under the Adults with Incapacity (Scotland) Act 2000.

[8]Section 328 Mental Health Act.

of 'mentally disordered offenders' although this chapter will focus on civil compulsory psychiatric care and treatment.

The Act is underpinned by ECHR informed principles,[9] which must be followed when considering whether compulsory psychiatric treatment is appropriate and implementing such treatment. These principles require respect for the individual's wishes and feelings and emphasise the importance of the individual's participation in care and treatment decisions. Elsewhere in the Act, supports for such participation are recognised in the form of advance statements[10] and independent advocacy.[11] Advance statements setting out a person's wishes about their treatment (including refusal of it) must be made where a person has capacity and come into effect when they lack capacity to communicate these wishes. Clinicians and the Mental Health Tribunal must have regard to such wishes, but these wishes may be overridden albeit subject to certain criteria. A duty is placed on local authorities and health boards to provide access to independent advocacy for anyone with a 'mental disorder' whether or not they are subject to compulsory measures.

The principles also include that there is consideration of the range of options available, that any adopted measure is the least restrictive in the circumstances and provides maximum benefit to that person. Non-discrimination and respect for diversity are also required as well as an obligation on health and social care authorities to provide suitable care and support for those subject to compulsion (the reciprocity principle).

The Mental Health Act principles are supplemented by criteria which must be applied before shorter term measures, such as emergency detention (of up to 72 h) or short-term detention,[12] are authorised. These are the existence of 'mental disorder', 'significantly impaired decision-making ability', the necessity for the measure and the presence of a significant risk either to the person or to others are essential requisites. The significantly impaired decision-making ability requirement is a 'capacity test' which is limited to decisions about psychiatric care and treatment and must be a direct consequence of the individual's mental disorder. Almost identical criteria also apply to Compulsory Treatment Orders,[13] which are longer term measures and granted and periodically reviewed, or compulsory measures appealed, by the Mental Health Tribunal for Scotland.

The fact that these principles and criteria were largely informed by the ECHR is not surprising given the treaty's incorporation into the UK and Scottish legal framework at the time of the Act's enactment.[14] As already stated, however, their CRPD alignment is limited.

11.2.4 Reflecting the CRPD in Current Mental Health Law and Practice

For the CRPD to be given real effect in mental health law and its implementation for persons with mental disabilities certain characteristics are essential, and these are:

1. Equality and non-discrimination in the enjoyment and restriction of rights for persons with mental disabilities. This allows access to support and services for persons with mental disabilities on the same basis as others and not restricted on the basis of diagnosis of mental disability or related impairment.
2. Accessible support to ensure equal rights enjoyment. Such support must include supported decision-making to ensure that the person's will and preferences are prioritised on the same basis as others.

[9] ss 1 and 2 Mental Health Act.

[10] ss 275–276C Mental Health Act.

[11] ss 259–259A Mental Health Act.

[12] ss 36(4)–(5) and 44(4) Mental Health Act.

[13] s 64(5) Mental Health Act.

[14] Indeed, there were no judicial findings of ECHR incompatibility of any Mental Health Act provisions until 2022 when the Court of Session for the first time held in *X v Mental Health Tribunal for Scotland* (2022) CSOH 78 that an aspect of the Act's different treatment of civil and forensic patients was discriminatory therefore violating forensic patients' rights to liberty and autonomy (Articles 14, 5 and 8 ECHR).

The term 'supported decision-making' has been interpreted in different ways (Martin et al. 2016). In the CRPD context, it means enabling persons with mental disabilities to make and see through their own decisions as others without disabilities are able to (Committee on the Rights of Persons with Disabilities 2014).

3. Consideration and availability of alternatives to non-consensual psychiatric care and treatment.
4. Enforceable civil, political, economic, social, and cultural rights.

For states who are also parties to the ECHR another consideration is the interaction between the arguably different approaches of the ECHR and CRPD in the context of mental health interventions. This different approach will be discussed later in relation to deprivation of liberty.

Whether the equality, supported decision-making and alternatives to coercion requirements can be fully achieved in the absence of a total abolition of psychiatric coercion, as required by the CRPD Committee, is a matter of ongoing debate. However, CRPD compliance does require these issues to be addressed and were all issues which the Scottish Mental Health Law Review was required to actively engage with.

11.3 The Mental Health Act and CRPD Rights Realisation

The Mental Health Act perpetuates the discrimination which the CRPD seeks to eschew by singling out those with a diagnosis of 'mental disorder' for compulsion. Its principles are non-hierarchical and the requirement to have regard to the person's wishes and feelings is therefore only one of a number of competing principles. The advance statements and independent advocacy provisions were strengthened in 2015 mainly in terms of recording and/or monitoring compliance.[15] However, wishes expressed in advance statements may, as already mentioned, be overridden and independent advocacy is woefully under-resourced (Scottish Mental Health Law Review (Scott Review) 2022).

The Act's focus on authorising compulsory psychiatric treatment also fails to address the wider needs of persons with mental disabilities. There is scant reference to the support and services which are essential to achieving the highest attainable standard of physical and mental health or independent living and no enforceable duties on state bodies to give effect to the underpinning social, economic, and cultural rights that enable this. For example, the Act requires local authorities to provide care and support services, services to promote wellbeing and social development and transport assistance in the absence of a specific enforcement mechanism underpinning such duties.[16]

11.3.1 The Scottish Mental Health Law Review (The Scott Review)

When originally enacted the Mental Health Act was regarded as world-leading in terms of its human rights-based approach to psychiatric care and treatment (Fischer 2006). However, over time it became clear that it was not fully meeting the needs and respecting all the rights of persons with mental disabilities (McKay and Stavert 2017). Developments in ECHR case law have reinforced the need to respect individual autonomy and, as already stated, the CRPD requirements go even further than this (Committee on the Rights of Persons with Disabilities 2014, 2015; Stavert 2021). In addition, despite the Act's principles being designed to promote autonomy, detention under it has been increasing (Mental Welfare Commission for Scotland 2021, 2022) although the reasons for this are currently unclear.[17] A re-evaluation of the Act was there-

[15] Mental Health (Scotland) Act 2015 amending the Mental Health Act.

[16] ss 25–27 Mental Health Act.

[17] Whilst the 2021/2022 report noted some decrease in Mental Health Act detentions it is uncertain at this stage whether this represents an end to what has been a yearly increase in such detention.

fore necessary. The Rome Review (2018–2019) considered whether persons with learning disabilities and with autism, as life-long conditions which are not of themselves susceptible to psychiatric treatment, should remain within the Act's definition of 'mental disorder'. However, in May 2019 the Scottish Minister for Mental Health established the Scottish Mental Health Law Review (the Scott Review)[18] which was a much more comprehensive review of the mental health, incapacity, and adult support and protection legislation.

The Scott Review's terms of reference included, importantly, consideration of how to give effect to the CRPD. It reported in September 2022 and most of its recommendations were directed towards greater CRPD alignment (Scottish Mental Health Law Review (Scott Review) 2022).[19]

11.3.1.1 Key Themes of the Final Report of the Scott Review

After extensive engagement with stakeholder groups, particularly those representing persons with lived experience of mental disability and their unpaid carers but also including practitioners, advocacy, and those in judicial and regulatory and monitoring roles, the Scott Review final report's recommendations fall under three key themes (Scottish Mental Health Law Review (Scott Review) 2022):

1. Strengthening the voice of people who use services and those who care for them.
2. Reducing the need for coercion in the system.
3. Securing rights to the help and support needed to live a good life.

These provide the basis for achieving CRPD alignment and, in pursuance of this, the report proposed a new model for mental health and capacity law, centred on the concepts of Human Rights Enablement, Supported Decision-Making, and Autonomous Decision-Making.

11.3.1.2 A Shift of Focus

The Review proposed a shift in mental health and capacity law away from a primarily focus on authorising and regulating compulsory measures which might limit a person's autonomy to law which allows for the needs of persons with mental disability to be met by ensuring that their underpinning rights are respected, protected, enabled, and fulfilled. There would be a move away from the perception of 'protection' requiring a limitation of a person's rights to one of protecting their freedom to enjoy their rights on the same basis as others.

11.3.1.3 The Purpose of Mental Health Legislation

Noting that mental health legislation needed to be supportive and meet individual needs as they arise on a non-discriminatory basis the Review recommended[20] that the:

> new purpose for mental health and capacity law should be to ensure that all the human rights of people with mental and intellectual disability (and otherwise included under [the Adults with Incapacity (Scotland) Act 2000] are respected, protected and fulfilled (Scottish Mental Health Law Review (Scott Review) 2022).

This effectively adopts the CRPD approach in Article 1 to disability:

> The purpose of the present Convention is to promote, protect and ensure the full and equal enjoyment of all human rights and fundamental freedoms by all persons with disabilities, and to promote respect for their inherent dignity.
> Persons with disabilities include those who have long-term physical, mental, intellectual or sensory impairments which in interaction with various barriers may hinder their full and effective participation in society on an equal basis with others.

11.3.1.4 Underpinning Principles

As with the existing *Mental Health Act year?*, the presence of expressly stated human rights-based legislative principles governing all support and

[18]Scottish Mental Health Law Review https://www.mentalhealthlawreview.scot/.

[19]The author was a member of the Scott Review Executive Team. However, any opinions expressed in this chapter are not necessarily attributable to the review team as a whole and remain those of the author alone.

[20]Recommendation 2.2.

intervention decisions and actions was considered by the Review to be integral to guaranteeing a human rights-based approach which incorporates the CRPD. The Review therefore recommended enhancing the *Mental Health Act* principles so that anyone discharging functions under future mental health, capacity and adult support, and protection law should have regard to the principles of dignity, inclusion, autonomy, equality, non-discrimination, respect for carers and for the rights of the child, benefit, the least restrictive alternative, and reciprocity (Scottish Mental Health Law Review (Scott Review) 2022).[21]

11.3.1.5 Thinking Beyond Civil Rights Towards Economic, Social, and Cultural Rights

Protecting an individual's civil rights may occasionally require positive action to be taken. However, generally speaking, respecting such rights normally only requires that the state avoids acting in ways that result in their violation. Ensuring economic, social, and cultural rights, on the other hand, invariably requires positive action on the part of the state, including, where necessary, sufficient allocation of resources.

Bearing in mind that resources are finite whilst at the same time acknowledging that persons with mental disabilities should not be disproportionately denied the benefit of these, the Review therefore recommended that changes to mental health law includes the establishment of minimum core obligations and progressive realisation of economic, social, and cultural rights. This is to be accompanied by clear and attributable duties on public authorities to provide or secure support and monitoring of these duties' as well as Scottish Ministers being under a duty to engage with the awareness-raising requirements of Article 8 CRPD in order to address attitudinal barriers including stigma (Scottish Mental Health Law Review (Scott Review) 2022).[22]

[21] Recommendation 3.3.

[22] Recommendations 6.1 and 6.12.

11.3.1.6 An Overriding Framework of Human Rights Enablement, Supported Decision-Making and Autonomous Decision-Making

In order to give effect to this new purpose and principles for mental health law, the Review recommended an overarching framework which encompasses Human Rights Enablement, Supported Decision-Making and Autonomous Decision-Making. It also emphasised that the development of these approaches would require sufficient resourcing by the Scottish Government, adequate training, and, importantly reflecting Article 4(3) CRPD, the active involvement of persons with lived experience in such processes.

11.3.1.7 Human Rights Enablement

The Review's recommendation (Scottish Mental Health Law Review (Scott Review) 2022)[23] that the Scottish Government should develop and adopt a Human Rights Enablement approach provides the opportunity for a person's specific and broader needs and underpinning civil, political, economic, social, and cultural rights to be considered, actioned, and protected where they come into contact with services.

Essentially, in any given situation Human Rights Enablement (a) maximises a person's ability to make autonomous decisions thus ensuring that priority is given to their will and preferences; (b) identifies what rights (meaning the full range of rights) need to be protected (including those of others); (c) balances the advantages of restricting certain human rights in order to protect the person's rights overall; and (d) allows for an action plan to achieve this to be put in place. Working in conjunction with the proposed Supported Decision-Making and Autonomous Decision-Making approaches, it would be accompanied by guidance, Codes of Practice and training. Importantly, the operation of Human Rights Enablement and Supported Decision-Making would transcend diagnosis and incapacity (or the inability to make autonomous

[23] Recommendations 8.1–8.4.

decisions) and apply at all times ensuring that the person's rights are considered and their voice heard at all times.

11.3.1.8 Supported Decision-Making

The Review identified the need for a better and common understanding of the rights and principles of Supported Decision-Making. It agreed that the purpose of such an approach would be to ensure that the person's will and preferences are heard and given effect on an equal basis with others including at times when the person is unable to express such will and preferences. It would involve not only assisting a person, where this is their wish, to make decisions but also communicating and putting into effect such decisions. It would be built into all relevant processes and training with a central point of development, promotion, and oversight, for example, this could be developed as part of the new mental health model within the National Care Service.

The types of support recommended by the Review included replacing the existing advance statement system with an advance choice document which would be more flexible and wide ranging and cover more than psychiatric care and treatment. It also recommended enhanced powers of attorney, the introduction of a Decision-Making Supporter appointed by the person, aids to communication and more widely available independent advocacy with independent advocates being trained, better funded, and subject to proper scrutiny, as well as national register established for Collective Advocacy (Scottish Mental Health Law Review (Scott Review) 2022).[24] Specialist support in legal and administrative proceedings was also recommended by the Review to ensure that people can participate as fully and meaningfully as possible in such proceedings (Scottish Mental Health Law Review (Scott Review) 2022).[25]

[24]Recommendations 4.1–4.12.

[25]Recommendations 5.1–5.7.

11.3.1.9 Reducing Psychiatric Coercion and Compulsion

The Review did not consider that there was sufficient evidence at present on alternatives to psychiatric coercion or the necessary stakeholder support in Scotland, importantly including those with lived experience of mental disability, to recommend the abolition of compulsory care and treatment at this stage although this should be the ultimate goal. However, it strongly agreed that psychiatric compulsion should be avoided where at all possible and always be a last resort, with a clearly defined pathway to reducing and eliminating psychiatric coercion and that alternatives should be actively explored and available. In this it was heavily influenced by the former United Nations Special Repporteur on the Right to Health's statement to this effect in 2017 (United Nations General Assembly 2017). It made 36 recommendations in this area requiring that active steps, led by the Scottish Government, be taken to reduce psychiatric coercion within mental health services and the wider care system including understanding the rising rates of detention (Scottish Mental Health Law Review (Scott Review) 2022).[26]

11.3.1.10 Autonomous Decision-Making

Despite the Review's decision that it was not yet the time to completely remove psychiatric compulsion, it did note the CRPD Committee's view on the use of capacity assessments and diagnosis as the threshold for involuntary interventions and the limitations of such assessments. Additionally, evidence collected by the Review confirmed widespread concerns in Scotland over the consistency, accuracy, and use of the existing capacity test under the *Mental Health Act* raising questions about whether capacity tests are the most appropriate means by which to meet the needs of persons with mental disability (Scottish Mental Health Law Review (Scott Review) 2022).

At the same time, the Review was conscious that there were several controlling influences, in

[26]Recommendations 9.1–9.36.

addition to decision-making challenges directly associated with a diagnosis of mental disability, which could prevent the making or communicating of an autonomous, or voluntary, decision-making so that it was impossible for others to know the person's authentic view. Such controlling influences might include, for example, the impact of another person or persons exerting coercive or undue influence, an illness, disability or health condition (including a health care crisis), and a situational or environmental factor or factors. It therefore recommended that the existing 'capacity' test in the Mental Health Act be replaced by an Autonomous Decision-Making test which could be used as a gateway to appropriate support and services provided either under mental health legislation or under other more appropriate policy, legislation, and services (Scottish Mental Health Law Review (Scott Review) 2022).[27]

It was proposed that Autonomous Decision-Making would work in conjunction with Supported Decision-Making and Human Rights Enablement allowing for rights to be proportionately weighed and balanced in routine and crisis situations and the person's voice to be heard and respected at all times. Importantly, the fact that a person cannot make an autonomous decision at a given time would not automatically lead to non-consensual psychiatric care and treatment being administered. This would only be the case where this was required to give the greatest effect to the person's rights overall. Moreover, whilst diagnosis will not determine whether an involuntary measure occurs, it may inform the nature of an intervention (Scottish Mental Health Law Review (Scott Review) 2022).

An Illustration of how the Review envisaged this new Human Rights Enablement, Supported Decision-Making, and Autonomous Decision-Making framework would work can be seen in the context of deprivation of liberty.

The CRPD Committee's criticism of the use of diagnosis to justify detention and other restrictions of autonomy has also been seen to be at odds with Article 5 ECHR. The reasoning behind this is that for detention to be lawful under Article 5 ECHR it must fall within one of the specified categories in Article 5(1). These exceptions include that of person being of 'unsound mind' (Article 5(1)(e) ECHR) which the 1979 *Winterwerp v the Netherlands*[28] European Court of Human Rights ruling established must be verified by objective medical evidence. Article 5(4) also requires that such detention is accompanied by regular review of the necessity for the detention and a practical and effective ability to challenge its lawfulness in a court.

The Review therefore had to attempt to reconcile the apparent inconsistency between CRPD and ECHR requirements in relation to deprivation of liberty. The need to address this issue arose primarily in Scotland as a result of the European Court of Human Rights *Bournewood*[29] and UK Supreme Court *Cheshire West*[30] rulings and in relation to persons who lack capacity who fall within the jurisdiction of the Adults with Incapacity (Scotland) Act 2000 which is currently considered sufficiently robust to protect a person's ECHR right to liberty. The Review made several recommendations in this respect (Scottish Mental Health Law Review (Scott Review) 2022).[31] It felt that the ECHR and CRPD dichotomy can be addressing through the Human Rights Enablement, Supported Decision-Making and Autonomous Decision-Making framework. This would allow for rights to be appropriately balanced in a diagnosis and disability neutral manner whilst still permitting detention when this is deemed the most appropriate means by which to protect and respect the person's overall rights and freedoms. Applying the same model to detention under the Mental Health Act would have the same effect.

[27] Recommendations 8.5–8.5.

[28] *Winterwerp v Netherlands* (6301/73) (1979) ECHR 4, para 39.

[29] *HL v UK* (45,508/99) [2004] ECHR 471.

[30] *Cheshire West and Chester Council v P* [2014] UKSC 19.

[31] Recommendations 8.9 and 8.10.

11.3.1.11 Ensuring and Enforcing CPRD Rights

Entrenching rights in legislation presents a solid means by which to ensure they are realised as this allows courts and tribunals to enforce them. However, the Review recognised that effective monitoring is also essential and therefore made recommendations that there be a comprehensive scrutiny and regulatory system for mental health legislation (Scottish Mental Health Law Review (Scott Review) 2022).[32]

The issue of allocation of finite resources when giving effect to economic, social, and cultural rights has been mentioned earlier and, as stated, the Review made the recommendations concerning core minimum standards which must be developed and applied. This was also accompanied by a recommendation strengthening 'recorded matters' which are care, treatment, or services the Mental Health Tribunal can direct as part of a Compulsory Treatment Order if it considers these to be essential to an individual's care.[33] Owing to the current difficulties in enforcing recorded matters the Review recommended that (Scottish Mental Health Law Review (Scott Review) 2022)[34] in the event of non-compliance with a recorded matter it would be empowered to direct the relevant service provider to provide such care and support within a specified time. When arriving at this decision the tribunal would be required to have due regard to the already mentioned core minimum obligations and any other relevant standards in place for the provision of mental health services, the Human Rights Enablement approach taken with the individual and the individual's wishes. The service provider would have a right of appeal against such a direction but continued non-compliance with a direction will be a breach of a statutory duty which may be referred to the Court of Session.

[32]Recommendations 11.1 11.10.

[33]S64(4)(a) *Mental Health Act*.

[34]Recommendation 11.16.

11.4 Other English-Speaking Jurisdictions

Throughout English-speaking countries mental health laws have tended to allow for compulsory psychiatric measures based on various criteria such as the presence of mental disability, risk, and/or decisional and/or functional incapacity thus presenting significant challenges for CRPD compliance, particularly Articles 5, 12, and 14. As has been the case in Scotland, in recent years many of these countries have sought to review these laws with CRPD compliance in mind, for example, all Australian states and territories have undertaken mental health legislation reviews and reforms[35] as have many Canadian provinces (Wilson 2022; Hoffman et al. 2016). Sometimes this has included considering the appropriateness of including certain categories of persons within the remit of mental health law, for instance in the case of England and Wales (UK Government (Department of Health and Social Care) 2018), Scotland (Independent Review of Learning Disability and Autism in the Mental Health Act (Rome Review) 2019; Scottish Mental Health Law Review (Scott Review) 2022), and New Zealand[36] relating to persons with intellectual disability. However, it appears that whilst most have recommended and/or sought to improve safeguards for individual autonomy, increase support, introduce forms of supported decision-making, and reduce psychiatric coercion none have completely abolished compulsory psychiatric care and treatment (Wilson 2022). Indeed, Canada and Australia, and other states, have made declarations that they do not interpret the CRPD as requiring such abolition. It has also

[35]For example, Mental Health Act 2013 (Tas), Mental Health Act 2014 (Vic) to be replaced by the recently enacted Mental Health and Wellbeing Act 2022; Mental Health Act 2014 (WA), Mental Health Act 2015 (ACT), Mental Health Act 2016 (Qld), Mental Health Amendment (Statutory Review Act) 2014 (NSW) and Mental Health (Review) Amendment Act (SA).

[36]The CRPD compatibility of New Zealand's Mental Health (Compulsory Assessment and Treatment Act) 1992 was reviewed as part of its Disability Action Plan 2014–2018.

been suggested that the UK did not make a similar declaration out of a belief that this was unnecessary to achieve the CRPD alignment (Donnelly 2010).

Scotland is a jurisdiction within the UK and in recent years, England and Wales and Northern Ireland (other parts of the UK) have undergone reviews of their own mental health law although neither of these have gone as far as the Scott Review recommendations in terms of giving effect to the CRPD.

The Mental Health Act 1983 in England and Wales underwent review (the Wessely Review) which reported in December 2018 (UK Government (Department of Health and Social Care) 2018). Although it advocated better tailored support and services, greater respect for individual autonomy and noted the CRPD's qualities it explicitly stated that it was not recommending fully implementing the CRPD and it disagreed with the CRPD Committee's requirement to abolish mental health legislation (UK Government (Department of Health and Social Care) 2018). It is also clear that the resultant Mental Health Bill,[37] progress of which has stalled (UK Parliament 2023; UK Government (Department of Health and Social Care 2024), whilst seeking greater ECHR alignment has little CPRD focus and merely seeks to achieve its objectives within the perimeters of traditional mental health legislation and substitute decision-making.

In Northern Ireland, the Bamford Review of Mental Health and Learning Disability (2002–2007) resulted in the enactment of the Mental Capacity Act (Northern Ireland) 2016 which was the first of its kind in the world in that it unified mental health and mental capacity legislation. The review considered that the presence of mental disability should not automatically lead to an assumption that a person lacks capacity and therefore denying a person with capacity the right to refuse treatment for physical or mental health conditions is unjust (Bamford Review (The) of Mental Health and Learning Disability (Northern Ireland) 2007).[38] Although the review's final report preceded the UK's ratification of the CRPD this notion of non-discrimination nevertheless adopts the CRPD approach. However, whilst the Mental Capacity Act (Northern Ireland) 2016 does not use the term 'mental disorder', unlike the Scott Review recommendations, it focuses on an absence of capacity as the threshold to interventions.[39] The Act also does not seek to provide a mechanism to ensure the realisation of economic, social, and cultural rights enforceable.

11.5 Conclusion

Recent reforms in English-speaking jurisdictions have sought to bring mental health law closer to CRPD requirements although not to completely abolish psychiatric compulsion as required by the CRPD Committee. The focus in this chapter on existing mental health legislation and its review in Scotland illustrates the challenges which many states face in bringing about CRPD alignment whether or not abolition of psychiatric compulsion is ultimately to be achieved. That is not to say, however, that the CPRD cannot be used within the limitations of the Mental Health Act to at least further enhance the autonomy and choices of persons with mental disabilities. Indeed, as stated, there is already evidence of practice attempting to align with its direction on the support for the exercise of legal capacity (Mental Welfare Commission for Scotland 2020) and policy around economic, social, and cultural rights (Scottish Government 2022).

The Scott Review's recommendations are far reaching and aspirational and offer a roadmap to full CRPD realisation. Cultural, environmental,

[37] UK Parliament, Draft Mental Health Bill, *https://www.parliament.uk/business/bills-and-legislation/draft-bills/*.

[38] In this it was influenced by the rulings in *Re T (Adult: Refusal of Treatment)* [1993] Fam 95 and *Re C (Adult: Refusal of Treatment)* [1994] 1 All ER 819.

[39] S 3 *Mental Capacity Act Northern Ireland 2016* states that a person lacks capacity where there is 'an impairment of, or a disturbance in the functioning of, the mind or brain' whatever the cause, whether permanent or temporary, and whether or not caused by a disorder or disability.

and institutional changes and adequate resourcing will of course, and importantly, have to accompany any legislative change established to give effect to these fundamental CRPD elements in order to secure its success. Clarity is also required around certain issues, such as how is it possible to ascertain with as much certainty as possible what are a person's authentic wishes at any given time, what works to reduce psychiatric coercion and what exactly are core minimum standards requirements which every person, including persons with mental disabilities, should be entitled to expect. The key themes identified in the report will therefore need to be developed and taken forward with full and equal participation of people with lived experience of mental or intellectual disability, including unpaid carers.[40] These are all things acknowledged by the Review (Scottish Mental Health Law Review (Scott Review) 2022).[41]

The Scottish Government responded in June to the Scott Review's final report. It broadly accepted the Review's recommendations and announced a programme of reform of mental health and capacity law over the next 6-10 years which will prioritise adults with incapacity law reform, supported decision-making, mental health law reform, human rights enablement, enhancing carers' rights and role, reducing coercion across the system and strengthening and scrutiny across the mental health system (Scottish Government 2023). However, at this stage it is not possible to know with any certainty the extent to which mental health law going forward will reflect CRPD standards although the Scottish Government's stated commitment, more broadly, to give legal effect to this treaty through wider human rights legislation within Scotland is encouraging. However, the role of legislation as a supporter and driver of change designed to improve the enjoyment of rights and lives of persons with mental disabilities is unquestionable.

[40] Article 4(3) CRPD states:

In the development and implementation of legislation and policies to implement the present Convention, and in other decision-making processes concerning issues relating to persons with disabilities, States Parties shall closely consult with and actively involve persons with disabilities, including children with disabilities, through their representative organizations.

[41] Recommendations 1.1–1.12.

References

Bamford Review (The) of Mental Health and Learning Disability (Northern Ireland) (2007) A comprehensive legislative framework. https://www.health-ni.gov.uk/sites/default/files/publications/dhssps/legal-issue-comprehensive-framework.pdf

Clough B (2018) New legal landscapes: (re)constructing the boundaries of mental capacity law. Med Law Rev 26(2):246–275

Committee on the Rights of Persons with Disabilities (2014) General comment no 1 (2014) article 12: equal recognition before the law. CRPD/C/GC/1 19 May

Committee on the Rights of Persons with Disabilities (2015) Guidelines on article 14 of the convention on the rights of persons: the right of liberty and security of persons with disabilities. United Nations, Geneva

Donnelly M (2010) Healthcare decision-making and the law. Cambridge University Press, Cambridge

Fischer J (2006) A comparative look at the right to refuse treatment for involuntarily hospitalised persons with mental illness. Hastings Int Comp Law Rev 29(2):153–186

Freeman MC, Kolappa K, Caldas de Almeida JM, Kleinman A, Makhashvili N, Phakathi S et al (2015) Reversing hard won victories in the name of human rights: a critique of the 473 general comment on article 12 of the UN convention on the rights of persons with disabilities. Lancet Psychiatry 2(9):844–850. https://doi.org/10.1016/S2215-0366(15)00218-7

Hoffman S et al (2016) Is the UN convention on the rights of persons with disabilities impacting mental health laws and policies in high-income countries? A case study of implementation in Canada. BMC Int Health Hum Rights 16(1):28–46

Independent Review of Learning Disability and Autism in the Mental Health Act (Rome Review) (2019) Final report of Scotland's independent review of learning disability and autism in the Mental Health Act. https://www.researchgate.net/publication/342314047_Final_report_of_Scotland's_Independent_Review_of_Learning_Disability_and_Autism_in_the_Mental_Health_Act

Martin W, Michalowski M, Jutton T, Burch M (2014) Achieving CRPD compliance. https://autonomy.essex.ac.uk/resources/achieving-crpd-compliance-is-the-mental-capacity-act-of-england-and-wales-compatible-with-the-un-convention-on-the-rights-of-persons-with-disabilities-if-not-what-next/

Martin W, Michalowski M, Stavert J, Ward A, Ruck-Keene A, Caughey C et al (2016) Three jurisdictions report: towards compliance with CRPD Art. 12 in capacity/incapacity legislation across the UK. https://autonomy.essex.ac.UK/wp-content/uploads/2017/01/EAP-3J-final-Report-2016.Pdf

McKay C, Stavert J (2017) Scotland's mental health and capacity law: the case for reform. Edinburgh Napier University. https://www.mwcscot.org.uk/sites/default/files/2019-06/scotland_s_mental_health_and_capacity_law.pdf

Mental Welfare Commission for Scotland (2020) Supported decision making. https://www.mwcscot.org.uk/sites/default/files/2019-06/mwc_sdm_draft_gp_guide_10__post_board__jw_final.pdf

Mental Welfare Commission for Scotland (2021) Mental health act monitoring report 2020/2021. https://www.mwcscot.org.uk/search?keys=monitoring+reports&op=submit

Mental Welfare Commission for Scotland (2022) Mental health act monitoring report 2021/2022. https://www.mwcscot.org.uk/search?keys=monitoring+reports&op=submit

Minkowitz T (2017) CRPD and transformative equality. Int J Law Context 13:77–86

National Taskforce for Human Rights Leadership (2021) Report. Scottish Government. https://www.gov.scot/publications/national-taskforce-human-rights-leadership-report/documents/

Scottish Government (2022) International covenant on economic social and cultural Rights (ICESCR): position statement. https://www.gov.scot/publications/international-covenant-economic-social-cultural-rights-icescr/pages/3/

Scottish Government (2023) Scottish Mental Health Law Review: Our Response, June https://www.gov.scot/publications/scottish-mental-health-lawreview-response/

Scottish Mental Health Law Review (Scott Review) (2022) Final report. https://cms.mentalhealthlawreview.scot/wp-content/uploads/2022/09/SMHLR-FINAL-Report-.pdf

Stavert J (2018) Paradigm shift or paradigm paralysis? National Mental Health and capacity law and implementing the CRPD in Scotland. Laws 7(3):26. https://doi.org/10.3390/laws7030026

Stavert J (2021) Supported decision-making and paradigm shifts: word play or real change? Front Psychiatry 11:571005. https://doi.org/10.3389/fpsyt.2020.571005

Stavert J, McGregor R (2018) Domestic legislation and international human rights: the case of mental health and incapacity. Int J Hum Rights 22(1):70–79. https://doi.org/10.1080/13642987.2017.1390307

United Nations General Assembly (Human Rights Council) (2017) Report of the Special Rapporteur on the right of everyone to the enjoyment of the highest attainable standard of physical and mental health, Thirty-fifth session, 6-23 June 2017, 28 March, A/HRC/35/21 https://digitallibrary.un.org/record/1298436?v=pdf

UK Government (Department of Health and Social Care) (2018) Modernising the mental health act: increasing choice, reducing compulsion. https://assets.publishing.service.gov.uk/government/uploads/system/uploads/attachment_data/file/778897/Modernising_the_Mental_Health_Act_-_increasing_choice__reducing_compulsion.pdf

UK Parliament Joint Committee on the draft Mental Health Bill (2023) Report of Session 2022-23 HC696 HL128 https://committees.parliament.uk/work/6888/draft-mental-health-bill/publications/#

UK Government (Department of Health and Social Care) (2024) Government response to the Joint Committee on the draft Mental Health Bill, Policy Paper, 21 March, CP 1036, ISBN: 978-1-5286-4428-0 https://www.gov.uk/government/publications/government-response-to-the-joint-committee-onthe-draft-mental-health-bill/government-response-to-the-joint-committee-on-the-draft-mental-health-bill

Wilson K (2022) The CRPD and mental health law: the conflict about abolition, the practical dilemmas of implementation and the untapped potential. In: Felder F, Davy L, Kayess R (eds) Disability law and human rights. Palgrave Macmillan, pp 171–198

Part IV

Responses to Issues Arising in the Application of the CRPD and Related Regulations

12 Human Rights and Mental Health Care: A Perspective from the World Psychiatric Association

Helen Herrman, Silvana Galderisi, John Allan, and Maria Rodrigues

Contents

The World Psychiatric Association (WPA) recommends implementing the provisions of the UN Convention on the Rights of Persons with Disabilities (CRPD) by adopting a rights-based approach across its range of activities. The WPA works with Member Societies in 145 countries and with other partners to protect and promote mental health in the populations of each country and to improve mental health care and support recovery among those people with lived experience of mental ill-health. Partners include people with lived experience and their families, and international and inter-governmental organizations with related interests. WPA works together with these partners to implement policies, actions, and research in and across countries as well as international norms and advocacy. The WPA has developed positions and programs on promoting mental health and preventing ill-health, and on supporting equity of access to high quality mental health care, especially for people living in adversity and scarce resource settings. This chapter will focus on the work of WPA on promoting alternatives to coercion in mental health care, and the concurrent program underpinning this on partnering with people with lived experience of mental health conditions and their families.

The rights-based approach taken and advocated by WPA sets out to respect and protect the rights of people in all situations, especially those living with mental health conditions: including the rights to autonomy and participation in

Supplementary Information The online version contains supplementary material available at https://doi.org/10.1007/978-3-031-52179-9_12.

H. Herrman (✉)
Orygen and Centre for Youth Mental Health, The University of Melbourne, Parkville, VIC, Australia

Kindred Collaborative, Cairns, QLD, Australia
e-mail: h.herrman@unimelb.edu.au

S. Galderisi
University of Campania Luigi Vanvitelli, Naples, Italy

J. Allan
Mayne Academy of Psychiatry, University of Queensland Medical School, University of Queensland, Brisbane, QLD, Australia
e-mail: john.allan@health.qld.gov.au

M. Rodrigues
Kindred Collaborative, Cairns, QLD, Australia

Community Works, Melbourne, VIC, Australia
e-mail: maria@communityworks.com.au

N. Gill, N. Sartorius (eds.), *Mental Health and Human Rights*, Sustainable Development Goals Series, https://doi.org/10.1007/978-3-031-52179-9_12

decision-making processes; and incorporating in all aspects of care for those that need it the principles of non-discrimination, inclusion, and accessibility. To achieve these ends, the WPA promotes the use of person-centered and evidence-based practices. It encourages early intervention as mental health problems emerge, and sustained support as needed for recovery and full inclusion in community and family living (such as support with housing, education, work, and meaningful activities). Including people with lived experience of mental health conditions and their families in the planning and evaluation of services and supports is integral to the success of this work.

The WPA has recommended an ethical as well as rights-based approach to improving mental health and health care through its history of ethical declarations dating from the 1970s, and the recent adoption of its Code of Ethics (Appelbaum and Tyano 2021), as well as the publication of the WPA Bill of Rights for Persons with Mental Illnesses (Bhugra 2019).

The WPA has paid particular attention to working in partnership with people with lived experience of mental health conditions and their families over recent years. Work supported by several leaders of the Association and their advisors culminated in a project to develop recommendations for the international mental health community on working in partnership with these groups (Wallcraft et al. 2011). Since then, WPA has advocated for involving each of them in the planning and delivery of mental health care services and the education and training of practitioners. It has done this by opening opportunities for these groups to influence the development of policies and programs and to build trust and mutual respect with practitioners. This needs the sharing of accurate and understandable information, and concerns and preferences, and adopting shared or supported decision-making in mental health care. WPA has emphasized that mental health practitioners benefit greatly from education and training on how to work in partnership with people with lived experience of mental health conditions and their family carers. It also encourages the use of peer support, which is support provided by people with lived experience of mental health conditions, to help people cope with their condition and improve their quality of life.

The WPA established systematic working relationships with people with lived experience of mental health conditions and their families in 2018 through an advisory committee (later termed working group) that has had an important role since then in the functioning of the Association. It participated recently in drafting the *WPA Position Paper on developing partnerships with persons with lived experience of mental health conditions and family and informal carers* which will be considered for ratification in 2023. The committee has contributed to several initiatives including planning and participating in WPA congresses and thereby changing the face of these congresses. It has had an influential role as WPA develops its program on supporting and implementing alternatives to coercion in mental health care.

The WPA has developed this program recently. A position statement with a call to action was adopted in 2020 (Herrman et al. 2022) and revised in 2023: *Implementing Alternatives to Coercion: A Key Component of Improving Mental Health Care (Appended).* The work began in 2018, with the goal to develop practical and accountable rights-based and person-centered policies and practices that then result in realistic alternatives to coercion in mental health care. The program is conducted and supported by a growing list of Member Society and other partners.

The program recognizes that the use of coercion in mental health care has long been subject to controversy, and the call for viable alternatives is growing both within the profession and among people with lived experience of coercion in mental health care. There is diversity of opinion among people with lived experience of mental health conditions, families and carers, and mental health professionals about the degree to which and the speed with which coercive practices can be eliminated. Rather than be caught up in that debate, the program advocates for a pragmatic approach to finding alternatives to coercion that promote good practices and avoid the potential harms to individuals and services. It aims to demonstrate how shared experiences and outcomes assessments can encourage the spread of actions across countries, while being mindful of the legislative arrangements and cultural norms in each place. Changes are required not just to treatment and care but to policy, legislation, human and financial resources, culture and attitudes, involvement of people with lived experience and their families, and training and research, as well as the open and transparent access to data about coercive practices. Positive experiences in countries as disparate as Colombia, India, and Australia (described in three case studies published by WPA and linked here) illustrate the value of setting out on the journey of mental health reform.

This can have extraordinary results despite the awareness that partners in the process in many places have different views on how to frame the ultimate aims: a statement examined in the appended WPA position statement and call to action (Version 2, 2023). The strengthening of bonds between people with lived experience of mental health conditions and their families and mental health practitioners is a valued consequence of the process as well as a critical prerequisite for it.

References

Appelbaum PS, Tyano S (2021) The WPA code of ethics for psychiatry. World Psychiatry 20:308–309. https://doi.org/10.1002/wps.20861

Bhugra (2019) Bill of rights for persons with mental illnesses. https://www.wpanet.org/position-statements. Accessed 24 Jan 23

Herrman H, Allan J, Galderisi S, Javed A, Rodrigues M (2022) WPA task force on implementing alternatives to coercion in mental health care. Alternatives to coercion in mental health care: WPA position statement and call to action. World Psychiatry 21(1):159–160. https://doi.org/10.1002/wps.20950

Wallcraft J, Amering M, Freidin J, Davar B, Froggatt D, Jafri H, Javed A, Katontoka S, Raja S, Rataemane S, Steffen S, Tyano S, Underhill C, Wahlberg H, Warner R, Herrman H (2011) Partnerships for better mental health worldwide: WPA recommendations on best practices in working with service users and family carers. World Psychiatry 10:229–236

Non-Governmental Organizations Promoting Human Rights of People with Lived Experience of Mental Health Conditions

13

Charlene Sunkel and Nasser Loza

Contents

13.1 International: Global Mental Health Peer Network

Charlene Sunkel

GLOBAL MENTAL HEALTH PEER NETWORK

Unapologetically Experts By Experience

The Global Mental Health Peer Network (GMHPN) is an international peer-led organization that builds capacity among people with lived experience of a mental health condition through empowerment, mentorship and support. The organization has an established Experts by Experience Consultancy Services unit that is unique in that it involves only persons with lived experience in the delivery of its services and ensure diverse perspectives within required contexts.

GMHPN values the voices and experiences of people with mental health conditions and whose platform creates a safe and engaging communication environment for individuals to share their experiences, opinions and recommendations related to mental health. It provides for a global network of peer led leadership and advancement in individuals' advocacy journeys and/or career paths. It embodies ideals of empowerment, enablement and development from local towards global advocacy efforts in changing the status quo of mental health around the world. It advocates for the meaningful and authentic inclusion and participation of persons with lived experi-

C. Sunkel (✉)
Department of Global Office, Global Mental Health Peer Network, Paarl, Western Cape, South Africa
e-mail: charlene.sunkel@gmhpn.org

N. Loza
The Behman Hospital, Cairo, Egypt
e-mail: n.loza@behman.com

N. Gill, N. Sartorius (eds.), *Mental Health and Human Rights*, Sustainable Development Goals Series, https://doi.org/10.1007/978-3-031-52179-9_13

ence in all matters related to mental health, by which they are directly affected.

GMHPN is exclusively and completely represented by persons living with mental health conditions, whose expertise is invaluable. Collectively, and across six world regions, our organization and its members work towards the common goal of uniting perspectives and recommendations from our members to inspire change. Our expertise brings about practical solutions which derive from our own lived experiences in mental health. We aim to improve mental health and human rights literacy, transform policies and practices, and with the main objective of destigmatising mental health and reducing discrimination against persons living with mental health conditions.

GMHPN fills the gap that exists in global mental health reform, policy and practice, in that its members provide the most honest and forthcoming opinions and solutions on themes trending across the world as far as mental health is concerned. People with lived experience are experts by their own right stemming from their personal journeys in navigating mental health systems, care and treatment towards recovery.

International human rights instruments call for equality and recognition of the value of all people, including people with psychosocial disabilities/mental health conditions, towards advancing socio-economic and sustainable development.

International strategies and related documents emphasize the same by acknowledging the importance of placing people with lived experience of mental health conditions at the centre of policy and practice, thereby ensuring that people with lived experience and their representative organizations are meaningfully and authentically included in engagement and decision-making processes.

The UN Convention on the Rights of Persons with Disabilities notes the commitment to "recognizing the valued existing and potential contributions made by persons with disabilities to the overall well-being and diversity of their communities, and that the promotion of the full enjoyment by persons with disabilities of their human rights and fundamental freedoms and of full participation by persons with disabilities will result in their enhanced sense of belonging and in significant advances in the human, social and economic development of society and the eradication of poverty".

WHO World Mental Health Report: Transforming Mental Health for All (2022) notes that "People with lived experience are crucial stakeholders in mental health. Their participation is vital to improve mental health systems, services and outcomes. Such participation includes full empowerment and involvement in mental health advocacy, policy, planning, legislation, programme design, service provision, monitoring, research and evaluation".

Based on the above, the GMHPN aligns its work on the evidence of the value of lived experience integration into research, policy, service development and delivery, stigma reduction and training of healthcare professionals, of which the benefits are evident on multiple levels.

13.2 National—The Egyptian Society for the Rights of People with Mental Illness

Nasser Loza

The Egyptian Society for the Rights of People with Mental Illness was born in 2009, the revolution of mental health, with the ratification with Egypt's mental health act of 2009. The main focus was to advocate for the rights of people with mental illness, as well as, to fight stigma to patients and their families. This was done in collaboration between the Egyptian Ministry of Health and the World Health Organization, and the Royal College of Psychiatrists along with other human rights entities to work on a new draft legislation that would protect the rights of people with mental illness and set guidelines for clinical practitioners. The goal was to push for a more liberal approach for the treatment of people with mental illness respecting their rights and providing for community-based mental health care. The Egyptian culture is traditional middle eastern and spiritual beliefs have always protected sufferers of mental illness. Over the centuries, they were cared for in the community, by the community. Although, the new law helped to evolve the concept of care in Egyptian hospitals and the treatment institutions became less stigmatized, there was a huge need for Egyptian societies to bear the responsibility for promoting the concept and fostering the rights of people with mental illness. The Egyptian Society for the Rights of People with Mental Illness was established to change this general attitude towards people with mental illness. The aim is to help integrate people with mental illness in the community and combat the stigma associated with mental illness.

The change of mental health legislation in Egypt enabled professionals and protected their steps in discharging patients. This was a huge step in the direction of liberal care for persons with mental illness. Nevertheless, it was clear that a powerful awareness campaign was crucial in advocating for the rights of that significant portion of our society.

This campaign was launched with the help of a grant from the ministry of foreign affairs in Finland. It was felt at the time that in conjunction with the work of the ministry of health in Egypt, it was important for the civil society to take part in this cultural change. The civil society can make a more sustainable effort, whereas governments change, NGOs are less affected by political factors.

In recent years, the Egyptian society for rights for people with mental health has worked closely with the World Federation for Mental Health. The Society hosted the World Congress of Mental Health in 2015 in Cairo. This was an opportunity for the exchange of the experience on a global level. It became clear that much of what we were calling for in the Egyptian mental health system was echoed in other parts of the world.

Throughout the past 15 years, the society has prioritized the advocacy and protection of the rights of people with mental illness. The Egyptian Society for the Rights of People with Mental Illness aims to advocate for the rights of those affected by mental illness in Egypt. Our vision is for fair treatment with dignity, respect and better quality of life for all those affected by mental illness, their carers, families and friends. The society has been supported by local and international donors, and it works in close collaboration with the mental health services in psychiatric hospitals in Egypt and more recently activities with the Fahem Foundation, an Egyptian NGO supporting the carers of people with mental illness. It is refreshing to see how civil society in Egypt is taking its role seriously in supporting the needs of people with mental illness. For decades the evolution of mental health policies, legislations and service organization was prioritized. In recent years, the role of advocacy, awareness campaign and anti-stigma messages are a priority that is having a clear impact in Egypt.

Part V

Conclusion

Impact of the Convention on the Rights of Persons with Disabilities on Mental Health Care: Way Forward

14

Neeraj Gill and Norman Sartorius

Contents

14.1 Introduction

The United Nations Convention on the Rights of Persons with Disabilities (CRPD) is a landmark international treaty based on the central idea of respect for an inherent dignity of every human being (United Nations 2006). It aims to protect and promote the human rights of people with disabilities including the right to dignity, autonomy, liberty, integrity, social inclusion and participation, and non-discrimination. The implementation of the CRPD requires the States Parties to undertake legislative amendment and administrative measures to enhance the human rights of people with disabilities. The CRPD adopts a social model of disability wherein disability resulting from interactions between person with impairment and environmental barriers leads to the hindrance of his/her full and effective participation in society. Therefore, the full realization of the principles of the CRPD requires a change of all sectors of government and the whole of community in a manner which will ensure the protection of human rights of people with disabilities.

N. Gill (✉)
School of Medicine and Dentistry, Griffith University, Gold Coast, QLD, Australia

Mental Health Policy Unit, Health Research Institute, University of Canberra, Canberra, ACT, Australia

Mental Health and Specialist Services, Gold Coast Health, Gold Coast, QLD, Australia
e-mail: neeraj.gill@griffith.edu.au

N. Sartorius
Association for the Improvement of Mental Health Programmes, Geneva, Switzerland
e-mail: sartorius@normansartorius.com

N. Gill, N. Sartorius (eds.), *Mental Health and Human Rights*, Sustainable Development Goals Series, https://doi.org/10.1007/978-3-031-52179-9_14

We decided to explore issues that arise in the application of the principles of the CRPD in practice by asking psychiatrists, legal experts, people who have experienced mental illness and their carers to recommend action in a series of events concerning people with mental illness. The description of the events in each of the case histories and of the reactions of those surrounding the person with a mental health condition have been modelled on real-life stories.

We have invited most of the main actors in the process of application of the Convention, including persons with lived experience, family members, psychiatrists, directors of health services, and specialists in legal matters and ethical issues. They are from many different continents and work in different legal traditions. We examined the responses of these specialists in live sessions and by asking them to write up their opinion after studying the cases.

We did not invite the ministers of health, representatives of insurance agencies, heads of foundations or others who make decisions about the allocation of resources for the promotion of mental health and the provision of help to people who experience mental illness and their families or informal carers. They should be the next target of mental health care efforts because they will have to provide the resources for the implementation of effective care, with the full and effective participation of the people who experience mental health problems and their carers. At this stage, the main target of efforts has to be the development of a consensus among all stakeholders about the methods, implementation steps and roles of participants in the care process, and we hope that the information contained in this book will serve as a stimulus and provide support to the development of this consensus.

Action to implement the principles of the CRPD (and other recommendations concerning the provision of care to people with mental health conditions) depends on four sets of factors:

First, the knowledge about the most effective ways for prevention and treatment of the mental health disorders while protecting the human rights of all those involved.

Second, the translation of this knowledge into the work schedules of the participants in the care process—including the people who have mental health conditions and their carers, community workers, professionals working in mental health services, lawyers, and key decision-makers in the community.

Third, the introduction of appropriate provisions into the laws relevant to health promotion and rules governing the functioning of mental health and other related health services.

Fourth, the provision of resources which are necessary to make the other three prerequisites to care a reality. Without additional resources, none of the other steps is likely to be successful.

The development of plans to achieve the first three of these requirements is an important part of the process of improving care, and we wanted to see whether the case history method could be helpful in this respect and whether it could can give us an estimate of the level of agreement among stakeholders about some of the key issues emerging in the provision of care. We found that the use of the case histories method gave us good information about the level and areas of agreement and disagreement among representatives of the stakeholders in the process of improving care. We hope that the method will be used at the service level and help to obtain consensus of stakeholders in settings characterized by different legal traditions, prevalent cultures, and styles of organizing mental health care.

The cases considered in this volume are from low-, middle-, and high-income countries from different continents, and from different socio-economic backgrounds, age groups and genders. The human rights issues raised include the right to autonomy, liberty, integrity, dignity, employment, highest attainable standard of health, social inclusion, and freedom from stigma and discrimination. The case histories presented situations in which these rights were at stake and in which the CRPD principles would have to be considered. The case history method produced wonderful results in this exercise. There was remarkable agreement among representatives of persons with the lived experience of mental illness, family members, and psychiatrists, including those who were experts in legal and ethical matters. The general agreement about the action to take in the situations described in the case histories demonstrated the importance of education of all those involved in the care for people with mental illness about matters concerning the promotion of human rights of those with mental health problems. This would include a clear interpretation and education about the nature and requirements of the CRPD and the contemporary human rights framework in general. An urgent task in this respect is to develop training materials and introduce relevant training into medical, nursing, law, and other training programmes as well as part of in-service training.

Despite general agreement on key issues, there were some points of divergence, which we noted in the concluding remarks of individual case histories and note again in this chapter. They illustrate the need for a discussion among mental health professionals and all the others involved in the care for people with mental illness. Such discussion will help to identify points which should receive particular attention in the process of training, and in communicating with the general public.

The analysis of the case history commentaries showed that the clear consensus about actions to take was not reflected in the legislation, organization of care, or cultural traditions in different countries around the world. To highlight this issue, we included an additional section into the volume describing the impact of the CRPD on mental health legislation in different regions of the world. We included countries with different legal traditions that utilised the most widely used first or second languages in the world. We hoped that this would illustrate the usefulness of introduction of the CRPD principles into mental health legislation in countries with different legal traditions.

Finally, we added a third section describing action by some of the international and national organizations engaged in efforts to protect the human rights of people with mental illness. The reason for their inclusion was to remind the reader of the many organizations—national and international, governmental and non-governmental which play an important role in the provision of care to people with mental illness. It is to be expected that these organizations will be actively involved in the promotion and use of principles of the CRPD.

14.2 Conclusion from Case History Commentaries

The case histories displayed that the most common violation of rights of persons with mental illness is that they do not have access to social and health services. The lack of services is in part due to the poverty prevailing in some countries and in part to the low priority that is given to the provision of mental health care to those who need it. The experts emphasized that the right to the provision of mental health care included much more than the provision pharmacological treatment and that mental health care involves psychosocial interventions, support to the carers, activities leading to the primary, secondary or tertiary prevention of mental illness. It also includes the promotion of mental health understood as action aiming to raise the value of mental health on the scales of value of individuals and societies. Furthermore, in case of an acute relapse of psychosis or agitation, the commentators repeatedly highlighted the need for de-escalation techniques directly with the person with mental illness, as well as training of family/carers and agents of society in de-escalation techniques.

The commentators highlighted the need to respect dignity, autonomy, and liberty of persons with mental illness. They unanimously criticized gross violations of human rights described in some case histories, for example, long-term incarceration of a woman in a stand-alone mental asylum, the chaining and physical abuse of a young man with acute mental illness, and the exposure to physical and sexual assault of a young man placed in a prison leading to mental illness related to trauma. They emphasized autonomous decision-making supported decision-making and the development of practice of using advanced directives.

The commentators highlighted that persons with mental illness and their family members and informal carers must be educated about mental illness and about its treatment. The responses highlighted that the family members and other informal caregivers are often neglected in the discussion on human rights, despite the burden of mental illness they bear by proxy. It is difficult to subscribe to the notion of 'community care' in situations in which the classic communities have vanished due to rapid urbanization and family units getting smaller. The health and capacity of carers did not receive sufficient attention although psychiatric services clearly rely on the massive investment of carers, often sacrificing their time and all else to provide care (Sartorius 2023). Therefore, efforts for promotion of human rights of people with mental illness must increase their focus on supporting families and informal carers (Sartorius et al. 2023).

In some instances, the commentators differed from the generally accepted principles of treatment in psychiatry; for example, they felt that where a person with mental illness wished to cease their medication, this should be accepted as an expression of their autonomy and should be respected. Some commentators highlighted that the right to autonomy must be balanced against the right to health, for example, when the right to refuse treatment was in direct conflict with the right to the highest attainable standard of physical and mental health.

While emphasizing the need to respect autonomy, will, and preference of the person with mental illness, there was consensus among all the commentators that involuntary psychiatric treatment was sometimes required to respect the right to health. This would be a measure of last resort, for a short period, with strong safeguards and monitoring. This unanimous response of the service-user and carer representatives, as well as psychiatrists was at odds with the stance taken by the CRPD Committee as well as of the World Health Organization who have called for an absolute ban on all involuntary interventions regardless of circumstances (United Nations Committee on the Rights of Persons with Disabilities 2014; World Health Organization 2019, 2023). However, the position of the CRPD Committee and the WHO is an interpretation of the Convention, but not written in the text of the Convention and hence is not legally binding on ratifying countries.

In cases where the person with a mental illness committed an offence due to symptoms of mental illness, all the commentators agreed with the need for placement in the health system rather than in criminal justice system. This is important considering the CRPD Committee's General Comment 1 on Article 12 that there must be no exceptions to the exercise of universal legal capacity (United Nations Committee on the Rights of Persons with Disabilities 2014; Freeman et al. 2015)]. The discussion of the case histories demonstrated general support for diversion from the criminal justice system to health system when an alleged offence was committed directly due to behaviour caused by mental illness. In fact, there was consensus that not diverting individuals to mental health system/psychiatric care in such instances was a violation of their right to justice as well as access to the highest attainable standard of health. One commentator argued that diversion from the justice/correctional system to health system was totally in line with the 'accommodation' by society that the CRPD encourages.

To conclude, the case histories exercise has shown that the CRPD is an effective instrument to help promote mental health care and the rights of people with mental illness. However, to realise these aims, there must be a realistic and balanced interpretation of the text of the Convention. Therefore, different organizations working in the field of mental health must record their experience, discuss these with experts, and find formulations which are generally acceptable, in line with the intention of the CRPD. Such formulations of the way in which the CRPD should be implemented based on experiential learning and must be included in the education and training of postgraduate training of doctors in psychiatry, other mental health professionals, and all other stakeholders including the police, lawyers, the justice system, and policymakers.

It is important to underline that the provisions of the CRPD are unlikely to be met unless governments decide to change their view about the importance of the promotion of mental health and provision of support to people with mental illness and their carers and provide for it in the national budgets. The resources currently made available for mental health care are far below the minimal requirements for care in most countries of the world. The fact that four fifths of people with serious mental illness in the low- and middle-income countries do not receive treatment for their illness and that even in high-income countries a quarter of those who have serious mental disorders and need mental health care are not given care should be remembered in each of the discussions concerning CRPD and other instruments protecting the rights of people with mental illness.

14.3 Conclusion from the Section on Mental Health Legislation in Countries Influenced by Different Legal Traditions

The chapters regarding the impact of the CRPD on mental health legislation in countries with different legal traditions and languages show that most countries have revised their legislation or are in the process of revising their mental health laws and related provisions to bring it in harmony with the CRPD. Most of the laws in these countries have incorporated the language of CRPD, for example, the protection of human rights, dignity and autonomy, and supported decision-making. However, most of the laws, while in harmony with the principles of the CRPD, fall short in mapping an implementation pathway and do not have the tools for estimation of resource requirements for implementation of the CRPD-compliant legislation.

None of the countries included in our review reported any move or plans to completely abolish substitute decision-making regimes like involuntary psychiatric treatment and guardianship. While provisions like supported decision-making and advance health directives have been included in many countries' mental health laws, there are inadequate resources for the operationalization of those provisions, which means that they remain concepts without much application in practice. Additional resources are necessary to make this happen.

Often, there is a tension between the local legal tradition and culture and the international human rights framework. For example, the *General Civil Law and Mental Health Law* of China continues to rely heavily on substitute decision-making in the form of a guardian. The medical facility can impose inpatient treatment if the guardian agrees and must discharge the patient if the guardian requests discharge. These provisions neither rely on the individual's capacity to provide informed consent nor respect their right to autonomy or participation in decision-making.

In large countries like China with a population over a billion people, as well as in very small countries like Fiji with population less than a million, the impact of the CRPD and WHO Comprehensive Mental Health Action Plan 2013–2030 (World Health Organization 2021) could be observed in the form of transition from stand-alone mental institutions to community-based mental health facilities. However, a lack of resources for community-based services and lack of adequate staffing levels was identified in many countries including China, Mexico, Egypt, and Fiji. Similarly, socio-economic issues such as the unemployment of people with mental illness were common to many countries.

The amended legislations in most countries either did not incorporate the right of access to and help from health services, or did not account for the resources required to improve mental health services. The right to treatment of mental illness was first recognized as a human right by the UN Principles for Protection of Persons with Mental Illness and for the Improvement of Mental Health Care (MI Principles) in 1991 and the right to the highest attainable standard of health is affirmed by the CRPD, Article 25 (United Nations 1991). While compliance with the human rights framework adopted by the CRPD requires government action to improve resources in social and healthcare sector, almost all the countries, including high-income countries reported significant under-investment in social and healthcare sector, and there seems to be no indication of intention to change this and provide more resources.

14.4 Conclusion from Human Rights Documents by International Agencies in Mental Health

A sub-section on responses to the issues arising in the application of the CRPD provides examples of how national and international agencies in the field of mental health can advocate for and promote the human rights of people with mental illness. This section can guide other national and international agencies in their efforts towards promotion and protection of human rights of people with mental illness.

The World Psychiatric Association (WPA) is an international organization with 145 member psychiatric organizations bringing together some 250,000 psychiatrists, around the world. The WPA has issued a position statement to implement alternatives to coercion in mental health care (World Psychiatric Association 2020; Herrman et al. 2022). The WPA views and action concerning this matter are included in the book. We hope that the position statement by WPA will encourage other professional organizations as well as other stakeholders in the field of mental health to question the status quo and raise their voices for promotion, resourcing, and implementation of alternatives to coercion in mental health care. These stakeholders include, first and foremost, the people with lived experience of mental illness and their family members and informal carers.

The World Health Organization's Quality Rights Initiative is an initiative by the WHO to improve quality of care and protect human rights of people with mental health conditions, psychosocial, intellectual, and cognitive impairments which may lead to disabilities (World Health Organization 2019, 2021). The Quality Rights initiative asks governments to put in place legislation, policies, and strategies to promote human rights in social and mental health services in line with the CRPD. Its stated objectives are to combat stigma and discrimination, promote social inclusion and participation of persons with lived experience of mental health conditions, create recovery-oriented and community-based services, and align national policies and laws with the principles of the CRPD.

A resolution adopted by the UN on 26th June 2023 on Mental Health and Psychosocial Disabilities is discussed in Chap. 2 (United Nations 2023). This resolution draws upon the CRPD and the Sustainable Development Goals (SDGs) (United Nations General Assembly 2015). This is the first time that the UN General Assembly has adopted a resolution on mental health, recognizing the importance of psychiatry and other mental health professions in providing quality treatments and support to people with psychosocial disabilities and actively combating stigma, discrimination, and coercion.

14.5 Concluding Remarks

The CRPD is an important addition to the international binding legal frameworks safeguarding the human rights of people with a mental illness. In order for the CRPD to be practically useful, it is crucial that it be interpreted in a realistic, balanced, and unbiased manner and that the required resources are provided to implement it. While the Convention is binding, the countries which ratify the Convention are not obliged to stick to its radical interpretations. There is general agreement that autonomy, will, and preference of people with mental illness must be respected, and that alternatives to coercion and supported decision-making must be implemented. On the other hand, no national legislation has accepted the CRPD Committee's insistence on abolishing substitute decision-making. It is generally accepted that involuntary psychiatric treatment must be minimized but is sometimes required as the last resort to promote the right to highest attainable standard of health, and sometimes even the right to life of people with mental illness (when the true wish and preference of an individual has been invaded and violated by mental illness). A need for a balanced interpretation is further highlighted by the so-called Geneva Impasse because agencies within the United Nations are divided in their opinion about completely abolishing involuntary treatment. As noted earlier, the UN Human Rights Committee (HRC) and the UN Subcommittee on Prevention of Torture (SPT) acknowledge the need for coercive measures as the last resort with strong safeguards in place (Guilloud 2019). The WHO and WPA have called for moving beyond this 'Geneva Impasse' by finding common grounds to work towards shared goals of promoting human rights and quality of care in social and mental health services and promoting alternatives to coercion (Gill et al. 2024). The WHO Quality Rights initiative and the WPA position statement and discussion paper on promoting alternatives to coercion in mental health care provide practical guidance to work towards these goals. A systematic operationalization of alternatives to coercion requires the definition of action such as provision of community-based services free of charge, arrangements for early intervention, open doors services, general use and insistence on the formulation of advance health directives, supported decision-making, co-produced individual recovery plans, and participation of people with mental disabilities and their carers in mental health policy and planning (Mezzina et al. 2019).

The CRPD affirms the indivisibility and interdependence of all human rights by placing equal emphasis on the rights included in the International Covenant on Economic, Social, and Cultural rights and the International Covenant on Civil and Political Rights (United Nations 1966a, b). Economic, social, and cultural rights (also called positive rights) include the right to housing, food, education, employment, health and social inclusion, and cultural participation. Civil and political rights (sometimes called negative rights) include the right to liberty; freedom from torture, cruel or degrading treatment; freedom from exploitation, violence, or abuse; and the right to equal recognition before the law. While this dichotomy helps in the conceptual understanding of human rights, it is well-recognized that all human rights are interdependent, interrelated, and indivisible (Donnelly 2013; United Nations 1993).

Despite ratification of the CRPD by 191 States Parties by April 2024 (including ratification by the European Union in 2010), mental health legislation in most countries continues to focus on the civil and political rights of safeguarding the rights of individuals being treated against their will. The CRPD advocates for a strong emphasis on rights by including articles related to the right to independent living and inclusion and participation in community (Article 19), home and family (Article 23), education (Article 24), health (Article 25), habitation and rehabilitation (Article 26), work and employment (Article 27), adequate standard of living and social protection (Article 28), and participation in cultural life (Article 30). All these 'positive rights' are social determinants of health (including mental health) and their violation can predispose, precipitate, or exacerbate mental illness. Therefore, adherence to the principles of the CRPD requires the involvement of the whole of government action and of all of the communities work to promote and protect the rights of people with mental illness and social equity. This could be conceptualized as a health ecosystem approach to mental health care and training encompassing nano to macro levels ranging from individual/clinical interaction, through individual services and local health catchment area to regional and national health system and social policy (Rosen et al. 2020). It is important to realize that the promotion of economic, social, and cultural rights paves the way to the protection of civil and political rights of people with mental illness (Gill 2019).

Most countries' mental health laws do not mention economic, social, and cultural rights, nor the right to access to health services. Government investment into health care, particularly mental health care continues to be grossly inadequate in a majority of countries of the world. It is important to emphasize that most of the violations of human rights of people with mental illness occur because of a lack of resources and inadequate investment in social and healthcare sectors in general, and in the mental health care facilities in particular. The Lancet series on global mental health, in 2007, highlighted that mental disorders affected the poor, disadvantaged, and vulnerable populations disproportionately; that there was a scarcity of resources and inefficiency of their utilization, leading to significant treatment gap especially in low- and middle-income countries; and that low cost-effective treatments could be delivered through primary care workers (Patel and Sartorius 2008; Saxena et al. 2007). Today, nearly two decades later the situation does not seem to have improved.

In 2015, the UN adopted the *2030 Agenda for Sustainable Development* outlining 17 Sustainable Development Goals (SDGs) to drive urgent action in areas such as poverty, equality, health, education, sustainability, and the environment (United Nations General Assembly 2015). Within the SDGs, there are both direct and indirect goals, targets, and indicators relating to mental health. The SDG 3 details the goal to ensure healthy lives, including promotion of mental health and wellbeing, prevention and treatment of substance abuse, including narcotic drug abuse and harmful use of alcohol; and universal health coverage. A resolution adopted by the UN General Assembly in 2023 reaffirms the human rights of people with psychosocial disabilities and urges the Member States to recognize the promotion of mental health and wellbeing is an essential component of universal health coverage (United Nations 2023).

The stakeholders who need to be involved in implementation of the principles of the CRPD include service-users, family/carers, peer support workers, nurses, social workers, psychologists, occupational therapists, general practitioners, policemen, lawyers, judges, directors of hospitals and health services and the governments, non-government organizations (NGOs) and the media. They should all consider what they must and can do to respond to the requirements of the CRPD. This then requires education and training of mental health professionals and all those stakeholders in the principles of the CRPD. The training programmes for psychiatrists and other mental health professionals should include macro-level skills of public advocacy, positive use of the media, social movements, and working with organizations of people with lived experience of mental illness and their families and informal carers (Rosen et al. 2020). Therefore, merely ratifying the Convention and amending the mental health legislation is not enough. The States Parties to the Convention must plan and allocate resources for training and education, in addition to legal and administrative mechanisms to comply with the Convention. As mentioned above, this must go side by side with resourcing social measures, (for example, housing, employment, social inclusion, and tackling stigma); and healthcare resourcing including mental health promotion, early intervention, and implementing voluntary recovery-oriented community-based mental health services.

There is a mosaic of principles that guide the future and each of the participants in the process of care, recovery, and inclusion in the community would be one of the stones making the mosaic. While there is considerable disagreement and divergence among various stakeholders regarding post-CRPD interpretations, our book has shown that harmony of action and congruence with the prescription of the CRPD can be achieved by focusing on the needs and specific circumstances of individuals and the training and education of all stakeholders leading to the understanding of the principles defined in the CRPD and by the provision of resources necessary to organize and provide care. International professional organizations and organizations bringing together people with lived experiences and of those who provide care to them should take on the task of producing documents that present a realistic and balanced interpretation of the CRPD and provide education regarding principles of the CRPD and guidance on application of the Convention in social and healthcare sectors. These documents must be created with active participation of people with lived experience of mental illness, their family members and informal carers, psychiatrists and other mental health professionals, and lawyers and human rights experts. The production of these agreements and guidelines must go hand in hand with the provision of resources for care.

References

Donnelly J (2013) Universal human rights in theory and practice. Cornell University Press, Ithaca

Freeman MC, Kolappa K, De Almeida JMC, Kleinman A, Makhashvili N, Phakathi S, Saraceno B, Thornicroft G (2015) Reversing hard won victories in the name of human rights: a critique of the general comment on article 12 of the UN convention on the rights of persons with disabilities. Lancet Psychiatry 2:844–850

Gill NS (2019) Human rights framework: an ethical imperative for psychiatry. Aust N Z J Psychiatry 53:8–10

Gill N, Drew N, Rodrigues M, Muhsen H, Morales G, Savage M, Pathare S, Allan J, Galderisi S, Javed A, Herrman H, Funk M. (2024) Bringing together the WHO QualityRights Initiative and the WPA position statement on implementing alternatives to coercion in mental health care – A common goal for action.

Guilloud SD (2019) The right to liberty of persons with psychosocial disabilities at the United Nations: a tale of two interpretations. Int J Law Psychiatry 66: 101497

Herrman H, Allan J, Galderisi S, Javed A, Rodrigues M, WPA Task Force on Implementing Alternatives to Coercion in Mental Health Care (2022) Alternatives to coercion in mental health care: WPA position statement and call to action. World Psychiatry 21: 159–160

Mezzina R, Rosen A, Amering M, Javed A (2019) The practice of freedom: human rights and the global mental health agenda. In: Advances in psychiatry. Springer

Patel V, Sartorius N (2008) From science to action: the lancet series on global mental health. Curr Opin Psychiatry 21:109–113

Rosen A, Gill NS, Salvador-Carulla L (2020) The future of community psychiatry and community mental health services. Curr Opin Psychiatry 33:375–390

Saxena S, Thornicroft G, Knapp M, Whiteford H (2007) Resources for mental health: scarcity, inequity, and inefficiency. Lancet 370:878–889

Sartorius N (2023) Community care for people with mental illness: challenges emerging in the 2020s and consequent recommendations. World Psychiatry 22(3):388

Sartorius N, Gill N, Virani S, Salvador-Carulla L (2023) Fighting for human rights and social justice and the promotion of mental health: complementary efforts. World Social Psychiatry 5(2):97–100

United Nations (1966a) International covenant on civil and political rights. United Nations. New York.

United Nations (1966b) International covenant on economic, social and cultural rights. United Nations. New York.

United Nations (1991) Principles for protection of persons with mental illness and for the improvement of mental health care (MI Principles). United Nations, New York

United Nations (1993) United Nations general assembly: Vienna declaration and program of action. United Nations, New York

United Nations (2006) Convention on the rights of persons with disabilities, adopted on 13 December 2006, GA res 61/106, UN doc a/res/61/106 (entered into force 3 may 2008). New York. https://www.un.org/development/desa/disabilities/convention-on-the-rights-of-persons-with-disabilities.html

United Nations Committee on the Rights of Persons with Disabilities (2014) General Comment No. 1 (2014). Article 12—Equal recognition before the law. 11th session, March 31–April 11, 2014, New York. https://documents-dds-ny.un.org/doc/UNDOC/GEN/G14/031/20/PDF/G1403120.pdf?OpenElement. Accessed 03 June 2018

United Nations General Assembly. (2015). Transforming our world: the 2030 Agenda for Sustainable Development. Retrieved from https://sdgs.un.org/2030agenda

United Nations. (2023). UN General Assembly Resolution A/RES/77/300. Adopted 26th June 2023: Mental Health and psychosocial support. Retrieved from https://digitallibrary.un.org/record/4014613?ln=en#record-files-collapseheader

World Health Organization (2019) WHO QualityRights initiative—improving quality, promoting human rights. World Health Organization, Geneva. https://www.who.int/mental_health/policy/quality_rights/en/

World Health Organization (2021) Guidance on community mental health services: promoting person-centred and rights-based approaches. World Health Organization, Geneva. https://www.who.int/publications/i/item/guidance-and-technical-packages-on-community-mental-health-services

World Health Organization (2021) Comprehensive mental health action plan 2013–2030. World Health Organization. https://apps.who.int/iris/handle/10665/345301

World Health Organization (2023). Mental health, human rights and legislation: guidance and practice. In Mental health, human rights and legislation: guidance and practice

World Psychiatric Association (2020) Implementing alternatives to coercion: a key component of improving mental health care. Position statement. https://www.wpanet.org/_files/ugd/e172f3_635a89af889c471683c29fcd981db0aa.pdf

GPSR Compliance

The European Union's (EU) General Product Safety Regulation (GPSR) is a set of rules that requires consumer products to be safe and our obligations to ensure this.

If you have any concerns about our products, you can contact us on ProductSafety@springernature.com

In case Publisher is established outside the EU, the EU authorized representative is:

Springer Nature Customer Service Center GmbH
Europaplatz 3
69115 Heidelberg, Germany

Batch number: 09533929

Printed by Printforce, the Netherlands